MAKE IT EASY

QUICK & EASY
COOKING

KNACK®

QUICK & EASY
COOKING

A step-by-step guide to meals in minutes

LINDA JOHNSON LARSEN

PHOTOGRAPHS BY LIESA COLE

Guilford, Connecticut
An imprint of The Globe Pequot Press

Copyright © 2009 by Morris Book Publishing, LLC

Editor-in-Chief: Maureen Graney
Editor: Katie Benoit
Text Design: Paul Beatrice
Layout: Kevin Mak
Cover photos by Liesa Cole
All interior photos by Liesa Cole with the exception of p. 1 (right): Bret Kerr/Globe Pequot Press; p. 6: PanPan/shutterstock; p. 13 (right): godrick/shutterstock; p.14 (right): courtesy of Oneida Ltd, photo by James Demarest; p. 16 (left): Constant/shutterstock; p. 17 (right): Edward Hardam/shutterstock; p. 19 (left): HomeStudio/shutterstock; p. 19 (right): Layland Masuda/shutterstock; p. 20 (right): Jo Williams; p. 21 (right): Anthony Berenyi/shutterstock; p. 25 (right): © Joe Gough |Dreamstime.com; p. 26: Justin Paget/shutterstock; p. 28: bluehill/shutterstock; p. 29 (left): jocicalek/shutterstock; p. 32: George Peters/istockphoto; p. 43 (right): Bratwustle/shutterstock; p. 65 (left): Debi Harbin; p. 148-149: Debi Harbin; p.223 (right): Anthony Berenyi/shutterstock

CIP DATA: A catalogue record for this book is available from the British Library.

Larsen, Linda, 1958-
  Knack quick & easy cooking : a step-by-step guide to meals in minutes / Linda Johnson Larsen.
       p. cm.

  ISBN 978-0-7627-5928-6
1. Quick and easy cookery. I. Title. II. Title: Quick & easy cooking.
TX833.5.L374 2009
641.5'55—dc22

Globe Pequot Press International
Footprint Handbooks
6 Riverside Court
Lower Bristol Road
Bath
BA2 3DZ
UK
T+44(0)1225 469141
F+44(0)1225 469461

The following manufacturers/names appearing in *Knack Quick & Easy Cooking* are trademarks: Crock-Pot®, eBay®, George Foreman®, Ritz®, Tabasco®

The information in this book is true and complete to the best of our knowledge. All recommendations are made without guarantee on the part of the author or The Globe Pequot Press. The author and The Globe Pequot Press disclaim any liability in connection with the use of this information.

Printed in India by Replika Press Pvt Ltd

About the author

Linda Johnson Larsen is the author of many cookbooks, including *Knack Grilling Basics*, and is the Guide for Busy Cooks at About.com. She has created and tested recipes for major food companies since 1987. Linda has written articles for *Woman's Day*, and her recipes appeared regularly in America's *Quick & Simple* magazine. She lives in Minneapolis, Minnesota, USA. Visit the author at www.busycooks.about.com.

CONTENTS

INTRODUCTION

Quick and easy cooking is all the rage these days, epitomized in 30-minute meals and five-ingredient recipes. But there's more to quick cooking than short cooking times and tiny ingredient lists. You need to have an organized kitchen, understand basic cooking concepts and be proficient in some easy kitchen skills.

The first thing you need to learn is how to read a recipe. If this is your first foray into the kitchen, read through some simple recipes and make sure that you understand all the terms and directions. You should read and understand every recipe completely before you begin.

There are lots of large cookbooks that define cooking terms, or you can look for information on the Internet. Never assume that you know what a term means; if you're unsure, look it up. Start by making some simple dishes, preferably those that can be completed in a short amount of time, with a short ingredient list, and with little or no cooking. Once you're comfortable using basic kitchen tools and working with food, you can proceed.

Then you'll need to organize your kitchen. Any kitchen can be made more efficient by knowing exactly what you have on hand and where it's stored. Every utensil, pan, spice jar and can of tomatoes should have a 'home' in your kitchen. And when a utensil is used and washed up, it should be put away in that home. If you have to stop and search for a tool or an ingredient, you're wasting valuable time in the kitchen.

Kitchen basics include a refrigerator, freezer, store cupboard or shelf space, appliances and worktop. Take a good, hard look at the kitchen and see if there are some things you can change. Many kitchens benefit from adding a table or freestanding butcher's block to increase the work space. Each appliance should have landing space nearby to hold hot pans and dishes. You can't move your appliances, but you can re-assign equipment to different spaces around the kitchen, making each item more accessible to the appliance it's used with.

Food safety is the next lesson. If your food isn't wholesome and safe, it doesn't matter how good it tastes or how perfectly it's cooked. There are some important rules you must follow. Always wash your hands before and after handling food. And wash your hands and utensils again with hot soapy water after you've handled perishable foods that need cooking before serving, such as raw beef, pork, chicken, seafood and eggs.

Never let cooked perishable food stand out of refrigeration for more than two hours, or one hour if the ambient room temperature is above 30°C. Those same perishable foods should be refrigerated promptly after cooking if they aren't going to be served immediately.

Never partially cook meat and refrigerate or freeze it. That will put it through the danger zone of 5–60°C too many times. Always cook meat completely if you plan to keep it for later consumption or freeze it for later use, and don't reheat food more than once.

Pork, poultry and meat products such as burgers and sausages may carry pathogens such as campylobacter or salmonella, and must be cooked all the way through to ensure that the bacteria are destroyed; cut into the middle to check there is no pink meat. Whole cuts of lamb or beef are safe to eat rare, provided the whole surface has been seared at high heat.

Finally, keep cooked and uncooked foods separate. Never place cooked meat on the same dish that was used to hold the uncooked food. And be sure to wrap raw meats well and don't let their juices drip through fridge shelves on to foods like fruits or vegetables.

There are many appliances that will help you cook food quickly and easily. When you buy a new appliance, whether it's a dual-contact grill, an electric steamer or a hand blender, make sure that you read the manufacturer's instruction booklet from beginning to end before

you use it. The booklet will include lots of safety information, and there are usually some easy recipes that will get you started using the appliance.

Now that you have an organized kitchen arranged for maximum efficiency, and you understand the basics of cooking and food safety, it's time to concentrate on filling the store cupboard, freezer and fridge. Everyone should have basic items like oil, flour, salt, pepper, butter, eggs, milk, and canned and frozen fruits and vegetables. The items you choose beyond that will depend on the recipes you make.

Salads and simple side dishes are probably the easiest foods to make. Salads, which are just combined and tossed with a dressing, can be an entire meal. Following these easy recipes will give you a lot of confidence. And a side dish, such as roast potatoes or steamed broccoli, is perfect for accompanying a rotisserie chicken from the supermarket or one of those marinated salmon fillets you just bake and eat.

If your family loves beef, start by cooking simple beef recipes. Marinated and grilled or griddled steaks, beef stir-fries and casseroles are good recipes to choose. A meat pasta sauce, served over linguine or penne, and a classic meatloaf are easy to make too.

For chicken lovers, look for recipes using baked, pan-fried, or grilled boneless, skinless chicken breasts. This cut of poultry is the easiest to work with: it cooks very quickly, and it's adaptable to many cuisines and flavours. For fish lovers, boneless fillets are the easiest to handle and cook. They cook very quickly, and fillets of fish such as salmon, hake, cod or halibut can be used in many different recipes. Baked and grilled fish fillets make quick and simple meals. And for pork lovers, look for simple recipes that use pork tenderloin and pork chops. Both these cuts of meat cook quickly, are easy to work with, and again pair well with lots of different flavours.

Once you've become comfortable making the basic recipes for each different cut of meat and the different categories of recipes, you can start having fun. Use the same type of food, proportions and cooking times as in the original recipe but add your own touches. Use your family's favourite ingredients, or change the seasonings, spices and herbs to the ones you like best.

For instance, once you've mastered grilling fish fillets with a simple mustard glaze, try making your own glaze using Tex-Mex ingredients such as chilli powder or fresh chopped chillis and salsa. Or add a Spanish flair with a glaze made from paprika, ground almonds, some chopped olives, lemon juice and sour cream. Substitute mushrooms and green peppers for cherry tomatoes and courgettes in a chicken quiche, or add some jalapeño peppers and spicy salsa to a salad for some extra zing.

When you create a recipe that you and your family love, remember to write it down. It's hard to recreate a successful recipe from memory, even if it's very simple. Keep notes as you work and your cooking skills will get better and better as your repertoire increases.

Now let's start cooking! The initial work and preparation that may be involved in transforming your kitchen into an efficient work space for quick and easy cooking may seem daunting, but once you've accomplished that, you'll be able to get an excellent and delicious dinner on the table in about 30 minutes, from start to finish.

THE QUICK AND EASY KITCHEN

An organized work space, from an efficient work triangle to well-planned cupboards, is the key to speedy cooking

A well-stocked and organized store cupboard, fridge and freezer make cooking easy and pleasurable. With a good supply of food on hand in an organized space to make tried-and-trusted recipes, you'll be able to whip up great breakfasts, lunches, snacks and dinners at a moment's notice. Even if you have a less than desirable kitchen, you can arrange your working space and equipment to help you prepare food quickly and efficiently. You can add a small freestanding table for extra work surface, clear paths between appliances and set up mini work stations. A large kitchen can be broken down into several preparation areas to allow more than one person to work comfortably in the space.

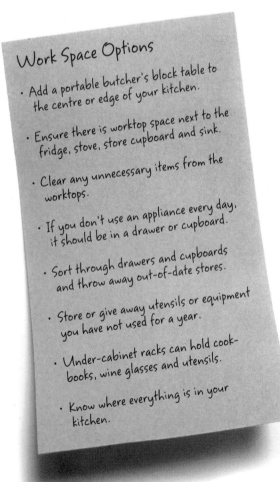

Work Space Options

- Add a portable butcher's block table to the centre or edge of your kitchen.

- Ensure there is worktop space next to the fridge, stove, store cupboard and sink.

- Clear any unnecessary items from the worktops.

- If you don't use an appliance every day, it should be in a drawer or cupboard.

- Sort through drawers and cupboards and throw away out-of-date stores.

- Store or give away utensils or equipment you have not used for a year.

- Under-cabinet racks can hold cookbooks, wine glasses and utensils.

- Know where everything is in your kitchen.

Work Triangle

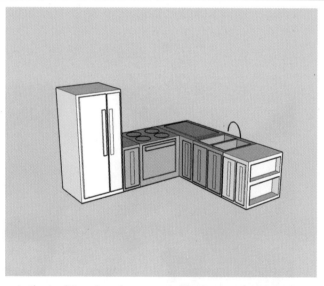

- In the traditional work triangle, the sink, stove and fridge are the three points.

- The distance between the points of the triangle should be 1.2–3 m. Any closer, and there isn't enough worktop space. Any further, and cooking will be tiring.

- That's a good arrangement, but some larger kitchens may have two or even three work triangles so more than one cook can perform tasks in comfort.

- An island can break a large kitchen up to make the work triangle a more convenient size.

It's important to keep the worktops free of clutter; if you find that your work surfaces are used for everything from homework to bill paying, find other areas of the house for those tasks and keep the worktops free for cooking.

Keep the kitchen, refrigerator, freezer and store cupboards clean and well organized. Everything, from foil to canned beans, should have a 'home': that way, you can always find what you need. And make sure that every utensil, piece of equipment, food item and tool is returned to its home after it is used and cleaned.

Shopping and Organizing Tips

- Shopping efficiently can save you money, and also saves time. Make a list every time you go shopping and stick to it, but take advantage of special offers.

- Go to your local supermarket at times when it's not crowded, and plan your list according to its layout.

- Try not to take children with you when shopping. Use coupons as much as possible, and come straight home from the shop.

- Your store cupboard should be organized by food category. Make sure you can see all the food; use risers for the backs of shelves.

Organized Fridge and Freezer

- Clean out the refrigerator once a week, so you know what foods need to be used and replenished.

- Remove everything, check the use-by dates, throw away any old food, and clean the shelves with soapy water.

- Clean your freezer every three to four months. For most energy efficiency, the freezer should be full.

- A notebook placed next to the freezer will help you remember what's inside, what you should use by certain dates, and what you need to replenish.

FRIDGE STAPLES

These staples are used in almost every recipe

Many of the ingredients used in the recipes in this book need to be stored in the refrigerator after opening. All packaged foods should have use-by or best-before dates stamped on the packaging.

Most staples such as salad dressings, mayonnaise and cheeses should be used within one to two months of opening. Fresh fruits and vegetables can be stored for only a few days until they lose quality or start to wilt or develop soft spots. Meats should be used or frozen within one to three days; seafood is best eaten on the day of purchase, pork, chicken and beef a bit later. Dairy products are marked with sell-by dates and use-by dates a few days later.

Organize your refrigerator by using the shelves to group the foods. Keep all dairy products on the top shelf, use the

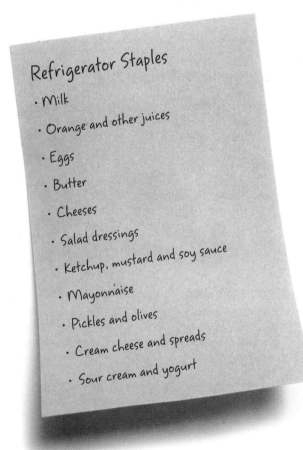

Refrigerator Staples

• Milk

• Orange and other juices

• Eggs

• Butter

• Cheeses

• Salad dressings

• Ketchup, mustard and soy sauce

• Mayonnaise

• Pickles and olives

• Cream cheese and spreads

• Sour cream and yogurt

Dairy Products

- It is very important to follow the use-by dates on dairy products. Throw away any product past its date.

- Keep dairy products in the body of the refrigerator, not the door (except for butter and milk), because the door area is warmer.

- Think about using the drawers to hold these products, which can be stored for longer periods of time.

- Keep milk, cream, buttermilk, yogurt and cheeses tightly wrapped or sealed, because they can easily pick up stray refrigerator odours.

second shelf for salad dressings and cheeses, and the third and fourth shelves for the perishable products you buy and use frequently. The door is a good place to store ketchup, mustard, pickles and olives. Oddly enough, the door, which often has those cute little indentations to hold eggs, is not the best place to store them; it's too warm. Keep eggs in their original carton in the body of the fridge.

A notepad with a magnetic back and attached pencil should be on your refrigerator to keep track of foods you need to add to your shopping list.

Condiments

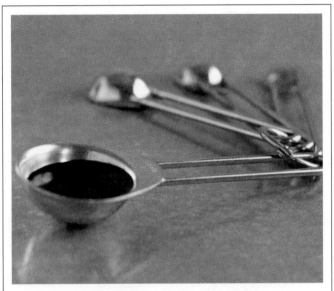

- Even condiments such as soy sauce, hoisin sauce, ketchup and mustard eventually need to be replaced.

- Read labels carefully. Many condiments instruct you to store them in the refrigerator once opened; others do not need chilling.

- The use-by date on the label applies to the unopened jar.

- In the door, arrange the bottles by height, placing the taller products at the back. It's easier to see what you have at a glance.

Eggs and Butter

- Keep eggs in their carton, even if your fridge door has a special compartment for holding eggs. The jostling from opening and closing the door is too much.

- Eggshells are porous, and will absorb strong smells from other foods in the fridge. Keep everything well wrapped to avoid eggs and dairy foods being contaminated.

- Butter lasts for a long time as long as it is properly wrapped. Keep it in the butter shelf in the door.

3

STORE-CUPBOARD STAPLES

A well-stocked store cupboard helps you make delicious meals at very short notice

The store cupboard can act as a mini grocery store when it's complete and well stocked. Once you have the staples, buy the fun foods that you want to add flavour and character to your dishes.

Flour, sugar, vinegar, oil, pasta and rice are all basic store-cupboard staples. Depending on what you cook and bake,

other staples can include canned fruits and vegetables, special seasonings such as stir-fry sauces and spice blends, and pasta and cooking sauces.

Have fun and expand your repertoire by buying flavoured oils and vinegars, different shaped pastas, unusual dried herbs and spices and exotic canned produce. Take some

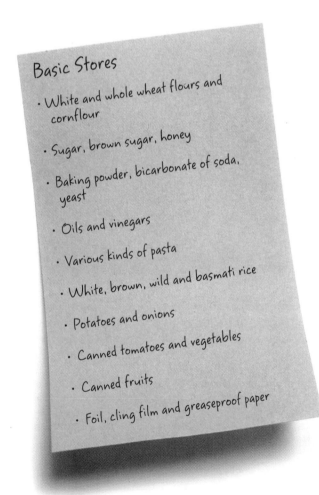

Basic Stores

- White and whole wheat flours and cornflour

- Sugar, brown sugar, honey

- Baking powder, bicarbonate of soda, yeast

- Oils and vinegars

- Various kinds of pasta

- White, brown, wild and basmati rice

- Potatoes and onions

- Canned tomatoes and vegetables

- Canned fruits

- Foil, cling film and greaseproof paper

Organizing Store-Cupboard Staples

- Just as you do in the refrigerator, organize your stores according to food categories.

- On one shelf, keep baking staples such as flour, sugar, brown sugar, baking powder, spices and extracts. Decant dry ingredients into tightly sealed containers.

- On another shelf, store pasta, grains and rice, along with canned fruits and vegetables, juices and fizzy drinks.

- And on the other shelves store measuring equipment, mixing bowls, baking and cake tins, and foil.

time every month to go along the aisles of the supermarket and look for new products you may want to try.

Clean out your store cupboard every month or two. Remove all items, reorganize if necessary, wash down the shelves and replace food. Take the time to look at all of the expiration and use-by dates on the products. Use foods close to the dates, or throw them away if you know you won't use them. Use wire shelf organizers, if necessary, so you can see all the way to the back of the shelves.

ZOOM

Insects like moths, fruit flies and other pests love munching on dry foods such as flour, pasta and rice, and spilled foods such as honey and juices. You can buy traps that will control any pests but they must be labelled food-safe. Keep all food in sealed containers and clean cupboard shelves regularly to reduce the risk of attracting mice.

Storing Pasta

- Dried pasta keeps well for a long time at room temperature. Have a good selection of different shapes and sizes on hand.

- You can decant the pasta into glass or plastic containers with a tight seal. This is also decorative!

- If you do decant the pasta, remember to make a note of the cooking time in a small notebook kept on the pasta shelf.

- Well-sealed containers will reduce the chance of infestation by pests.

Canned Vegetables and Fruits

- A good stash of canned tomato products, plus pasta, means you can always make a meal in minutes.

- Canned chopped tomatoes, tomato juice, purée, passata and tomato sauce all belong on your store-cupboard shelves.

- Canned vegetables are also important staples. Look for flavoured vegetables, such as corn with peppers and artichokes packed in a spicy marinade, for double duty.

- Canned fruits add interest to salads and can be the basis for quick and simple desserts.

FREEZER STAPLES

Your freezer can become your own in-house store, with ingredients to inspire delicious meals

A stand-alone freezer is a real luxury and the perfect aid for quick and easy cooking. But with just the freezer attached to your refrigerator, you can stock a great selection of foods that will help you get food on the table in a flash.

Any freezer has to be well organized. You need to know what's in it. No packages of mystery meat are allowed! Wrap and label everything, and keep a notebook with a running tab of what the freezer contains. When you use an item, cross it out on the running tab. If it's a staple, make a note of it on your shopping list so you can replace it.

You can freeze almost anything as long as it's prepared and wrapped properly. Be sure to use freezer wrap, paper or

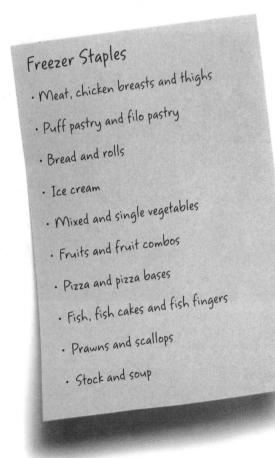

Freezer Staples

- Meat, chicken breasts and thighs
- Puff pastry and filo pastry
- Bread and rolls
- Ice cream
- Mixed and single vegetables
- Fruits and fruit combos
- Pizza and pizza bases
- Fish, fish cakes and fish fingers
- Prawns and scallops
- Stock and soup

Frozen Meat and Fish

- Meat and fish freeze very well. You should have a good supply of meats, including beef, pork and chicken, in your freezer.

- Well-wrapped meat and fish should be clearly labelled and dated. Use them within six months, otherwise the flavour will deteriorate.

- To thaw meat, leave it in the refrigerator overnight, or if you're going to cook it immediately use the micro-wave. Never thaw meats at room temperature.

- You can cook some meat and fish from frozen, especially commercially prepared products.

freezer bags; ordinary wraps and foils aren't thick enough to protect the food from the harsh freezer environment.

Just as with the store cupboard, you must mark and label every food that goes into your freezer. Use a chinagraph pencil. As a general rule, use the food within one year.

Stock your freezer with purchased and homemade foods for your own in-house mini supermarket. Keep in mind that a freezer thermometer is an essential tool. Your freezer should always be at −18°C or lower.

· · · · · · · · · · · · *RED ● LIGHT* · · · · · · · · · · · ·

Never freeze meats in their original packaging. Freezer burn is the number one cause of meats spoiling when frozen. It is caused by dehydration. The freezer is a very dry place. Improperly wrapped foods will dry out. Remove meat from the original packaging (retaining any labels or cooking instructions) and wrap in freezer bags.

Freezer Tips

- Every freezer is more efficient and freezes food more evenly when it's full. But don't pack food tightly. There should be about 25 mm of airspace around each package so the cold air can circulate.

- Most foods should be thawed in the refrigerator, but some, like breads, can safely thaw at room temperature.

- You can refreeze some foods, like filo pastry or previously frozen food that has been thoroughly cooked. Food thawed in the refrigerator can be refrozen, but may lose quality.

Freezing Homemade Foods

- When you add homemade foods to the freezer, they should already be cool, to avoid raising the temperature in the freezer.

- Refrigerate hot foods or place them in an ice water bath so they cool quickly, then wrap well and freeze.

- You want foods to get quickly out of the danger zone of 5–60°C.

- If your electricity supply is interrupted, don't open the freezer. The food should stay frozen for 24 hours. If it still has ice crystals, it is safe to eat.

FRESH FOODS

Shop for fresh foods a few times a week to supplement your stores

Once you have a good stock of food on hand in the store cupboard, fridge and freezer, it's time to shop for fresh foods. Shop once or twice a week for these products. Be sure to store perishable foods in the refrigerator immediately and wrap according to the needs of the food.

When you shop for perishable foods, plan your trip so you return home immediately. Refrigerate these foods within two hours; one hour in the summer.

Designate a special shelf or spot in your refrigerator and store cupboard for fresh foods. Since waste is the biggest food budget-buster, you need to know what you have on hand and use it or freeze it while the food retains quality. Look through these shelves every day and rotate foods so you use the older foods first, before they deteriorate.

Since the atmosphere in the refrigerator is very dry, unwrapped fresh foods will quickly dry out, shrivel or

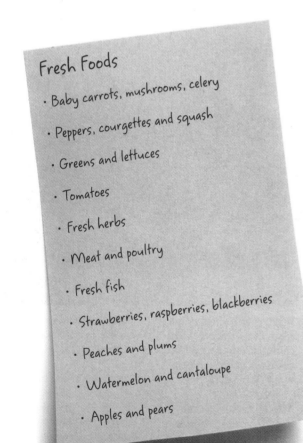

Fresh Foods

- Baby carrots, mushrooms, celery
- Peppers, courgettes and squash
- Greens and lettuces
- Tomatoes
- Fresh herbs
- Meat and poultry
- Fresh fish
- Strawberries, raspberries, blackberries
- Peaches and plums
- Watermelon and cantaloupe
- Apples and pears

Fresh Meat and Fish

- Fresh meat should last about two to three days in your refrigerator. Freeze it after that time. Always buy fresh fish on the day you're going to cook it.

- Read your refrigerator manual to discover the coldest part of the appliance, then store fresh meat there.

- Packaged meat will have expiration dates that tell you to use or freeze by that time. If you buy meat from the butcher, mark the date of purchase on it.

- Use the meat within three days, including marinating time. And always marinate meat in the fridge.

8

otherwise spoil. More delicate foods can also absorb the flavours of other foods. It's a good idea to keep everything in your fridge sealed in plastic boxes or wrapped in good quality bags or wrap.

Meats should always be refrigerated. Leafy greens and tender fruits and vegetables should be refrigerated too. Others, such as apples and pears, store well at room temperature. Don't refrigerate bananas, tomatoes, potatoes or onions. The chill changes cell structures, reducing quality and altering flavour in these foods.

ZOOM

You may have come across 'green storage bags', which claim to keep produce from becoming overripe by absorbing ethylene gas. Tests have shown that they help, but food doesn't stay fresh as long as is claimed. The best way to prevent waste is to keep an eye on food and use it at its peak.

Fresh Fruit

- Fresh fruit should be refrigerated unless it isn't quite ripe. Most fruits ripen well at room temperature.

- Berries are very perishable. They should be stored in the refrigerator, and should never be washed until you're ready to use them.

- If you like to bite into a cold, crisp apple or juicy pear, refrigerate the fruit for a few hours before eating.

- Keep fresh fruit well wrapped. The refrigerator is a very dry place, and delicate fruit can shrivel easily.

Fresh Vegetables

- Fresh vegetables that are high in water content, including peppers, courgettes and celery, should be well wrapped.

- Some refrigerator drawers have special controls that help regulate temperature and humidity, perfect for fresh produce.

- Be sure to use the produce in those drawers every day. Examine the food for any sign of decay, and keep the drawers impeccably clean.

- Read your manual to learn how to use the temperature and moisture controls in the drawers.

VALUE-ADDED FOODS

Foods that combine more than one ingredient save steps in preparation and cooking

One of the best ways to eliminate time in cooking is to use foods that replace two or more steps. Ready-made pasta sauces, marinades, salad dressings and mixes save time in the kitchen.

Be sure to choose value-added foods carefully. Read labels and pick the products that are closest to fresh, with as few artificial ingredients as possible. You may also be able to choose low-fat and low-sodium versions of these improved products, and sometimes organic varieties are available.

Value-added foods for the store cupboard include marinades, salad dressings, bread and cake mixes, cooking sauces, and flavoured vinegars. Freezer value-added foods include frozen pastas, pasta and vegetable combinations, mixtures

Value-Added Foods

- Tortellini and ravioli
- Classic and flavoured pesto
- Prepared fruits and vegetables
- Marinated meats
- Marinades and salad dressings
- Cake and dessert mixes
- Ready-made tart cases
- Frozen pasta and vegetable combos
- Pasta and stir-fry sauces
- Seasoned canned vegetables
- Fresh stocks

Filled Pasta

- Filled pasta shapes include tortellini, ravioli and cappelletti, with a range of fillings.

- You can freeze the pasta on the day of purchase and cook them from frozen.

- They can be quickly made into a meal with a simple butter sauce.

- They make delicious additions to soups and salads, or can be mixed with vegetables in a sauce.

- Cook the pasta according to the package directions. They usually need just a couple of minutes, so don't overcook them.

of soft fruits, and prepared meat and fish. And within the past decade, supermarkets have added lots of refrigerator value-added foods, from prepared carrot sticks and fruit combinations to stir-fry blends and salad mixes.

With a good supply of these foods on hand, you'll be able to whip up a pasta supper or a meal on the barbecue in minutes, without having to set foot out of the front door. When you find a product that you like and use, always pick up a can or a package or two when you see them in the supermarket, so you're prepared.

GREEN ● LIGHT

There are always new value-added foods coming on to the market. Take some time each month to look through the canned food, frozen food and dry goods aisles of the supermarket. Try these new foods and add them to your regular shopping list if you and your family like them. Be sure that the value that is added works for you and really does save time.

Prepared Pasta Sauces

- The greatest advances in prepared sauces have been in the pasta sauce department. Pesto and tomato sauces are essentials.

- These sauces are great straight out of the jar, or you can add your own twist with herbs, spices or liqueurs.

- Bottled sauces can be high in sodium, so read labels carefully and choose wisely.

- Combine these sauces with prepared vegetables and value-added pastas to save time and serve delicious meals quickly.

Dessert Products

- Desserts can be made in a flash using value-added products like ready-made pastry cases, whipped toppings and chocolate chips.

- These products have expiration dates, so follow them closely and store them according to the package directions.

- You can make your own value-added products and freeze them for later use. Good choices include biscuit dough, flan cases and bread and pizza dough.

- Store a variety of dessert products, such as tartlet cases, pie fillings and pudding mixes.

POTS AND PANS

Sturdy, well-made pots and pans in a variety of sizes will help you cook most foods

A good-quality, heavy-duty set of pans is essential for quick and easy cooking. You don't need to buy a complete set; buy individual pieces to suit the way you cook.

Look for stainless steel, anodized aluminium, heatproof glass or enamelled cast iron equipment that is solidly made. You may spend more for a good set of pans, but they will last for a lifetime. It's a good idea to look for pans that are also ovenproof. That means the handles can be placed in the oven or under the grill without danger of melting.

Always lift and handle equipment before you buy it. Make sure that the handles of the pans feel good in your hand; that the weight is evenly balanced, and that the pans aren't too

Cookware Set

- A cookware set should include one 22-cm frying pan, one 20-cm sauté pan, one 3-litre and one 2-litre saucepan, a large stockpot and a 20-cm omelette pan.

- Vary this collection depending on your cooking needs. Look for 18/10-gauge steel.

- If you cook pasta, buy a pasta or steamer insert for the stockpot, which will enable you to easily drain cooked pasta and vegetables.

- All the pans should have close-fitting lids and solid, well-attached handles.

Wok and Steamer

- A wok is a good addition to your collection. Its sloping sides help you keep the food moving when you stir-fry.

- A wok should have a sturdy handle that doesn't conduct heat so you can hold it while you cook. Do not purchase nonstick woks because they can scratch easily.

- A steamer addition makes cooking vegetables and fish very easy. Collapsible steamers take up less storage space.

- Separate steamers, especially when made of bamboo, also look beautiful and can be used to serve food at the table.

heavy. Some large pans can be very heavy, especially if they are made of cast iron.

Saucepans are about 10–13 cm deep and have straight sides. Frying pans have sloping or flared sides, and sauté pans have fairly low, straight sides and a thick base. Saucepans and sauté pans come with lids.

Some manufacturers combine different sizes of pans into sets. If you find one that includes the pans you need, at a good price, buy it. You can always add more pans as you need them in the future.

ZOOM

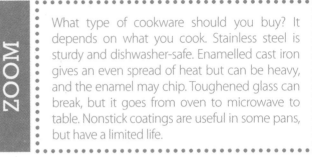

What type of cookware should you buy? It depends on what you cook. Stainless steel is sturdy and dishwasher-safe. Enamelled cast iron gives an even spread of heat but can be heavy, and the enamel may chip. Toughened glass can break, but it goes from oven to microwave to table. Nonstick coatings are useful in some pans, but have a limited life.

Ovenproof Cookware

- Glass cookware can be used on the hob, in the oven, in the microwave and even in the freezer.

- Ovenproof pans can be made of tempered glass but it conducts heat unevenly so isn't the best choice if you do lots of pan-frying.

- Cast-iron casseroles are ideal for long, slow cooking in the oven. Ovenproof ceramic casseroles are more limited because they can- not be used on the hob.

- Enamel-coated cast iron chips or cracks fairly easily so must be handled gently.

Baking Sheets

- Baking sheets are used for more than baking biscuits. Look for sturdy equipment that will conduct heat evenly and won't buckle in the heat of the oven.

- Buy at least two baking sheets so you always have one ready to use and for baking large batches.

- Baking sheets can be used to flash-freeze food and hold foods going out to the barbecue. Purchase some baking sheets with sides and some without.

- Buy some half-size and some full-size baking sheets for different-sized batches of biscuits.

UTENSILS FOR PREPARATION

Utensils from knives to mandolines to assist in food preparation

Low-tech preparation equipment includes tools and utensils that don't use electricity and usually have only one purpose. Many have been around for years. Some of these utensils have been updated with the latest materials, but they have always been an essential part of the quick and easy kitchen.

Buy the best quality preparation equipment you can afford. A good set of knives is essential to a good kitchen experience; and they have to be kept sharp. Tools such as graters, microplanes and mandolines make food preparation easy. And when you have an easy time in the kitchen, you'll be encouraged you to spend more time there.

You can buy this equipment in kitchenware shops, hardware and department stores, large supermarkets and online. You'll find apple corers, swivel-bladed vegetable peelers, and other tools in many styles and levels of quality. And once you start looking you'll find a host of specialist gadgets.

Knives

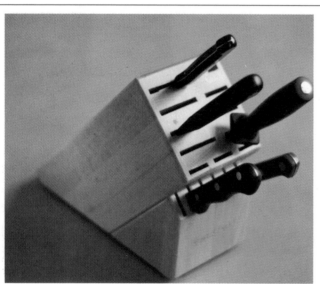

- Whether you buy knives individually or in sets, there are certain basic knives every kitchen needs.

- A chef's knife, two paring knives of different sizes, a utility knife, a bread knife, scissors and a sharpening steel are essentials.

- Purchase other knives, such as boning knives, as you need them. A knife block keeps them stored safely.

- Be sure that any knife you buy is heavy duty, with a full tang, or steel shaft, running the length of the handle.

Mandoline

- A mandoline is a slicing tool that can speed preparation and allow you to make fancy cuts. The mandoline is sharp and should have good safety features.

- You can julienne vegetables or cut potatoes into chips or waffle slices with a mandoline.

- The price range for this tool is very wide. You can find a mandoline for under £5, while others retail for nearly £100.

- Read reviews online to find the best tool for you. Then make sure you understand how to use it before you start slicing.

Store the equipment in drawers separated by type. But it's not a good idea to store knives in drawers because it's too easy to cut yourself reaching for one.

Having bought your equipment, you need to take care of it. Clean using hot soapy water, and dry each item thoroughly after each use. If the tool is dishwasher-safe, that's the best way to clean it. Be sure to follow the manufacturer's instructions for cleaning and storage. Your tools should last a lifetime with proper care.

MAKE IT EASY

When you've been cooking for a while in your kitchen, clean out your drawers. The most efficient kitchen will have only those tools that you use, plus duplicates of your favourites. If there are tools you haven't used for a year, put them in a box and store them elsewhere. If you haven't looked for that tool in another year, give it away or throw it out.

Graters

- Graters are excellent tools, whether you're grating 200 g for a pizza or just a small amount for a garnish.

- Have several different sizes of grater in your kitchen drawers. Box graters can also serve as measuring tools, while microplane graters are good for garnishing.

- Buy microplane graters in hardware and kitchen shops. You can also use them for grating nutmeg and zesting citrus fruit.

- Be careful with your fingers when using graters. Work slowly, and discard the last bit of food.

Wire Whisks

- Wire whisks are essential for making lump-free batters and puddings.

- They can be used to whip cream and egg whites, though an electric hand whisk is much faster.

- During cooking a wire whisk can get into the corners of a pan so sauces and custards don't burn.

- Large whisks shouldn't be too big or they can become unwieldy. Look for a whisk about 20 cm long.

- Small whisks can be very handy when making a small amount of sauce.

HIGH-TECH PREP EQUIPMENT

From hand blenders for puréeing to electronic scales, these tools are like kitchen assistants

There are many wonderful appliances that truly do cut down on food preparation time. Mixers, blenders and food processors make quick work of chopped fruit, grated cheese and julienned vegetables.

Scales are essential if you do a lot of baking, as it's important to weigh ingredients accurately. And the newer blenders are very powerful machines, with special actions that make the appliance very efficient.

As with pans and utensils, the sturdier and more well-made the equipment you buy, the longer it will last. Heavy-duty food processors, blenders and mixers are serious appliances. Study online recommendations before you buy.

Food Processors

- If you have a large family and often prepare large quantities of food, a full-size food processor is probably for you.

- But if you only make small quantities, think about a mini food processor. This smaller appliance can be very versatile.

- Be very careful of the food processor blades because they are razor sharp. Choose a processor that has dishwasher-safe blades and attachments.

- Clean the food processor casing regularly and inspect the flex before each use.

Blenders

- Blenders can do everything from mixing drinks and smoothies to chopping vegetables and blending soups.

- The newest blenders have large motors and specially shaped blades to move the food around.

- 'Wave action' technology moves the food from the top to bottom, so stopping to scrape down the sides is a thing of the past.

- Hand blenders can be used to purée soups directly in the pan on the stove or in a slow cooker.

The appliances you buy will depend on the food you make. If you use lots of shredded vegetables and grated cheese in your cooking, a food processor will come in handy. If you make lots of soups, a hand blender is a good choice.

Small versions of larger appliances may be just what you need. A mini food processor, for instance, can be just as powerful as a full-size processor, but is less expensive, takes up less worktop space and is easier to clean.

Read through the manufacturer's instruction booklet completely before using the equipment.

Mixers

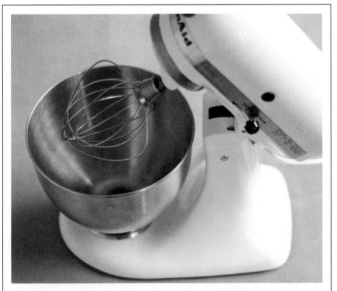

- Stand mixers and hand mixers are both useful. If you make lots of bread and cakes, consider investing in a stand mixer.

- With a stand mixer and several bowls and paddles, you can quickly make several batches of dough.

- Hand mixers are more powerful than ever. They can't knead dough, but can easily mix cake batters and whip cream and egg whites.

- Hand mixers work well for almost every kitchen need, and are much less costly.

Scales

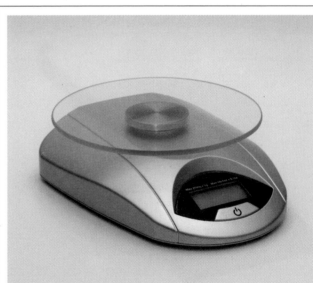

- Scales, whether manual or digital, measure ingredients accurately and can help to control portion sizes.

- When baking, measuring ingredients by weight is the most accurate way and will give you the best results.

- High-tech scales can have the nutritional content of the food you are weighing programmed into them. You can add up to 1,000 foods to the programmes in these dietary computer scales. You can also record food intake and keep track of total calories.

COOKING UTENSILS
Find tools you can trust when handling food while cooking

Well-made cooking utensils are like extensions of your hands. They have to be comfortable and easy to use and must be sturdy. Hold them in your hand before you buy.

A good quality utensil will last for many years; you don't want to buy something flimsy. There's nothing more frustrating than stirring a thick icing and having the handle snap off the spatula.

Essential equipment includes heatproof spatulas, wooden spoons, slotted spoons, a measuring jug, wire whisks, a sieve with a handle, a ladle, and rubber spatulas for scraping mixtures out of food processors and mixing bowls.

Take some time and browse through a kitchen shop or a well-equipped department store. There are lots of specialized utensils that you may want to buy if it will make your

Spatulas

- There are two kinds of spatulas: the ones with a slight curve that are used for scraping, and stiff, flat spatulas used for lifting.

- Silicone spatulas are the newest addition to the spatula family. These utensils are heatproof and durable.

- You can find different sizes and shapes of these spatulas for every need. Fish spatulas are very wide and shallow.

- Round spatulas work well for transferring cookies to cooling racks and flipping eggs or fish cakes.

Silicone Tools

- There are many kitchen tools made of silicone. This material stands up well to high heat and cleans beautifully.

- Silicone basting brushes are great for basting foods on the barbecue. They are dishwasher safe and easy to clean.

- Silicone pot holders and oven gloves can stand up to very high heat, protecting your hands from pans and hot food.

- Most good quality silicone products, such as spatulas and brushes, have steel handles or steel cores.

18

cooking chores easier. Not everyone needs a prawn deveiner or an egg slicer, but if you do, you shouldn't feel guilty about buying one.

You may want to keep some of these utensils in a decorative ceramic or stoneware pot sitting on the worktop for easy access. That way it's easy to see what you have on hand while you're busy cooking.

Wooden Spoons

- Wooden spoons and spatulas are indispensable for stirring and moving food around when cooking in a pan on the hob.

- Wood is a poor conductor of heat, so the handle of the spoon stays cool while you stir.

- Wooden tools will not scratch nonstick pans.

- Build up a collection of spoons and spatulas in different shapes and sizes.

- Wood has natural antibacterial properties and is safe to use with food.

Specialized Tools

- A number of kitchen tools are essential for specific tasks in cooking. A masher is the best tool for mashing vegetables.

- Apart from serving soup, a ladle works as a measure when adding stock to risotto, or pouring pancake batter on to a griddle.

- Tongs are essential if you do a lot of grilling, as is protection for your hands: invest in a pair of oven mitts.

- Every kitchen shop stocks hundreds of handy gadgets, but what you need depends on the type of food you cook. Buy things as you need them.

TIME-SAVING COOKING DEVICES

Small appliances from microwave ovens to rice cookers can make quick work of cooking meals

Small appliances make quick and easy cooking very simple. A rice cooker makes rice perfectly while you are stir-frying the chicken and vegetables it will accompany. A microwave oven is great for preparing food and making complete meals. And a breadmaker can work away all night making you a delicious fresh loaf in time for breakfast.

Many of these appliances have multiple uses. A rice cooker can be used to cook other foods; the Internet has lots of recipes. A dual-contact grill can be equipped with different plates to cook everything from a grilled panini to pancakes.

There are many different models on the market, all with different pros and cons, so when you're looking for a small appliance

Dual-Contact Grill

- Dual-contact grills are worktop appliances that cook food on both sides at the same time.

- George Foreman is one leading brand of this type of grill.

- The large versions of these grills can cook enough food for four to six people at once. Grease and fat drain away during cooking, so the food is healthy too.

- The food cooked on these grills has lots of flavour without the hassle of dealing with charcoal or gas in an outdoor barbecue.

Automatic Breadmaker

- A programmable automatic breadmaker allows you to enjoy fresh-baked bread every day.

- The ingredients are measured into the pan and once the programme is set the machine mixes and kneads the dough, waits for it to prove and then bakes it.

- Breadmakers use instant yeast, which is activated only when it comes in contact with the liquid in the recipe.

- Modern breadmakers can also be set to prepare dough without baking (for pizzas), and to add ingredients such as fruit and nuts.

it's helpful to read reviews online or in consumer magazines. Compare products in the store to see which one has the features you want.

Always fill out warranty cards, and keep the purchase information, together with the instruction and care booklets, in a drawer or cupboard. Even these things should have a 'home'.

Be sure that you understand how the machines function and read the safety precautions before you start using them. With care, these appliances, which aren't inexpensive, can last for years.

Rice Cooker

- A rice cooker can do more than just cook plain rice! You can cook rice pudding, macaroni cheese, potatoes and main dishes.

- Look for a rice cooker with the largest capacity you can afford. The capacity is measured in terms of the amount of raw rice it holds.

- You can brown foods, cook and keep them warm in a rice cooker.

- The easiest way to extend the use of the cooker is to cook rice to which you have added other ingredients, such as spices, herbs and vegetables.

Microwave Oven

- The microwave oven hasn't transformed the kitchen as much as some people at first thought it would. Most cooks use it mainly as a preparation tool.

- Microwave ovens cook by making molecules vibrate, creating heat in the food.

- The waves the oven uses are radio waves; they are not radioactive.

- Follow cooking, covering, stirring, venting and standing times to the letter for best results.

STIR-FRYING

Learn the basics of stir-frying, one of the quickest cooking methods on the planet

Stir-frying is a method of cooking food quickly. The wok or frying pan is heated until very hot, then a small amount of oil is added. The food, cut into small pieces, cooks very fast and is kept moving by a stirring action, hence the name.

Stir-frying was originally developed in Asian cuisines as a cooking style for use over wood-fired stoves, in order to conserve precious fuel. Since the food cooks so quickly, less fuel can be used.

This method of cooking helps preserve nutrients and colour in vegetables. A sauce, sometimes a marinade that has been used to tenderize the meat, is usually added during the last few minutes to blend the ingredients and add flavour.

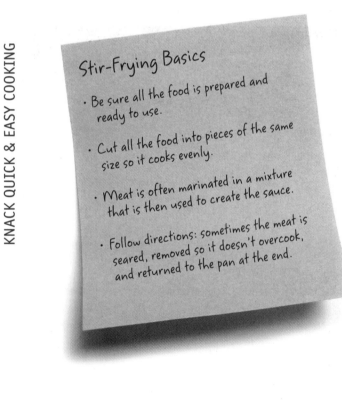

Stir-Frying Basics

• Be sure all the food is prepared and ready to use.

• Cut all the food into pieces of the same size so it cooks evenly.

• Meat is often marinated in a mixture that is then used to create the sauce.

• Follow directions: sometimes the meat is seared, removed so it doesn't overcook, and returned to the pan at the end.

Wok on Heat

• Preheat the wok on the hob before you add the oil and the rest of the ingredients.

• It's not necessary to buy a nonstick wok. If you pre-heat the wok and add the oil, then let the oil get hot before adding the food, the food won't stick.

• If you're adding eggs, as in stir-fried rice, make a well in the centre of the food and add egg; cook until done.

• Do not interrupt the cook-ing when stir-frying, or the food will overcook.

22

Stir-frying isn't difficult, it just takes a bit of practice to turn all the food evenly. After a minute or two, you will fall naturally into a pattern.

You don't need a wok to stir-fry. A large frying pan with sloping sides is a good substitute.

Meat and vegetables can be prepared ahead of time and quickly cooked just before serving. Use ready-prepared stir-fry vegetable mixtures for an even quicker meal.

Stir-fried food is often served with rice: cook that in your rice cooker to make serving these healthy meals easy.

Stir-Frying in Wok

- The food has to be kept moving as it cooks. You can use a metal, wooden or silicone rubber spatula.

- Use your dominant hand to stir the food, and your non-dominant hand to hold the wok as the food cooks.

- Have all the ingredients lined up by the stove, in the order in which they will be added to the wok.

- The whole cooking process should be done in about 6–8 minutes.

Stir-Frying in Frying Pan

- Add the vegetables to the pan in the order of cooking time. Add vegetables that need longer cooking, like carrots and potatoes, first.

- Then add more tender vegetables. The harder vegetables continue to cook while the soft vegetables become crisp-tender.

- If you add a sauce at the end of the cooking time, stir it thoroughly so the seasonings and any thickening are well blended.

- This type of dish should be served immediately, while the ingredients are still piping hot.

COOKING METHODS

23

PAN-FRYING

There are rules to learn about pan-frying to create juicy and delicious meals

Pan-frying, which is also known as sautéing, is a quick cooking method that uses the hob or an electric frying pan.

A small amount of fat is placed in the pan, and then the food is added, quickly cooked and then lifted out and drained. The fat left in the pan can be poured off and the residue used to make a sauce to finish the dish.

It's important to preheat the pan and get the fat hot before adding the food. If it's not hot enough, the food will steam instead of frying and will absorb some of the oil. If the oil is too hot, the food can burn.

You need to know the smoking point of the oil you use. This is the temperature at which the oil begins to break down

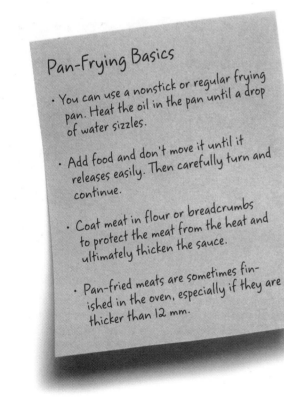

Pan-Frying Basics

- You can use a nonstick or regular frying pan. Heat the oil in the pan until a drop of water sizzles.

- Add food and don't move it until it releases easily. Then carefully turn and continue.

- Coat meat in flour or breadcrumbs to protect the meat from the heat and ultimately thicken the sauce.

- Pan-fried meats are sometimes finished in the oven, especially if they are thicker than 12 mm.

Pan-Frying Bacon

- Rashers of bacon are good candidates for pan-frying.

- When you pan-fry meat, you must let the pieces cook until they release easily. If you try to move the meat by force, it will tear.

- When the meat is done on one side, it will release easily. Bacon should be turned often so it browns evenly. Other meats and fish need to be turned only once.

- Cook until the outside is golden brown. You can check doneness with the point of a knife.

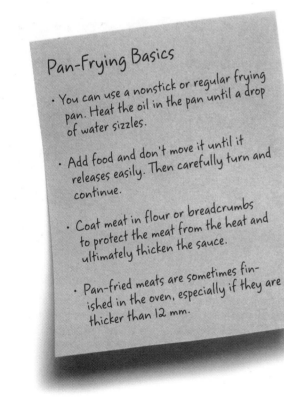

KNACK QUICK & EASY COOKING

24

and starts to smoke. When the oil reaches this temperature, byproducts can add an unpleasant taste to food.

Regular olive oil can be used for pan-frying since its smoking point is around 215°C, but extra-virgin olive oil can have a lower smoking point. Since the temperature of the pan is around 175–200°C, any oil with a smoking point above 215°C will work well.

The sauté pan or frying pan you use has to be heavy, with a thick base so it transfers heat to the food evenly.

• • • • • • • • • • • • • • • *RED●LIGHT* • • • • • • • • • • • • • •

Many foods are pan-fried in flavoured oils: that is, oil that has been flavoured with garlic or onion. If the flavouring agents burn, remove the pan from the heat, carefully drain off the oil, and start again. A burned flavour will permeate the entire dish. It's better to start afresh early in the process so you waste less food.

Cooking Scotch Pancakes

- Scotch pancakes or griddle cakes are the perfect breakfast food to cook in a pan. They cook in a few minutes.

- Use a packet mix or make your own batter from scratch: it's easy. Lightly grease the pan and add the batter in 50 ml amounts.

- Let the pancakes cook, undisturbed, until the edges start to look dry and bubbles form on the surface and just begin to pop.

- Carefully slide a spatula under the pancake and turn, using your wrist to flip. Cook for 2–3 minutes on the second side.

Pan-Frying Steak

- Steaks, especially thinner, tender steaks like skirt and flat iron steaks, are good candidates for pan-frying.

- When the meat is cooked, remove it and place on a warmed dish, covered, to rest and keep warm in a very low oven, while you make a sauce.

- Add beef stock, seasonings and herbs to the pan and stir over the heat, scraping up the residue in the pan.

- Swirl in a little butter and pour the sauce over the meat; serve immediately.

GRILLING

Grilling is a simple and quick cooking method that produces delicious results

Cooking food under an overhead grill is a dry heat method. The food is placed 10–15 cm from the hot upper burners in the oven, and is cooked quickly. The food browns easily and caramelizes well, giving lots of flavour.

You can grill everything from chicken fillets to fish steaks, from peppers to frittatas. All you need is a grill in your oven,

and ovenproof pans that will withstand the high heat. If you don't have a grill pan, you can wrap a double layer of heavy-duty foil around the handle of a frying pan so that it can be used under the grill.

There are two keys to grilling: the placement of the food and the cooking time. Don't step away from the food even

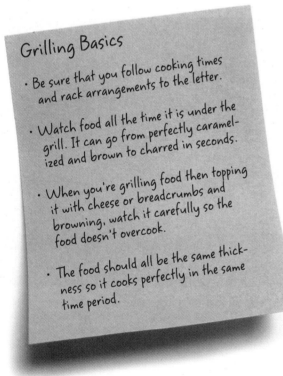

Grilling Basics

- Be sure that you follow cooking times and rack arrangements to the letter.

- Watch food all the time it is under the grill. It can go from perfectly caramelized and brown to charred in seconds.

- When you're grilling food then topping it with cheese or breadcrumbs and browning, watch it carefully so the food doesn't overcook.

- The food should all be the same thickness so it cooks perfectly in the same time period.

Preheating Gas Grill

- In some older stoves, the grill may be at eye-level at the top of the stove.

- Follow the manufacturer's directions for your grill; they are different for every model of stove.

- Removable handles may have been supplied with your oven for use with a grill pan. Always use oven mitts to protect your hands.

- You can cover the rack with foil to make cleaning easier: cut slashes in the foil so the fat can drain.

for a moment, because it can go from beautifully browned to burned in seconds. Adjust the top oven rack to place the food at the right distance from the grill according to the recipe.

On some ovens, the oven door has to be open for the grill to be at its highest heat, but on newer models grilling is done with the door closed. Some older stoves have a dedicated grill above the hob, at eye level. Some grills have a variable temperature control, but most operate at just one temperature: high. Grill steaks, hamburgers, chicken breasts, chops, fish fillets and the toppings of gratins for a crunchy caramelized finish.

Grilling is a low-fat form of cooking. Trim excess fat from foods and use marinades that are low in fat.

Grill Racks

- Grill racks are specially made to withstand the high heat of the grill, and to allow fat to drain away from the food.

- The pan is usually in two parts: a slotted or wire rack, and a bottom pan with sides to hold fat.

- You can use the rack or the bottom pan to hold the food while grilling.

- Depending on the style of your stove, the grill pan may double as a roasting tin in the oven. Removable handles will be supplied for use when grilling.

Position Food Carefully

- Some foods need to be turned during grilling; others will cook through perfectly under the intense heat.

- Use a spatula or tongs, not a fork, to turn the food so it doesn't lose any juices.

- If the food you are grilling has been marinated, drain the marinade from the food before cooking to avoid flare-ups and fat fires.

- Always have a fire extin-guisher or box of bicarbon-ate of soda or salt nearby when using this intense heat, to extinguish fires.

COOKING METHODS

BARBECUING AND GRIDDLING

Cooking food on an outdoor barbecue or a kitchen griddle are among the best fast cooking methods

You can chargrill outside over live coals, or cook on a indoor griddle, depending on the weather and the equipment you have. Barbecuing is an event in itself, requiring equipment and utensils specialist to that cooking art.

There are two basic types of barbecues: gas and charcoal. Gas barbecues are more expensive and simpler to use; you

just push a button and wait for the grill to heat. Charcoal barbecues require more finesse: you have to light the fire and maintain it throughout the cooking process. As always, read and follow the manufacturer's instructions

For indoor use you can buy a griddle pan with ridges that will fit on to your hob to mimic the effect of a barbecue.

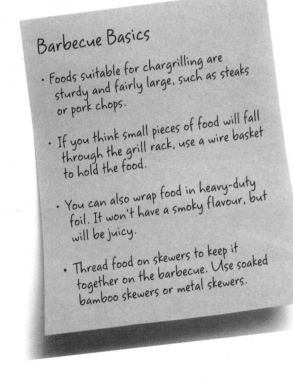

Barbecue Basics

- Foods suitable for chargrilling are sturdy and fairly large, such as steaks or pork chops.

- If you think small pieces of food will fall through the grill rack, use a wire basket to hold the food.

- You can also wrap food in heavy-duty foil. It won't have a smoky flavour, but will be juicy.

- Thread food on skewers to keep it together on the barbecue. Use soaked bamboo skewers or metal skewers.

Outdoor Barbecue

- Take care when choosing a location for your barbecue. Don't site it too near wooden fences, and keep clear of overhanging trees and shrubs.

- Find a sheltered position out of wind and draughts, and away from major thoroughfares in the garden.

- Make sure the barbecue is stable, and keep children and pets under control while it's hot.

- Preheat a gas barbecue for at least 10 minutes before you start cooking. If using charcoal, wait until the fuel is completely covered in grey ash.

A barbecue must always be preheated before the food is added. It takes about 30 minutes for charcoal to reach the proper cooking temperature, but gas barbecues and indoor grills and griddles preheat in 10 minutes.

Never leave a barbecue unattended. Keep kids and pets away from the cooking area. And also think about food safety. Perishable foods must be refrigerated after two hours; one hour if the ambient temperature is over 27°C. Separate cooked and uncooked foods, and wash hands and equipment in hot soapy water before and after cooking.

Dual-Contact Grill

- Dual-contact grills and griddles are a great addition to any kitchen. They cook quickly and fat drains away, lowering the fat content of your food.

- Look for the largest grill you can afford so you can cook an entire meal at once.

- A dual-contact grill should have a floating hinge so it will accommodate thicker foods.

- These grills have to be preheated before the food is added. You should hear a sizzling sound when you place the food on the grill.

Grill Marks

- Grill marks are beautiful and add a lot of flavour to the food. You can make crosshatch marks with this method.

- Place the food at a 45° angle to the rack and leave it to cook until the food releases.

- Lift the food completely off the grill, then turn it through 90°, and place it down again, still on the same side.

- Lift the food off when it releases and repeat on the other side.

COOKING METHODS

MICROWAVING

Your microwave is more than a butter melter, so use it to its fullest capacity

The microwave can do more than just pop popcorn, melt butter and defrost foods; you can cook an entire meal in this appliance, with a bit of attention and by following a few rules.

There are several types of microwave ovens. You can buy very basic models that are low wattage, but remember that it can be difficult to cook in those appliances. High-end microwave ovens, which are usually mounted over an oven, can have 1100 watts, with lights and vent fans. Whichever type of oven you buy, be sure that you understand how to use it before you start cooking.

Most microwave ovens have about 600–800 watts of power, and that's the range that recipes are developed for. If your

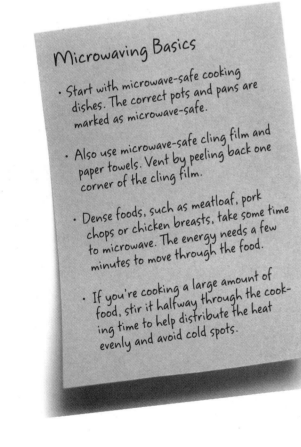

Microwaving Basics

- Start with microwave-safe cooking dishes. The correct pots and pans are marked as microwave-safe.

- Also use microwave-safe cling film and paper towels. Vent by peeling back one corner of the cling film.

- Dense foods, such as meatloaf, pork chops or chicken breasts, take some time to microwave. The energy needs a few minutes to move through the food.

- If you're cooking a large amount of food, stir it halfway through the cooking time to help distribute the heat evenly and avoid cold spots.

Microwave-Safe Containers

- Not all glass is microwave-safe. To determine if a container is microwave-safe, fill it with water.

- Microwave on high power for 1 minute, then leave to stand for 1 minute.

- If the container is hot but the water isn't, you shouldn't use it in the microwave oven.

- Never use glass or ceramic dishes with metallic trim or decorations. You'll know if the dish isn't meant for the microwave; there may be sparks or arcing in the appliance.

microwave is more or less powerful, reduce or increase the cooking time by 30–40 per cent, then write down the changes on the recipe. With some experimentation, you'll be able to estimate cooking times accurately.

Microwave recipes are written with venting, stirring, rotating and standing times included; follow all of them to the letter for best results.

Foods don't brown in the microwave unless it has a built-in grill, but you can compensate for that by searing food in a pan or under the grill in your conventional oven.

ZOOM

When microwaves (which are in fact radio waves) are absorbed by fat, liquid or sugars they activate the atoms and produce heat. The waves are not absorbed by glass, ceramics or most plastics, and containers made in these materials will not heat up. Metal reflects the waves so nothing made of metal should ever be placed in a microwave oven, including metal handles and twist ties.

COOKING METHODS

Standing Time

- Standing time is an important part of microwave cooking. The food should stand on a solid surface after cooking.

- This allows heat to move throughout the food, finishing cooking and eliminating hot and cold spots.

- The food must stand on a solid surface, not a wire rack, or heat will escape from the top and bottom, cooling the food.

- If possible, stir the food halfway through the cooking time to distribute the heat effectively.

Microwave a Quiche

- Yes, you can cook a quiche in a microwave oven. This is where you can use a browning trick.

- Brush the pastry with soy sauce, or another sauce such as hoisin, teriyaki or Worcestershire sauce to add colour. A dusting of paprika will also help.

- Microwave the pastry case first before adding the filling, to prevent a soggy bottom crust.

- Standing time is very important when cooking main dishes in the microwave, so don't skimp on it.

SLOW COOKING

Slow cookers take care of all of the work for you, after just a little bit of advance preparation

The slow cooker (sometimes called by the name of a well-known brand, Crock-Pot) doesn't cook food quickly, but it does all the work for you once the food has been added.

Slow cookers come in a range of sizes and have various additional features, such as programmable timers and ultra-low settings designed to keep cooked food warm.

There's really no trick to using a slow cooker. Add the food, usually in a precise order, then turn the slow cooker on and get on with the rest of your life. Some recipes call for stirring or adding extra ingredients towards the end of the cooking time; be sure that you read the entire recipe before leaving the slow cooker to do its work.

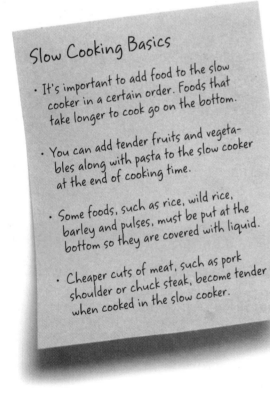

Slow Cooking Basics

- It's important to add food to the slow cooker in a certain order. Foods that take longer to cook go on the bottom.

- You can add tender fruits and vegetables along with pasta to the slow cooker at the end of cooking time.

- Some foods, such as rice, wild rice, barley and pulses, must be put at the bottom so they are covered with liquid.

- Cheaper cuts of meat, such as pork shoulder or chuck steak, become tender when cooked in the slow cooker.

Small Slow Cooker

- Small slow cookers are perfect for appetizer dips, chutneys and ketchups. They cook just like their larger counterparts.

- If you need to stir the dish, don't do this more frequently than the recipe requires or the slow cooker will lose too much heat.

- For every time the lid is lifted, you will need to cook the food for 20–30 minutes longer.

- You can make batches of preserves in the slow cooker and freeze them for later use.

Newer models, brought out over the last four to five years, cook hotter than the slow cookers of the 20th century. With recipes written in that era, you should reduce the cooking time so food doesn't overcook or burn. Newer recipes are written with the hotter temperatures in mind, but still you should check to see if the food is done at the earliest time.

Foods that cook best in a slow cooker include soups and stews, roasts, casseroles and vegetable dishes. You can also cook sandwich fillings, ingredients for salads and some desserts in them.

ZOOM

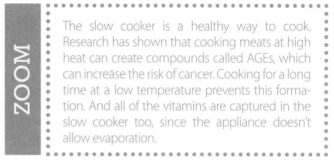

The slow cooker is a healthy way to cook. Research has shown that cooking meats at high heat can create compounds called AGEs, which can increase the risk of cancer. Cooking for a long time at a low temperature prevents this formation. And all of the vitamins are captured in the slow cooker too, since the appliance doesn't allow evaporation.

Large Slow Cooker

- Add ingredients in order as the recipe directs. Some foods need to be covered with liquid to cook evenly.

- It may seem surprising, but hard vegetables take longer to cook than meats, so onions and potatoes go on the bottom.

- You can brown meat before adding it to the slow cooker. This will add flavour and colour to the dish.

- Remember that no evaporation takes place when using the slow cooker, so use one-third less liquid when converting recipes.

Stirring Food

- Some recipes need to be stirred during the cooking time. Do this quickly, so not much heat escapes.

- Dry beans and pulses should be soaked for 18–24 hours before cooking in the slow cooker.

- To thicken soups, chillis or stews, combine 2 tablespoons cornflour with 75 ml water in a small bowl.

- Stir into the slow cooker at the end of cooking time; cook for 20–30 minutes on high until thickened.

DIPS

Creamy dips are the perfect appetizer, served with crudités, grissini or crackers

An appetizer can be a great tool for the host or hostess. With ingredients for an appetizer or two in your store cupboard or fridge, you can be ready to entertain at a moment's notice.

These foods will keep your guests occupied while you put the finishing touches to dinner. They are also great for getting appetites going, and can set the tone for the evening.

Dips are the easiest type of appetizer. You can make one with some crème fraîche and a packet of onion dip mix, but recipes can be a lot more interesting than that.

And the foods you serve with your dips can be varied and inventive, from baby vegetables to crisp, savoury biscuits, breadsticks and exotic fruits.

Ingredients

Serves 6

225 g cream cheese

75 ml half-fat crème fraîche

50 ml mayonnaise

1 tablespoon lemon juice

25g freshly grated Parmesan cheese

2 tablespoons chopped fresh basil

2 tablespoons fresh thyme

2 tablespoons finely chopped celery leaves

Creamy Herb Dip

- Place cream cheese in microwave-safe bowl. Microwave on medium power for 1 minute, then remove and leave to stand.

- Beat cream cheese with electric whisk until very smooth. Gradually beat in crème fraîche, mayonnaise and lemon juice until smooth.

- Add cheese, basil, thyme, and celery and beat well. Cover and refrigerate for 4–5 hours to blend flavours.

- When ready to serve, let dip stand at room temperature for 20 minutes before serving with toasted French bread, breadsticks, apple slices and baby carrots.

Blue Cheese Dip

In a large saucepan, combine 450 g cream cheese with 150 ml crème fraîche, 100 ml garlic mayonnaise, 3 tablespoons Tabasco sauce, 50 g blue cheese, crumbled, and 115 g Emmental cheese, grated. Cook and stir until cheese is melted and dip is smooth. Serve with celery sticks, baby carrots and cooked chicken strips.

Enchilada Dip

Soften 450 g light cream cheese in the microwave oven for 1 minute on medium power. Drain 1 (400-g) can chopped tomatoes and add the juice gradually to the cream cheese, beating until smooth. Stir in tomatoes, 1 chopped red onion, 2 cloves garlic, 1 tablespoon chilli powder and ½ teaspoon dried oregano.

Chop Herbs

- It's easy to chop fresh herbs using a chef's knife. First, rinse the herbs well and shake off excess water.

- Then pull or cut the leaves from the stems. Gather the leaves in a tight bundle and cut, rocking the blade across them.

- Then fluff up the pile and continue cutting with the knife, changing direction to produce even, small pieces.

- Parsley, basil and sage can be cut from the stem, while rosemary, oregano, and thyme leaves should be pulled off by hand.

Soften Cream Cheese

- You can soften cream cheese by just letting it stand at room temperature for an hour or two.

- Another way to soften it is to place the cream cheese on a microwave-safe plate and microwave on medium power for 1 minute.

- When combining cream cheese with other ingredients, beat the cream cheese well and add liquids gradually so no lumps form.

- Cream cheese dips harden when chilled; leave at room temperature for 15–20 minutes before serving.

APPETIZERS

PARTY DIPS

You can add a world of flavours to basic dips with these easy recipe variations

Dips can span the world from Greece, to Japan, to Buffalo, New York. Once you have a basic dip base that you like, change it by varying the herbs, spices and relishes you add.

The flavours typical of different cuisines make characterful dips. Tex-Mex flavours include chilli peppers, onion and tomato. For a Greek flavour, put together a dip using lemon, yogurt, olives and tomatoes. Spanish dips characteristically include almonds and oregano, while Asian dips would use soy sauce, hoisin sauce, five-spice powder, lemongrass and citrus juices. Mix and match these flavours to create your own special dip recipes.

Classic dips include fruit and vegetable salsas, mixtures of different types of cheese and yogurt, and recipes based on pulses and grains.

Layered Greek Dip

Ingredients

Serves 8

225 g cream cheese

350 ml Greek yogurt

115 g sun-dried tomatoes in oil, drained and chopped

225 g prepared hummus

1 cucumber, peeled and chopped

2 tomatoes, chopped

75 g kalamata olives, chopped

50 g feta cheese, crumbled

3 tablespoons toasted sesame seeds

- Soften cream cheese in microwave oven. Beat until smooth, and then gradually beat in yogurt until smooth.

- Stir in the sun-dried tomatoes. Spread in even layer on serving dish.

- Stir the hummus and spread over the cream cheese layer, leaving a small border of cream cheese dip exposed.

- Cover and refrigerate for up to 24 hours. When ready to serve, prepare cucumber, tomatoes and olives and sprinkle over dip. Top with feta and sesame seeds and serve.

Greek yogurt is strained to reduce its liquid content, so has more milk fat than even full fat ordinary yogurt and is much thicker and richer. You can buy Greek yogurt in any supermarket, or you can strain plain yogurt as a substitute. Just place plain yogurt in a sieve over a bowl and leave to stand in the fridge for 12–24 hours.

• • • • RECIPE VARIATION • • • •

Creamy Sesame Dip: Use 250 ml Greek yogurt or drained plain yogurt. Combine in small bowl with 2 tablespoons soy sauce, ½ teaspoon five-spice powder, pinch of cayenne pepper, 2 teaspoons sesame oil, and 65 g toasted sesame seeds. Mix well and chill for 1–2 hours before serving.

Prepare Vegetables

- The cucumber should be peeled and seeded. To seed, cut peeled cucumber in half lengthwise. Use a spoon to scoop out the seeds, then chop the flesh.

- Sun-dried tomatoes bottled in oil are ready to use. Just drain them on paper towels and cut into small pieces.

- Because the tomatoes are so strongly flavoured, the dip will be better balanced if they are finely chopped.

- You can vary this recipe by adding chopped green peppers, red onion or courgettes.

Assemble Dip

- Make sure that you leave some of the cream cheese mixture showing when you layer the hummus on top.

- To toast sesame seeds, place them in a dry pan over medium heat. Toast, shaking the pan frequently, until the seeds are fragrant.

- Let the seeds cool completely before adding them to the dip.

- Serve this dip with toasted pitta chips. Cut pitta breads into wedges, brush with olive oil, sprinkle with salt, and bake at 200°C for 10 minutes.

SPREADS

A spread or two, some knives and chunks of hearty bread make appetizers a breeze

Spreads are just thick appetizer dips that you can spread on anything from toasted French bread, to breadsticks, to tiny bagels, crackers or apple slices.

Use your prettiest dishes for serving appetizer spreads. Layered spreads are fun to make, too, and can look very beautiful. Think about investing in some small knives with decorative handles to make it easy for your guests to use the spread. For best results, all the ingredients should be at the same temperature. You want the base of the spread to be as smooth as possible. Then you can add ingredients like chopped nuts, herbs, spices, chopped onion and garlic, grated cheese, or chutneys and preserves.

Roasted Garlic Herb Spread

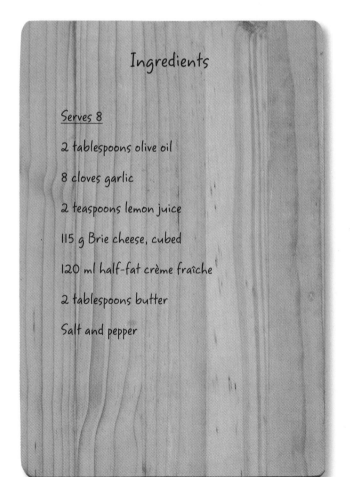

Ingredients

Serves 8

2 tablespoons olive oil

8 cloves garlic

2 teaspoons lemon juice

115 g Brie cheese, cubed

120 ml half-fat crème fraîche

2 tablespoons butter

Salt and pepper

- Place oil in small pan over medium heat. Add garlic cloves; cook, watching carefully, until the cloves turn brown.

- You can also roast the whole head, cut in half, in the oven at 180°C for 1 hour until soft.

- Remove garlic from oil and leave to cool, then squeeze out of skins. Combine garlic with lemon juice; season with salt and pepper.

- In food processor, combine garlic mixture with remaining ingredients; process until smooth. Cover and chill for 2–3 hours before serving.

Roasted Garlic Spread
Roast 1 head of garlic as described below, leave to cool and pop the cloves out of their skins. Combine in food processor with 1 (150-g) jar of roasted red peppers, drained, 3 tablespoons lemon juice, 120 ml crème fraîche, and 115 g crumbled goat cheese. Process until smooth, then chill for 2–4 hours.

Spicy Prawn Spread
Thaw 225 g cooked frozen prawns. Place in food processor with 225 g softened cream cheese, 100 ml seafood cocktail sauce, 3 tablespoons orange juice, ½ teaspoon salt, pinch of cayenne pepper and 2 teaspoons chilli powder. Process until almost smooth. Chill for 2–4 hours before serving.

Roast Garlic

- Garlic, that pungent and fiery vegetable, becomes unbelievably sweet and mild when roasted or toasted.

- It's easy to roast 6–7 heads of garlic all at once, then remove the sweet flesh from the skins and freeze it for future use.

- Then when you need it, you can just remove the amount you need, defrost in the microwave, and proceed with the recipe.

- You can also toast garlic in oil in a pan over medium heat for 7–9 minutes until brown. Discard the oil and leave the cloves to cool.

Remove Flesh from Skins

- Removing the garlic from the skins is a messy process, but it's not difficult.

- Just try to get all of the tender roasted flesh out of the skins. Discard the skins.

- You can serve the roasted garlic heads all by themselves, as a side dish with roasted or grilled meat, or as an appetizer.

- Let your guests remove the cloves from the heads and spread the soft garlic directly on toasted bread or grilled steak.

APPETIZERS

KEBABS

Grilled or not, kebabs are the perfect little appetizer for a barbecue

Kebabs don't have to be meal-sized. Tiny kebabs are one of the best and most elegant quick and easy appetizers.

They can be made of meat and fruit, or meat and vegetables, or all vegetables, or fruit and cheese. Marinades, salad dressing and simple oil mixtures can be brushed on these little treats while they're being chargrilled.

Bamboo skewers are ideal for making these little kebabs because they don't need to cook for long on the barbecue.

Using bamboo makes them easier to handle, too, since the skewers cool off in seconds.

Soak bamboo skewers in water for at least 30 minutes before you thread the ingredients on to them, so they don't burn to a crisp in the high heat. The skewers for these small kebabs should be about 20 cm in length.

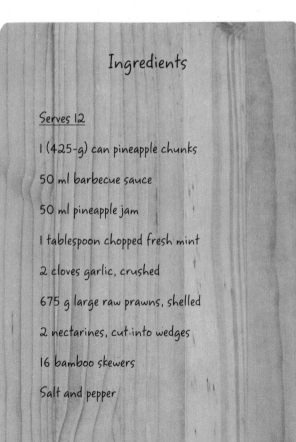

Ingredients

Serves 12

1 (425-g) can pineapple chunks

50 ml barbecue sauce

50 ml pineapple jam

1 tablespoon chopped fresh mint

2 cloves garlic, crushed

675 g large raw prawns, shelled

2 nectarines, cut into wedges

16 bamboo skewers

Salt and pepper

Fruit Prawn Kebabs

- Drain pineapple chunks, reserving 50 ml juice. Pat the pineapple dry and place in medium bowl.

- In small bowl, combine barbecue sauce, jam, mint, juice and garlic; season with salt and pepper.

- Thread prawns, pineapple

- and nectarines on skewers, nestling the fruit in the curve of each prawn. Brush with sauce; chill for 1 hour.

- Grill kebabs, turning and brushing frequently with sauce, until done, about 4–6 minutes. Discard any remaining sauce. Serve kebabs immediately.

Asian Chicken Kebabs
In medium bowl, combine 50 ml soy sauce, 2 tablespoons brown sugar, 2 tablespoons olive oil, 2 crushed garlic cloves and ½ teaspoon chopped ginger. Add 3 boneless chicken thighs cut into 2.5-cm pieces, 2 spring onions, sliced, and 175 g button mushrooms; chill 2 hours. Thread on skewers; grill for 9–12 minutes, turning once, until done.

Almond Salmon Kebabs
Combine 3 tablespoons each honey mustard, vegetable oil and lemon juice in bowl; mix well. Add 1 salmon steak, cubed, and 75 g small mushrooms. Leave to marinate in fridge for 2 hours. Thread on skewers, grill for 8–10 minutes; roll in chopped toasted almonds to coat before serving.

Prepare Prawns

- Large prawns are needed in this recipe because they will cook through in the same time as the other ingredients.

- If the prawns still have the shells and tail on, remove the shells by cutting down the back of the prawn.

- If you see a dark, thin vein running down the back of the prawn, cut along it and rinse to remove: this is the digestive tract.

- You can leave the tails on for a pretty appearance, or remove them for easier eating.

Skewer Food

- You can buy bamboo skewers in a range of lengths, for making kebabs in various sizes. Always soak them before use to stop them charring.

- You may also be able to find flat bamboo skewers, which hold food steady and are easier to turn on the grill.

- The fruit nestled into the curve of the prawns helps shield them from the heat so they don't overcook; also, it looks pretty.

- You could make this recipe into a main dish by using large skewers and adding more pieces per skewer.

APPETIZERS

41

MINI PIZZAS

Scaled-down pizzas aren't just for kids; these sophisticated recipes are elegant, too

Mini pizzas are an excellent appetizer. Once you know how to make and bake or barbecue the base, you can make these appetizers out of practically anything. For these tiny pizzas, you can use pizza dough cut out with biscuit cutters, little tortillas or mini pitta breads. Other choices for the crust include flatbreads and French toasts.

With small appetizers, you can splurge on more expensive ingredients, like exotic mushrooms, authentic cheeses and out of season fruits and vegetables.

To barbecue pizzas, place the bases on a grill basket. Grill until one side is crisp, then turn, top, and grill until the second side is crisp and the toppings are melted and blended.

Ingredients

Serves 8–10

2 tablespoons butter

1 tablespoon olive oil

2 onions, chopped

2 cloves garlic, crushed

1 teaspoon sugar

2 tablespoons fine cornmeal or flour

400 g uncooked pizza dough

2 plum tomatoes, chopped

50 g Emmental cheese, grated

50 g blue cheese, crumbled

Salt and pepper

Onion and Blue Cheese Pizza

- In a large pan, melt butter with olive oil over medium heat. Add onion and garlic; cook and stir for about 10 minutes, until translucent and very tender.

- Season with sugar, salt, and pepper; remove from heat.

- Preheat oven to 220°C.

- Sprinkle board with cornmeal and roll out pizza dough to 5-mm thickness. Cut into 7.5-cm rounds. Place rounds on a parchment-lined baking tray.

- Top with onion mixture, tomatoes and cheeses. Bake for 8–11 minutes, until crust is golden and cheese melts.

Mini Barbecued Greek Pizzas

Cook 1 chopped onion and 2 cloves garlic in 2 table-spoons olive oil. Remove from heat and add 75 g chopped kalamata olives. Divide among 12 picnic pitta breads; top with 60 g chopped sun-dried tomatoes, 75 g crumbled feta cheese, and 2 tablespoons grated Pecorino cheese. Barbecue on grill basket over medium heat for 6–8 minutes.

Tex-Mex Mini Pizzas

Top 12 (10-cm) tortillas with 250 ml salsa, then top with 175 g cooked crumbled pork sausage, 150 g cooked and drained black beans, and 115 g grated Pepper Jack or Cheddar cheese. Bake the pizzas at 220°C for 8–12 minutes, until the tortillas are crisp and the cheese has melted and browned.

Caramelize Onions

Roll and Cut Pizza Dough

- The onions are cooked for a long time so they caramel-ize. The mixture will turn light brown; stir constantly so the onions don't burn.

- That means the sugars and proteins in the onion break down and combine to form new compounds.

- These new compounds are very flavourful. The onion and garlic become sweet and nutty tasting.

- You can make the onion mixture ahead of time and freeze it. Thaw in the microwave at low power for 2 minutes.

- Anything you'd put on a big pizza can be added to a mini pizza. Use your imagination!

- Chilled pizza dough can be used for the base, or you can make your own dough or cut small circles out of ready-made pizza bases.

- Place the biscuit cutter right next to the round you just cut out so you waste very little of the dough.

- If you don't have a suitable biscuit cutter, use a large drinking glass instead.

QUESADILLAS

Quesadillas don't have to be Tex-Mex; try Greek or French variations

Quesadillas are thin sandwiches, usually grilled or pan-fried, that are made of a small amount of filling between two flour tortillas. These quick and easy sandwiches are simple to serve and eat, and they are very versatile.

You can cook quesadillas on a dual-contact indoor grill, on the outdoor grill, or in any frying pan. Cheese is always used to help hold the tortillas and filling together – *quesadilla* means 'little cheesy thing'.

It's important to not overfill the quesadillas, or the filling will just drop out as they are being eaten. Choose highly flavoured filling ingredients because of the proportion of filling to bread.

Have fun with your quesadilla creations, and be sure to write down the winners so you'll be able to reproduce them.

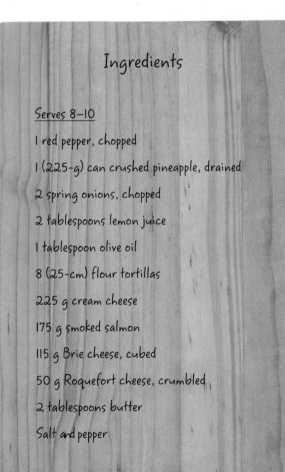

Ingredients

Serves 8–10

1 red pepper, chopped

1 (225-g) can crushed pineapple, drained

2 spring onions, chopped

2 tablespoons lemon juice

1 tablespoon olive oil

8 (25-cm) flour tortillas

225 g cream cheese

175 g smoked salmon

115 g Brie cheese, cubed

50 g Roquefort cheese, crumbled

2 tablespoons butter

Salt and pepper

Creamy Salmon Brie Quesadillas

- In small bowl, combine red pepper, pineapple, spring onion, lemon juice and olive oil; season with salt and pepper, mix and refrigerate.

- Place 4 tortillas on work surface and spread with cream cheese. Divide salmon, Brie and Roquefort cheeses on top. Top with remaining 4 tortillas and press gently.

- Heat butter in large frying pan. Cook quesadillas on both sides, turning once, for 4–5 minutes or until cheese melts. Cut into wedges and serve with pepper mixture.

Tex-Mex Quesadillas

Spread 6 large corn tortillas with 200 g refried beans. Top with 150 g browned spicy chorizo sausage, 75 g thawed frozen corn, 115 g grated Pepper Jack cheese and 50 g grated strong Cheddar cheese. Top with 6 more tortillas, then grill 15 cm from heat for 4 minutes. Turn and grill for 4–5 minutes longer. Serve with salsa.

Green Chicken Quesadillas

Spread 6 flour tortillas with 225 g softened cream cheese. Add 175 g chopped cooked chicken, 250 ml green salsa, and 1 chopped green pepper. Top with 175 g grated Monterey Jack or strong Cheddar cheese. Top with 6 more tortillas, brush with oil, and grill, turning once, for 7–9 minutes until cheese is melted.

Prepare Filling

- Chop all the filling ingredients for the quesadilla so that they are about the same size.

- Cheese is an essential part of the quesadilla. You could use lower fat cheeses, but if they are too low in fat they do not melt as well.

- Mix the ingredients gently but thoroughly so each bite of the quesadilla has all of the ingredients.

- Serve the finished quesadillas with a dip: a salsa, creamy salad dressing or a dip from this chapter would be delicious.

Cook Quesadillas

- The easiest way to cook quesadillas is in a nonstick frying pan. You can cook them in a dry pan, or you can brush or spray the pan with oil or butter.

- Use a spatula to press down on the quesadillas as they cook to help hold them together.

- A large, round spatula will hold the quesadilla and turn it easily.

- When it's browned on both sides and the cheese is melted, leave to stand for 3–4 minutes, then cut into quarters to serve.

APPETIZERS

45

SIMPLE FRIED EGGS
The perfect fried egg is a work of art if you follow a few simple rules

A fried egg seems like an easy dish to cook, but there are quite a few rules to follow. Whether you like your eggs sunny-side up or over easy or hard, follow these directions.

Fried eggs are best when they're cooked quite gently over low or medium-low heat. That way the white cooks through without becoming too brown or crisp at the edges. If you want to turn an egg, wait until the white is firm before flipping it over.

You can also cook the yolk by spooning some of the butter over the egg while it is cooking. With the heat low, you can cover the pan; the steam will help cook the yolk. Just don't overcook the eggs, or they will be rubbery.

Ingredients

Serves 2

2 tablespoons butter

4 eggs

Sea salt and black pepper

Classic Fried Eggs

- Heat a nonstick frying pan over low heat for 3 minutes. Add butter and let it melt.

- Break eggs into a shallow saucer one at a time, and slip into a shallow bowl, making sure that yolks stay intact.

- Add eggs, carefully and all at once, to the pan.

- Sprinkle with salt and pepper. Cover and leave to cook for 3 minutes.

- Uncover and spoon some of the butter over each egg. At this point you can flip them if you like. Cover and cook for 30 seconds longer until yolks are set, then serve immediately.

It's worth your while to search out free-range organic eggs, especially if you're cooking these for a special occasion. The yolk will be a deep orange colour, the white very thick, and the flavour very rich, nutty and smooth. You'll probably find the freshest free-range eggs at farmers' markets or direct from your local poultry farm, but they are available from all supermarkets.

Cheesy Eggs Over Hard: Melt 3 tablespoons butter in a pan over low heat. Break 4 eggs into a saucer and slip into the butter. Sprinkle with salt, white pepper, and 25 g finely grated Parmesan cheese. Cover and cook for 3–4 minutes until whites are firm. Flip the eggs, cover, and cook for a further 2–3 minutes until the yolks are no longer runny.

Break Eggs Individually

Cook Eggs

- Most people break eggs by tapping them on the side of the bowl.

- But this method sometimes results in broken egg yolks and can force the shell into the egg.

- The best way to crack an egg is to tap it quickly but firmly on the worktop. This will break the shell but keeps the yolk intact.

- Break each egg, one at a time, into a saucer, then combine them in a bowl and slip into the pan, so if one yolk breaks, it doesn't ruin the whole pan.

- Be sure that the butter is melted and slightly foamy before you add the eggs to the pan.

- Let the eggs set for a few minutes, then gently shake the pan to make sure they are not sticking.

- As the eggs firm, continue shaking them gently. If you are going to flip the eggs, use a large, round spatula.

- Gently slip the spatula under each egg, or all of them if the spatula is large enough, and flip them over using your wrist.

SCRAMBLED EGGS

Light and fluffy scrambled eggs are a delicious and healthy breakfast food

Scrambled eggs are the easiest eggs to make, but everyone has eaten dry, hard eggs. You can serve creamy, flavourful, moist eggs in minutes with these simple hints.

Adding air is the secret to fluffy scrambled eggs. Beat the eggs well, turning the mixture with a whisk to incorporate as much air as possible.

Once the eggs start to set on the bottom, it's time to move them around. Using a heatproof spatula, gently push the eggs around the pan, scraping the cooked egg from the bottom and letting the uncooked mixture flow underneath.

Serve your scrambled eggs immediately. They shouldn't have to wait any longer than an omelette.

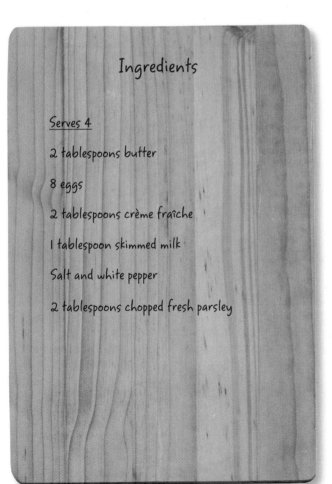

Ingredients

Serves 4

2 tablespoons butter

8 eggs

2 tablespoons crème fraîche

1 tablespoon skimmed milk

Salt and white pepper

2 tablespoons chopped fresh parsley

Creamy Scrambled Eggs

- Melt butter in large non-stick pan over medium heat. Meanwhile, combine eggs, crème fraîche, milk, salt and pepper in medium bowl.

- Beat eggs with wire whisk or egg beater for 2 minutes, until light and foamy. Add to butter in pan.

- Cook eggs over medium heat, moving a heatproof spatula through the eggs occasionally. When the eggs start to set, turn them over as you move them.

- When eggs are set but still creamy, turn out on to serving plate. Sprinkle with parsley and serve at once.

Scrambled Eggs with Cheese
Combine all ingredients as for basic scrambled eggs. Cook as directed, turning the eggs as they begin to set. When eggs are almost done, add 115 g grated Gouda cheese; cover the pan and remove from heat. Leave to stand for 3 minutes, then serve.

Scrambled Eggs with Smoked Salmon
Combine all ingredients as for basic scrambled eggs. Cook as directed, turning the eggs as they begin to set. When eggs are creamy and just done, remove from the heat. Add 75 g smoked salmon, cut into small pieces, and stir very gently into the eggs. Serve immediately.

Beat Eggs with Milk

- You can use an egg beater or a wire whisk to beat the eggs. Never beat or season the eggs ahead of time, or they will be watery.

- The eggs should be cold, just out of the refrigerator, for best results.

- You can add everything from water to double cream to eggs. Use about 1 tablespoon of addition for each egg.

- Water or low-fat milk makes eggs fluffy, and crème fraîche or cream makes them creamy.

Cook Eggs

- Scrambled eggs have to be moved pretty constantly once they have started to cook.

- Scrape the bottom of the pan and let the uncooked egg flow into the spaces. Be careful to work the spatula right into the corners of the pan so that none of the mixture sets hard.

- The cooked egg will pile up in 'curds'.

- Remove from the heat just before you think the eggs are done, as the hot pan will continue to cook them.

EGGS

OMELETTES

Omelettes aren't difficult to make with these tips and tricks

A light, fluffy omelette is one of French cuisine's best contributions to the world of cooking. Omelettes aren't difficult to make with just a few tips.

Unlike fried or scrambled eggs, omelettes are cooked over high heat so the eggs set quickly, trapping the air that you have beaten into them.

Omelettes should be made one at a time, unless you're making an oven omelette, which is sturdier than pan omelettes.

The pan has to be hot, and the bottom coated with melted butter before you add the eggs. As the eggs start to set, lift up the edges to let uncooked egg flow underneath.

Then top with fillings, fold one half over the other, slide on to a plate, and eat!

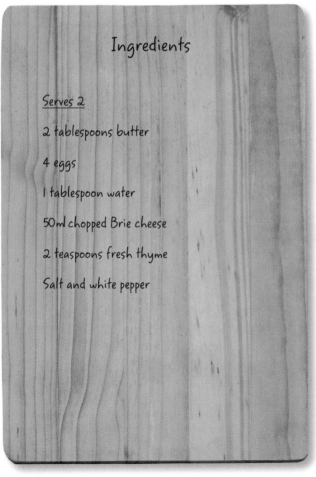

Ingredients

Serves 2

2 tablespoons butter

4 eggs

1 tablespoon water

50ml chopped Brie cheese

2 teaspoons fresh thyme

Salt and white pepper

Brie French Omelette

- Have all ingredients ready before you start. Heat butter in a nonstick omelette pan over medium-high heat.

- Beat eggs with water, salt, and pepper until foamy. Add to butter in pan and swirl the mixture in the pan.

- Leave to cook for 1 minute, then swirl the pan again. Gently lift the edges of the mixture and let uncooked egg flow underneath.

- When eggs are almost set, sprinkle with Brie and thyme. Cook for 1 minute, then slide half of omelette on to plate and flip other half on top. Serve immediately.

Spinach Gouda Omelette

Melt 2 tablespoons butter. Add 1 chopped onion and 50 g sliced mushrooms; cook until tender. Add 100 g fresh baby spinach leaves and cook until wilted. Add 5 eggs beaten with 2 tablespoons milk and seasoned with salt and pepper. Cook until moist, then top with 100 g grated Gouda cheese. Fold over and serve.

Baked Bacon Omelette

Preheat oven to 180°C. Cook 4 rashers of bacon until crisp; drain and crumble. Beat 9 eggs with 75 ml milk and 1 tablespoon Dijon mustard; season with salt and pepper. Add bacon and 50 g each grated Havarti and mild Cheddar cheeses. Pour into a greased gratin dish. Bake for 40–50 minutes until set.

Prepare Filling

- The filling ingredients must be fully cooked if you're using onions or meat.

- Or you can cook the food in the omelette pan, spread in an even layer, then add the eggs and cook as directed.

- Be sure to chop all of the filling ingredients to about the same size so nothing stands out and the omelette is easy to eat.

- A nonstick pan is the best choice for omelettes. The finished omelette should slide out of the pan.

Finish the Omelette

- Add the filling when the omelette is set and there is no more runny egg, but the top is very moist and shiny.

- Don't overfill an omelette. You want to be able to taste the egg as well as the cheese or meat in the filling.

- Omelettes have to be served the second they are made. They will start to deflate almost immediately.

- That means you have to stand at the stove making each omelette individually, but it's worth it.

EGGS

FRITTATAS

A frittata is like a sturdy omelette and can be seasoned in so many ways

A frittata is the perfect last-minute dish for a late supper or brunch. Frittatas are delicious and easy to make. They are a sturdier version of an omelette and aren't as finicky to make.

One of the best things about them is that they can be served warm or cold. The eggs are cooked for a longer period of time over lower heat, and the frittata is cooked on both sides, creating a thick, firm-textured omelette that can be cut into wedges to serve.

Use any meat, cheese or vegetables to fill your frittata. This recipe is a great way to use up leftover pasta, meats and breadcrumbs. You can use more filling than in an omelette because you use more eggs.

Spanish Frittata

Ingredients

Serves 4

2 links chorizo sausage, diced

2 tablespoons olive oil

1 onion, chopped

400 g frozen rosti potatoes

8 eggs, beaten

½ teaspoon dried oregano

50ml grated Manchego cheese

Salt and pepper

- In large nonstick pan, cook chorizo over medium heat until crisp. Remove; drain on paper towels.

- Wipe out pan and add olive oil. Cook onion and potatoes until tender.

- Preheat grill. Mix remaining ingredients and pour into pan with reserved chorizo. Cook, lifting mixture to let uncooked egg flow to bottom, until set.

- Sprinkle frittata with cheese and place pan under grill; cook until top is lightly browned and set. Cut into wedges to serve.

Breadcrumb Frittata

Melt 2 tablespoons butter and add 50 g breadcrumbs with 2 cloves crushed garlic; cook until crumbs are toasted. Beat 8 eggs with 120 ml milk, salt, pepper and 4 tablespoons chopped parsley. Melt 2 tablespoons butter in pan and cook egg mixture until partially set. Add breadcrumbs and 150 g grated Emmental cheese. Brown under a hot grill.

Mini Frittatas

Soften 1 chopped onion in 1 tablespoon butter. In a medium bowl, beat 8 eggs with 75 ml cream and 40 g pecorino cheese. Season with salt and pepper. Add onion and divide mixture among 48 nonstick muffin tins, lightly oiled. Bake at 190°C for 9–11 minutes.

Cook Until Set

Finish under the Grill

- The filling can be cooked in the pan before you add the eggs, or you can cook the eggs until partially set, then add the filling.

- Be sure to move the eggs continually in the pan, allowing the uncooked egg to flow underneath the cooked parts.

- A heatproof silicone spatula is the best tool for this job, since it won't scratch a nonstick pan.

- A frittata is always cooked on both sides. To flip the frittata, turn it on to a baking sheet, then slide it back into the pan.

- Instead of flipping the frittata in the pan, you can set and brown the top under a preheated grill.

- Watch the frittata carefully when it's under the grill. You may need to rotate the pan a bit so that the top browns evenly.

- You can serve the frittata immediately, or leave it to cool for 10 minutes and eat warm, or chill it.

- Frittatas are delicious cold, or you can warm them in the microwave at medium power for 1–2 minutes until hot.

EGGS

BAKED EGGS

Egg, sausages, fruits and vegetables combine in tasty baked dishes

Egg bakes are a great choice for brunch or informal lunches and suppers. Whether you choose a strata, which consists of bread layered with ingredients and baked in an egg custard, or an American-style casserole made with potatoes and bacon, these easy recipes are perfect.

Because they are usually better if put together ahead of time, baked egg dishes are a great asset for entertaining. You just pull the dish out of the fridge, bake, and you're ready to

eat! But you can also assemble them and bake them immediately. They take only about 20 minutes to prepare.

Think about your favourite flavour combinations when creating your own recipes. Ham and potatoes, sausage with cracked wheat bread, and leftover roast beef with spinach and cheese are all great ideas.

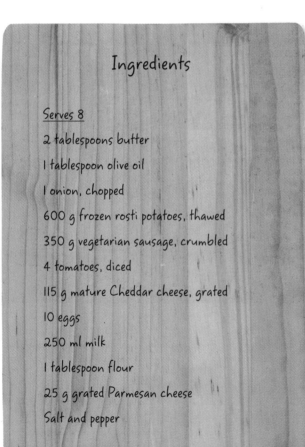

Ingredients

Serves 8

2 tablespoons butter

1 tablespoon olive oil

1 onion, chopped

600 g frozen rosti potatoes, thawed

350 g vegetarian sausage, crumbled

4 tomatoes, diced

115 g mature Cheddar cheese, grated

10 eggs

250 ml milk

1 tablespoon flour

25 g grated Parmesan cheese

Salt and pepper

Egg and Potato Bake

- Heat butter and olive oil in large frying pan. Cook onion until tender, about 6–7 minutes.

- Grease a 3-litre casserole dish. Layer in the grated potatoes, onion, crumbled sausages, tomatoes and Cheddar cheese.

- Beat eggs, milk, flour, salt and pepper until smooth. Pour over the layered ingredients and top with Parmesan. Cover and refrigerate for up to 12 hours.

- Preheat oven to 190°C. Bake for 30–40 minutes until set and turning brown.

Using partially cooked frozen potatoes in a bake saves a lot of preparation time. Try Southern-style cubed potatoes (which are sometimes mixed with chopped peppers), or coarsely grated potatoes designed for making rosti or hash browns. And frozen French fries and potato wedges can also be used in these recipes.

• • • • • RECIPE VARIATION • • • •

Croissant Egg Bake: Halve 4 large croissants; place bottoms in greased baking dish. Add 115 g grated Emmental cheese. Cook 1 chopped onion and 2 cloves garlic in 2 tablespoons butter; spoon over croissants; add tops. Beat 6 eggs with 250 ml milk, salt, pepper and dried thyme; pour over croissants; top with 25 g Parmesan cheese; bake at 180°C for 30 minutes.

Layer Ingredients

- It's important to drain thawed frozen ingredients very well before layering them in the dish.

- If you don't, the finished dish will have too much liquid, which will dilute the eggs. The cooked egg will be runny and won't cut nicely into squares.

- You can substitute just about any ingredients for the layered ingredients in this recipe.

- All raw ingredients, such as onions, garlic, peppers, fresh potatoes and meat, should be cooked before layering in the dish.

Add Egg to Dish

- Beat the egg mixture until well combined, but don't overbeat or the result will be tough.

- Pour the egg mixture slowly over the ingredients in the baking dish, allowing it to soak into the layers.

- You may need to push bread and other ingredients down into the mixture a few times until the egg is absorbed.

- Cover the dish tightly while it's in the refrigerator so it doesn't absorb flavours from other foods.

PANCAKES

Make pancakes like a professional, then fill them with wonderful healthy fillings

Making pancakes or crêpes can seem intimidating, but they are actually quite easy. The secret is all in the wrist. Once you've learned how to add batter to the pan and swirl it around, a pancake will take a couple of minutes to make.

Once made, you can freeze pancakes, separated by foil or greaseproof paper, then thaw and fill with anything you like.

Thaw pancakes by leaving them at room temperature for about 30 minutes, then fill and serve, or bake until hot.

Fillings for pancakes can range from leftover beef stroganoff to whipped cream and fruits. These thin pancakes are one of the best ways to use leftovers, so use your imagination and have fun!

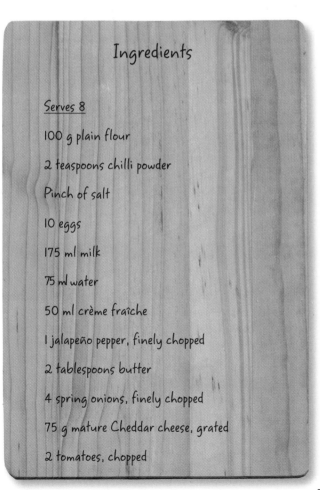

Ingredients

Serves 8

100 g plain flour

2 teaspoons chilli powder

Pinch of salt

10 eggs

175 ml milk

75 ml water

50 ml crème fraîche

1 jalapeño pepper, finely chopped

2 tablespoons butter

4 spring onions, finely chopped

75 g mature Cheddar cheese, grated

2 tomatoes, chopped

Tex-Mex Egg Pancakes

- Mix flour, chilli powder and salt. In small bowl, beat 2 of the eggs with milk and water; add to flour; whisk.

- Wipe a 20-cm pancake pan with oil and place on medium heat. Add 50 ml batter; swirl to cover bottom; cook until set. Repeat with remaining batter.

- In large bowl, beat remaining 8 eggs with crème fraîche and jalapeños. Melt 2 tablespoons butter in large pan; scramble eggs.

- Divide egg mixture among pancakes, and top with remaining ingredients. Roll and serve.

Plain Pancakes

Combine flour and salt in medium bowl. Beat eggs with milk and water and add to flour mixture; whisk until smooth. You can store the batter in the fridge up to 2 days. For sweet pancakes, add 2 tablespoons of sugar to the flour mixture. Cook as directed. Freeze pancakes, well wrapped, for up to 6 months. Thaw at room temperature.

Fruit-Filled Crêpes

Make sweet pancakes as directed and cool completely. For filling, combine 225 g chopped strawberries, 175 g raspberries, and 175 g blueberries with 2 tablespoons sugar; leave to stand for 5 minutes. Fold in 450 ml whipped cream, along with 115 g strawberry jam. Fill pancakes, roll up; sprinkle with icing sugar.

Make Pancake Batter

- You can use a blender or food processor to mix the batter instead of a whisk.

- Just put the eggs, milk, and water in the blender and blend until combined.

- Add the flour and seasonings and blend just until the batter is smooth; no longer.

- Leave the batter to stand for at least 5 minutes before making the pancakes.

- Don't overmix pancake batter, no matter which method you use. Overmixing will make the pancakes tough.

Cook Pancakes

- It's all in the wrist! Tip the pan back and forth as soon as you pour in the batter, so that it swirls and covers the bottom of the pan.

- Don't stack pancakes on top of each other when they come out of the pan or they will stick.

- Place the hot cooked pancakes on clean kitchen towels until they have cooled.

- Stack with foil, cling film or greaseproof paper between each pancake. They can be stored in the refrigerator for up to 4 days, or frozen.

EGGS

BEEF STIR-FRY

A speedy stir-fry with tender beef and savoury vegetables is an excellent quick supper

Stir-frying is a quick cooking method developed in Asian countries. The actual cooking time is about 5–10 minutes.

Have all the ingredients ready and waiting to go into the wok or frying pan before you start cooking. You can prepare the ingredients ahead of time; in fact, some ingredients, like meat in a marinade, benefit from time in the refrigerator.

You don't need a wok to stir-fry, but you do need a large sturdy frying pan and a heat-resistant spatula. Don't use non-stick equipment to stir-fry, since you need to scrape the bottom to deglaze the pan.

Almost any meat and vegetable combination is delicious, so enjoy experimenting.

Ingredients

Serves 6

3 tablespoons soy sauce

2 tablespoons white wine vinegar

1 tablespoon honey

120 ml beef stock

1 tablespoon finely chopped fresh ginger

1 tablespoon cornflour

1 teaspoon sesame oil

Pinch of pepper

450 g sirloin steak

2 tablespoons groundnut oil

150 g mangetout peas

6 spring onions, chopped

200 g baby corn cobs, halved

1 red pepper, chopped

Beef and Vegetable Stir-Fry

- In medium bowl, combine the first 8 ingredients.

- Slice steak into 1 x 10-cm strips, against the grain, and add to marinade. Cover and refrigerate for 12–24 hours.

- Heat wok or large frying pan over medium-high heat. Add oil. Drain beef, reserving marinade. Stir-fry beef until browned, then remove and reserve.

- Add vegetables to pan; stir-fry until crisp-tender. Return beef and reserved marinade to wok; stir-fry until beef is tender and sauce is thickened. Serve immediately with rice.

~ VARIATIONS ~

Beef Mushroom Stir-Fry

In resealable plastic bag, mix 2 tablespoons cornflour, 3 tablespoons teriyaki sauce, 1 tablespoon chopped fresh ginger, 2 cloves garlic, crushed, and 250 ml beef stock. Add 450 g rump steak, cut into strips; marinate for 2 hours in fridge. Stir-fry 2 onions, 3 sticks celery and 6 mushrooms, all sliced, in 2 tablespoons groundnut oil. Add drained beef, then marinade; stir-fry until done.

Beef Pepper Stir-Fry

Combine 1 tablespoon grated fresh ginger, 2 tablespoons cornflour, 250 ml beef stock, and 2 cloves garlic, crushed, with 450 g rump steak, cut into strips; marinate. Drain beef, reserving marinade. Heat 2 tablespoons oil; stir-fry beef until pink; remove. Stir-fry 1 onion, 1 red and 1 yellow pepper, all chopped. Add beef and marinade; stir-fry until sauce is thickened.

Prepare Ingredients

- Until you're experienced at cutting foods, work slowly and with a ruler to measure the size of the chopped ingredients.

- If you are preparing the food ahead of time, refrigerate each separately in a closed plastic bag.

- Don't refrigerate meat for longer than the recipe states, or it may become mushy.

- You can marinate the vegetables with the meat if you like, for even more flavour. Serve these stir-fry recipes with rice.

Stir-Fry

- The stir-fry technique isn't difficult to achieve. Be sure that you turn all of the foods with your spatula.

- Reach into the edges of the pan so no food overcooks. Be sure to remove foods when the recipe specifies.

- Always stir the marinade or sauce mixture before adding to the wok or frying pan, because the cornflour can settle to the bottom.

- Always serve stir-fried food immediately; have your guests waiting for the food.

PAN-FRIED BEEF

Cook beef for a few minutes, add some ingredients to the pan to create a sauce, and you have an elegant dish

Pan-frying is an excellent quick and easy cooking technique. For beef to cook in a short amount of time, it usually has to be pounded thin or cut into strips.

Very thin pieces of meat that have been pounded are known as paillards, escalopes or cutlets. Cook them as they are or coat them with a seasoned flour mixture or breadcrumbs.

This type of cooking automatically creates a sauce, whether or not the meat has been marinated. The residue left behind when the meat is cooked is full of flavour; add stock and stir vigorously to deglaze the pan, add a bit of butter, swirl and pour over the beef.

Ingredients

Serves 4

450 g sirloin steak

2 tablespoons olive oil

2 tablespoons red wine vinegar

½ teaspoon garlic salt

Pinch of pepper

1 tablespoon finely chopped fresh rosemary

1 tablespoon fresh thyme

2 tablespoons butter

120 ml beef stock

French Beef Paillards

- Cut steak into four serving pieces. Place on a sheet of cling film and sprinkle with a little water. Top with more cling film. Pound until 3 mm thick. Remove cling film.

- Mix oil, vinegar, salt and pepper in a shallow dish. Add beef, cover; marinate for 20 minutes.

- Remove steaks from marinade; rub rosemary and thyme into meat. Heat butter in pan over high heat.

- Add steaks; cook 1–2 minutes per side until browned. Remove meat and keep warm; add stock to pan. Cook for 2 minutes. Pour over steaks; serve.

~ VARIATIONS ~

Mustard Steaks
Rub 4 sirloin steaks with 2 tablespoons each olive oil and mustard; sprinkle with salt, pepper, 1 tablespoon dried thyme, 1 tablespoon mustard seed; leave to stand for 10 minutes. Heat 2 tablespoons oil in pan; cook steaks for 3–5 minutes on each side. Remove; add 120 ml broth and 2 tablespoons Dijon mustard; boil and pour over steaks.

Burgundy Tenderloin
Pound 4 fillet steaks until 12 mm thick; sprinkle with salt, pepper, and 1 teaspoon dried oregano; cover with 120 ml red burgundy and leave to stand for 10 minutes. Drain and cook in 2 tablespoons oil for 4–6 minutes on each side. Remove steak; add wine mixture; bring to the boil. Add 2 tablespoons butter, swirl and pour over steaks.

Pound the Beef

- When pounding beef, be fairly gentle. You don't want to tear or rip the meat.

- If you are pounding fillet steak, slice into individual serving pieces, then place cut side up on greaseproof paper.

- Start at the centre and work out toward the edges of the beef.

- You can use the flat side of a meat mallet or a rolling pin. It may help to sprinkle the meat with a little water before you start.

Pan-Fry

- After the steak has marinated, many of the fibres will have been weakened by the acid.

- This is the perfect time to add more flavour with dry rubs. Sprinkle on herbs, spices, peppers and sugar.

- Be careful with dry rubs that contain a large amount of sugar, because they can burn easily.

- When the beef is done, leave to rest for 5 minutes; then, if you have cooked it in a single piece, slice across the grain.

GRILLED STEAK
Cooking under a hot grill adds great caramelized flavour to simple steaks

The secret to successful grilling is to preheat the grill and cook with the oven door open to keep the heat high. Position the food about 10–15 cm away from the heat source and watch it carefully.

You may need to move the steaks around and turn the grill pan so the meat cooks evenly. Don't walk away from the grill while you are cooking, because the meat can go from caramelized to charred in seconds.

Marinades, dry rubs, basting sauces and pastes can add great flavour to grilled steaks. If these sauces contain sugar, they will caramelize on the meat, creating a delicious crust.

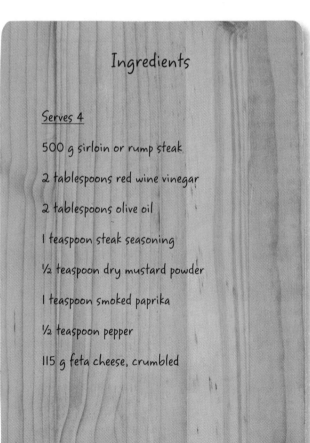

Ingredients

Serves 4

500 g sirloin or rump steak

2 tablespoons red wine vinegar

2 tablespoons olive oil

1 teaspoon steak seasoning

½ teaspoon dry mustard powder

1 teaspoon smoked paprika

½ teaspoon pepper

115 g feta cheese, crumbled

Spicy Grilled Feta Steak

- Place steak in shallow non-metallic dish. In small bowl, combine remaining ingredients (except cheese) and mix well. Rub into both sides of steak.

- Marinate at room temperature for 30 minutes or in the refrigerator for 8–24 hours.

- Arrange grill rack 10 cm from heat source and preheat grill. Drain steak, pat dry, and place on grill rack.

- Grill for 6–7 minutes per side, turning once, for medium-rare steak. Remove, top with cheese, cover with foil, and leave to rest for 5 minutes, then serve.

• • • • RECIPE VARIATION • • • •

Grilled Rib-Eye Steak: Brush 4 boneless rib-eye steaks with olive oil; rub with a mixture of 1 teaspoon salt, ¼ teaspoon pepper, ½ teaspoon dry mustard, 1 tablespoon brown sugar and 1 teaspoon dried oregano. Leave for 10 minutes. Grill 15 cm from heat source for 8–10 minutes, turning once, until done to your liking. Top each steak with a pat of butter and serve.

Marinate Steak

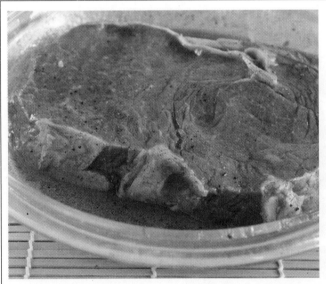

- Any marinade can be used for the steak. There are lots of bottled versions on the market.

- Salad dressings are also good choices for steak marinades. The tougher the steak, the longer it should marinate in the fridge.

- Rump steak and flank steak should be marinated. Fillet, rib-eye, sirloin and T-bone steaks don't need a marinade.

- Be sure to pat the meat dry after it's removed from the marinade so the surface caramelizes.

Grill Steak

- The steak should be 10–15 cm from the heat source for best results. Make sure to preheat the grill.

- Don't turn the steak until the top is browned and crusty. Use tongs or a spatula to turn the steak.

- To test whether the meat is cooked, cut a small slit into it to see the colour of the interior. Medium rare should be a deep pink. Medium steaks are a lighter pink colour.

BARBECUED STEAK

Juicy steak chargrilled on the barbecue is one of the classic recipes of summer

Your barbecue is an ideal quick-cooking appliance. If you own a gas barbecue, you can heat it up, start cooking and finish in under 20 minutes. A charcoal grill takes longer to start.

Chargrilled foods have a slightly smoky taste and develop wonderful caramelization on the surface. Sugars and proteins on the food break down, then recombine to form the hundreds of compounds that give barbecued foods their complex and delicious taste.

When barbecuing, always work with two levels of heat. On a gas barbecue, first heat all the burners, then turn one off so there's a cooler area to control cooking. On charcoal grills, leave a small space empty of coals.

Ingredients

Serves 4

2 tablespoons olive oil

3 tablespoons red wine vinegar

1 tablespoon honey

2 cloves garlic, crushed

1 teaspoon steak seasoning

Pinch of pepper

675 g sirloin steak

225 g button mushrooms, sliced

225 g chestnut mushrooms, sliced

Barbecued Mushroom Steak

- In large plastic bag, combine oil, vinegar, honey, garlic, seasoning and pepper and mix well.

- Cut steak into four portions. Add to marinade along with mushrooms, close bag, and turn it over several times to distribute marinade. Leave for 30–40 minutes.

- Prepare the barbecue. Drain steaks, pat dry and cook over direct heat for 8–10 minutes, turning once, until medium.

- At the same time, drain the mushrooms and arrange on a grill basket; cook, turning basket, until browned and juicy, about 7 minutes.

~ VARIATIONS ~

Rib-Eye Steak with Feta Butter
Brush 4 boneless rib-eye steaks with olive oil and sprinkle with salt, pepper and steak seasoning. Leave to stand for 10 minutes. Meanwhile, in small bowl combine 50 g butter, 50 g crumbled feta cheese, ½ teaspoon dried oregano, ½ teaspoon grated lemon zest, and 3 tablespoons chopped parsley. Barbecue steak until cooked as you like it, then top with butter mixture and serve.

Delmonico Steak
In a plastic bag, combine 3 tablespoons each olive oil, Worcestershire sauce, finely chopped onion, steak seasoning, pepper and salt. Add 4 rump steaks to the bag, turn to coat meat with the mixture, and leave in refrigerator for 18–24 hours. Prepare barbecue, drain steaks, pat dry, and grill until they are cooked as you like them. Discard the marinade.

Marinate Steak

- Marinade makes even tough steaks tender by breaking down the fibres in the meat. The acidic ingredient is key.

- Don't marinate the steaks longer than directed in the recipe, or the fibres will break down too much and the meat will be mushy.

- Always marinate meat in the refrigerator unless marinating time is less than 30 minutes.

- Pat steaks dry before you place them on the barbecue so that they brown nicely. Don't turn the steaks until they release easily; then turn with tongs.

Grill Mushrooms

- A grill basket is a great way to barbecue smaller foods that might fall through the grill rack.

- Add the ingredients and lock the basket; place over direct heat.

- Then shake and turn the basket occasionally as the

food cooks. Add the food in the basket after the steaks start cooking.

- If you like, you can boil the marinade for 2 minutes, add a knob of butter, and serve it as a sauce for the steaks.

STEAK WITH FLAVOURED BUTTER

Herby, garlicky butter melting into steak is one of the easiest ways to dress up the meat

We all know that a great way to finish off a grilled steak is to top it with a pat of butter as it comes off the barbecue. But did you know you can dress up the butter to make it even more special?

You can flavour butter in many different ways, by adding other ingredients such as cooked garlic, herbs, spices and cheeses. You can use flavoured butters to top grilled chicken, pork or seafood as well.

There's one caveat: this butter doesn't store well. You can freeze it for up to two weeks, but it's not advisable to store flavoured butters in the fridge for longer than two days for food safety reasons.

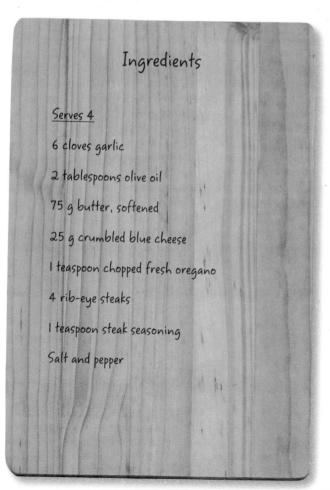

Ingredients

Serves 4

6 cloves garlic

2 tablespoons olive oil

75 g butter, softened

25 g crumbled blue cheese

1 teaspoon chopped fresh oregano

4 rib-eye steaks

1 teaspoon steak seasoning

Salt and pepper

Rib-Eye Steak with Roasted Garlic Butter

- Place unpeeled garlic cloves and oil in a small saucepan over medium heat until cloves turn golden brown.

- Remove cloves and leave to cool. Squeeze flesh from skins. In a bowl, combine with butter, blue cheese and oregano, season with salt and pepper; refrigerate.

- Preheat barbecue to medium. Brush steaks with the oil from the garlic and sprinkle with steak seasoning and pepper.

- Barbecue steaks over medium heat, turning at least twice – 12–14 minutes for medium rare. Top with butter; serve immediately.

~ VARIATIONS ~

Steak with Pesto Butter

Marinate 4 steaks in a mixture of 2 tablespoons lemon juice, 1 tablespoon olive oil, ½ teaspoon salt and ½ teaspoon dried basil for 2 hours in fridge. Meanwhile, combine 75 g softened butter, 15 g chopped fresh basil, 3 tablespoons grated Parmesan cheese, and 2 cloves of garlic, crushed. Mix well and chill. Drain steaks, pat dry; grill for 8–10 minutes; top with butter.

Steak with Lemon Herb Butter

For butter, combine 50 g softened butter with 1 tablespoon lemon juice, ½ teaspoon grated lemon zest, 2 teaspoons fresh thyme leaves and a pinch of pepper. Roll into a log, wrap in greaseproof paper and chill for 2–3 hours. Grill steaks as desired. Slice butter into rounds and place on steak; serve immediately.

Make Flavoured Butter

- You can make flavoured butter with just a bowl and a spoon. Well-softened butter is the key to this method.

- Or you can combine the butter with the other ingredients in a food processor. Pulse until well mixed.

- Form the butter into a log and chill, then cut rounds to top the steaks.

- Or just place the butter in a dish and spoon a dollop on to each steak for a more casual presentation.

Grill Steak

- The key to grilled steaks is to leave them alone when they first go on the heat. Don't move the steaks until they release.

- Clean and oil the rack or griddle before you add the steaks. Oil the steaks, or, if they have been marinated, pat them dry.

- Turn the steaks at least twice. The first turn should be when they release from the grill.

- The final turn finishes the steaks. If you are brushing with marinade, this will 'cook off' the marinade.

GRILLED BURGERS

You can flavour burgers any way you like, from classic American to French

Lean minced beef is one of the most versatile meats in the supermarket. It can be crumbled into a pasta sauce, made into a meatloaf, or formed into meatballs or burgers.

Burgers are easy to make and they can be flavoured in many different ways. As long as you keep to a basic proportion of 50–75 g additions per 450 g of beef, you will be able to shape the meat easily and the burgers will hold together well while they're cooking.

Handle the meat gently when making burgers. Combine all of the ingredients together except the meat and mix well. Then add the beef and mix gently with your hands just until combined. Less handling means juicier burgers.

Ingredients

Serves 4

40 g finely chopped onion

3 cloves garlic, crushed

3 tablespoons butter

2 tablespoons ketchup, plus more for serving

2 tablespoons mustard

500 g 80 per cent lean minced steak

4 burger buns, split

50 ml mayonnaise

4 slices Cheddar cheese

1 large tomato, sliced

Classic American Burgers

- Cook onion and garlic in 1 tablespoon of the butter until soft. Remove to large bowl and leave to cool.

- Stir in 2 tablespoons ketchup and mustard, then add beef and mix gently. Form into four patties. Press into the centres of each to make a depression.

- Preheat grill. Grill burgers 15 cm from heat source for 8–10 minutes, turning once.

- Spread buns with remaining butter and grill until toasted. Spread with mayonnaise and ketchup, and fill with the burgers and slices of cheese and tomato.

Bacon Burgers

Cook 4 rashers bacon until crisp; crumble; place in large bowl. Add 2 cloves garlic, crushed, 2 tablespoons Worcestershire sauce, salt, pepper and 1 egg. Add 500 g minced beef and mix gently. Form into 4 patties, make indentation in centre, and grill until done. Serve on toasted buns with ketchup, mustard and sliced tomato.

Greek Burgers

In small pan, cook 1 medium onion, chopped, and 2 cloves garlic, crushed, in 1 tablespoon olive oil. Place in large bowl. Add 1 tablespoon each lemon juice and mustard, ½ teaspoon grated lemon zest and 50 g crumbled feta cheese. Add 500 g minced beef; shape into patties and indent centre. Grill until done; serve in toasted muffins with feta and mayonnaise.

Mix Burger Ingredients

Form Patties

- The cooked ingredients should be cool before you add the minced beef so it doesn't start cooking.

- Don't handle the mixture too much after the beef has been added, and shape gently using your hands.

- You can shape the burgers ahead of time; cover and refrigerate for up to 4 hours before cooking.

- Preheat the grill before you add the hamburgers, and watch them carefully under the heat. Turn gently using a spatula.

- Many homemade hamburgers tend to puff up when they're cooked, making it difficult to add ketchup and mustard.

- Press down in the centre of each patty with a spoon or your fingers to prevent this.

- The meat will still swell during cooking, but because of the indentation, the finished burger will be flat.

- Never press down on the meat while it's cooking, or you'll press out all the juice and flavour.

MEATLOAF IN THE MICROWAVE

Microwave meatloaf stays moist and juicy when cooked in this special way

Yes, you can cook more in the microwave than popcorn and frozen dinners. Meatloaf, a traditional dish in many parts of Europe and one of the USA's best-loved meals, cooks especially well in a microwave oven because the mixture is dense. The energy moves easily through the meat, cooking it thoroughly but leaving it tender and juicy.

There are some special rules to follow when you're cooking in a microwave oven. It is important to follow turning, stirring and covering instructions to the letter. With all microwave recipes, standing time is essential. This means the dish must stand on a solid surface, not a rack, after cooking, to let the heat distribute so the food is evenly cooked.

Ingredients

Serves 6

4 rashers bacon

1 tablespoon olive oil

50 g finely chopped onion

3 cloves garlic, crushed

25g chopped chestnut mushrooms

10 g crushed crisp rice cereal

115 g grated Emmental cheese

1 egg

450 g extra lean minced beef

50 ml chilli sauce

2 tablespoons mustard

Salt and pepper

Swiss Bacon Meatloaf

- Cook bacon until crisp; drain, crumble and set aside. Wipe out pan and add olive oil, onion, garlic, and mushrooms; cook until liquid evaporates.

- Remove to large bowl, add bacon and cool slightly. Stir in cereal, salt, pepper, cheese and egg. Add beef.

- Form into loaf in a 1-litre microwave-safe dish. Cover; microwave on high for 10–11 minutes.

- Mix chilli sauce and mustard; pour over loaf. Microwave for another 5–7 minutes. Cover and leave to stand for 10 minutes. Slice and serve.

~ VARIATIONS ~

Spanish Meatloaf

In large bowl, combine 50 g chopped red onion, 50 g chopped olives, 2 crushed garlic cloves, 50 ml chilli sauce, 25 g ground almonds and ½ teaspoon paprika; season with salt and pepper. Add 450 g minced beef; form into loaf. Place in dish; cover with 3 tablespoons chilli sauce. Microwave as directed.

Sweet and Sour Meatloaf

Combine 50 ml chilli sauce, 1 egg, 30 g crushed Ritz crackers, 2 tablespoons sugar, 2 tablespoons cider vinegar and 2 tablespoons mustard; season with salt and pepper. Add 450 g minced beef and mix. Shape into loaf, place in microwave-safe dish. Brush with 50 ml ketchup and microwave as directed.

Cook Bacon and Onions

- Most ingredients should be cooked before being mixed into a meatloaf. The cooking time isn't long enough to make them tender.

- The bacon will soften when added to the minced beef, so make sure it's cooked very crisp and drained well.

- Cool the bacon and onion mixture before you add the cheese and meat, so everything mixes well.

- Mix gently but thoroughly by hand, just until all of the ingredients combine.

Finish the Meatloaf

- There are three tricks to making the best microwave meatloaf.

- One is to not overmix the ingredients.

- The second is to follow the cooking and standing times carefully.

- And number three: after cooking, cover the meatloaf and leave it to stand on a solid surface for at least 10 minutes before you slice it, to ensure that it is evenly and thoroughly cooked.

71

MICROWAVE CHILLI

Rich, thick chilli, made with minced beef and beans, is easy to make in the microwave

Chilli is a classic quick and easy dish that is usually cooked on top of the stove. But the microwave is a faster way to cook it, and the flavours blend beautifully. With this recipe, you can have chilli on the table in about 20 minutes.

Make sure you cook the minced beef fully with the onions before you add the other ingredients. Stir the beef from time to time to make sure it breaks up and cooks evenly.

Once you've mastered the basic recipe, you can start having fun with it. Use ground chicken or turkey, try spicy pork sausage, or even frozen vegetarian sausages. Make the dish spicier with jalapeño or serrano peppers and use different types of beans. The sky's the limit.

Ingredients

Serves 4

450 g minced beef

1 onion, chopped

3 cloves garlic, crushed

1 tablespoon chilli powder

1 teaspoon ground cumin

1 (400-g) can chopped tomatoes, undrained

1 (225-g) can tomato sauce

1 (350-g) jar salsa

1 (425-g) can kidney beans, drained

50 ml strong brewed coffee

2 tablespoons mustard

Salt and pepper to taste

1 tablespoon cornflour

75 ml water

Spicy Tex-Mex Chili

- Crumble beef into 2.5-litre microwave-safe dish. Add onion and garlic. Microwave mixture on high for 4 minutes.

- Stir, and microwave on high for 2–3 minutes longer until beef is cooked. Drain off fat.

- Add remaining ingredients except cornflour and water and stir well. Cover and microwave on high for 10–12 minutes until bubbly.

- Stir. Add mixture of cornflour and water; stir well. Microwave on high for 2–3 minutes longer until thickened. Leave to stand for 5 minutes before serving.

Vegetable Beef Chilli

Cook 450 g minced beef, 1 chopped onion, 150 g mushrooms, and 1 yellow summer squash, sliced, in microwave for 6 minutes; drain. Add 1 tablespoon chilli powder, 250 ml salsa, 400-g can chopped tomatoes, 250 ml beef stock, and 425-g can black beans; stir well. Cover; microwave on high for 10–12 minutes, stirring once. Serve with blue corn chips and grated cheese.

Beef Chilli with No Beans

Cook 450 g minced beef, 1 chopped onion, 3 cloves garlic, and 1 chopped green pepper in microwave for 5 minutes; drain. Add 1 tablespoon chilli powder, salt and pepper, 1 (225-g) can tomato sauce, 475 ml salsa, and 50 ml tomato purée. Cover and microwave on high for 10–12 minutes, stirring once. Serve with Parmesan cheese.

MINCED BEEF

Brown Minced Beef

- The ground beef won't really 'brown' in the microwave, but it will lose its pink colour. That's how you tell it's done.

- Onions, garlic and other vegetables cook very well in the microwave oven.

- Be sure to stir the beef at least once during the cooking time so it cooks evenly.

- When you drain off fat, pour it into a container and leave it to solidify before discarding it: don't pour it down the drain.

Stir Chilli

- When you stir the chilli, use a cloth to hold the dish because it will be hot.

- Stir gently, but be sure to get into the corners of the dish so food doesn't stick there and overcook.

- Always let the chilli stand, covered, on a solid surface

for at least 5 minutes after microwaving.

- Serve your finished chilli with bowls of crème fraîche, salsa, sliced avocados, chopped tomatoes and grated cheese.

DELUXE BARBECUED BURGERS

Grown-up burgers use good quality but easily available ingredients for a special recipe

Barbecuing gives burgers a wonderfully smoky taste. There's something primal about cooking meat over a fire.

Minced meat should be cooked to an internal temperature of 74°C to be completely safe. You can check the temperature of the burgers before you serve them using an instant-read thermometer; if you don't have one, push a knife into the centre of a burger to check that there is no pink meat. Keep an area of the barbecue at a lower heat, so that you can move the burgers from higher to lower heat as needed. You don't want the outside to burn before the inside is fully cooked.

Add indulgent ingredients to your burgers. Cheeses, bacon and caramelized onions are all delicious.

Deluxe Beef Burger

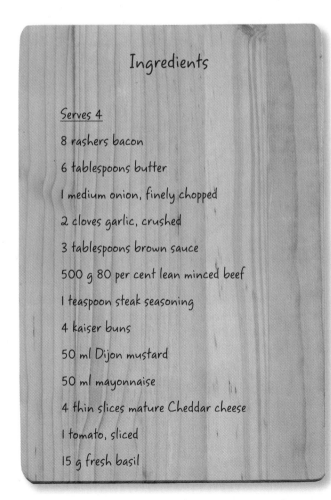

Ingredients

Serves 4

8 rashers bacon

6 tablespoons butter

1 medium onion, finely chopped

2 cloves garlic, crushed

3 tablespoons brown sauce

500 g 80 per cent lean minced beef

1 teaspoon steak seasoning

4 kaiser buns

50 ml Dijon mustard

50 ml mayonnaise

4 thin slices mature Cheddar cheese

1 tomato, sliced

15 g fresh basil

- Cook bacon until crisp; drain on paper towels. Drain pan but don't wipe. Add 2 tablespoons butter.

- Cook onion and garlic for about 7 minutes. Place in large bowl. Add steak sauce, then beef; mix gently.

- Form into 4 patties 12.5 cm in diameter. Make indentation in centre; top with seasoning and 2 teaspoons butter. Cook over direct medium heat 9–11 minutes.

- Butter buns and grill. Spread with mayonnaise and mustard. Top with burgers, cheese, tomato, bacon, basil, top half of bun; serve.

Onion Brie Burgers

Cook 1 medium onion, chopped, and 2 cloves garlic, crushed, in 2 tablespoons butter. Cool in large bowl. Add salt, pepper and 1 teaspoon thyme leaves; work in 450 g minced beef. Form into 8 thin patties. Top 4 with slices of Brie cheese; add remaining patties and seal edges. Grill over medium heat. Serve on muffins with lettuce.

Butter Burger

Put 3 tablespoons brown sauce in a bowl and stir in salt and pepper. Add 450 g minced beef and form into four patties, each around a pat of butter. Chill for 3–4 hours. Grill over medium direct heat until done; top with more butter. Serve on grilled burger buns with lettuce, tomato and avocado.

Mix Ingredients

- Just as with meatloaf, burgers are better if the meat isn't handled too much. Use a light touch.

- Combine all the other ingredients first before adding the meat. Work gently with your hands just until combined.

- The best beef for burgers has about 20 per cent fat. Any less and the burgers will be dry. Any more and the meat may fall apart.

- You can chill the formed burgers until you're ready to cook; just cook them for a couple more minutes.

Barbecue Burgers

- Make sure that the coals are burned down to a grey ash covering, or that the gas grill has been preheated, before adding the meat.

- For medium heat, you should be able to hold your hand over the grill for 5 seconds before you have to pull it away.

- Never press down on the burgers when on the grill. That will just press the juice and flavour out.

- Have fun garnishing burgers; use guacamole, salsa, basil leaves or flavoured mustards.

ONE-PAN BEEF

A one-dish meal cooked in a frying pan uses lean minced beef for a hearty recipe

One-dish meals are one of the best ways to save time in the kitchen. All you need to add to these recipes is some bread, perhaps a cool salad, and dessert.

One-pan meals are usually faster to make than oven meals. And you don't even need a kitchen! An electric frying pan and a spoon work just fine.

Lean minced beef is the perfect ingredient upon which to base this kind of meal. It's inexpensive, delicious and everyone loves it. It can be formed into meatballs or burgers, or browned with onions and garlic.

Recipes like this are great for impromptu entertaining. Keep ingredients on hand to make your own favourites.

Ingredients

Serves 5

30 g crushed Ritz crackers

1 egg

1 (275-g) can condensed French onion soup

¼ teaspoon pepper

500 g 80 per cent lean minced beef

25 g plain flour

2 tablespoons olive oil

2 tablespoons butter

1 onion, chopped

3 cloves garlic, crushed

225 g sliced mushrooms

120 ml chilli sauce

2 tablespoons Dijon mustard

2 teaspoons Worcestershire sauce

Minced Beef Patties

- Mix together crumbs, egg, 2 tablespoons of the soup and pepper, then add beef.

- Form into five oval patties. Dredge in flour, shaking off excess. Heat oil in large pan; brown patties on both sides over medium heat. Remove and reserve on a plate.

- Drain fat from pan; add butter; cook onion, garlic and mushrooms for 5 minutes.

- Add remaining soup, chilli sauce, mustard and Worcestershire sauce; mix well. Return patties to pan, bring to boil, cover, and simmer for 15–20 minutes until beef is cooked.

Homemade Meatballs

In medium bowl, combine 1 beaten egg with 2 table-spoons water, 25 g dry breadcrumbs, 25 g grated Parmesan cheese, 1 teaspoon dried basil, salt and pepper to taste. Add 500 g minced beef. Form into 2.5-cm meat-balls. Dredge in flour and pan-fry or bake at 180°C for 20–30 minutes until thoroughly cooked. Cool and freeze.

Steak and Potatoes in a Pan

Toss 450 g thinly sliced rump steak with 3 tablespoons flour, 1 teaspoon each paprika, salt and dried oregano, and a pinch of pepper; brown in 3 tablespoons butter. Add 2 potatoes, diced, 1 chopped onion, and 3 cloves garlic. Add 450 ml beef stock and diced tomato; simmer for 15 minutes. Add 150 ml cream and simmer until sauce is blended and thickened.

Shape into Patties

Add Sauce and Finish

- Like meatloaf and meat-balls, these patties must be handled gently or they will be tough.

- Mix the other ingredients for the patties first, then add the beef and mix just until combined; don't overmix.

- You can make the patties ahead of time; dredge them in flour and brown when you want to eat.

- When browning the patties, don't turn them until they easily release from the pan for the best colour and crust.

- After draining the fat from the pan, don't wipe it out or wash it. Not only does this save time, it adds flavour.

- You want the caramelized bits of meat sticking to the bottom of the pan to blend into the sauce.

- You can add more veg-etables to this meal for nutrition: green pepper, courgettes or squash are good choices.

- Serve the patties with rice or mashed potatoes to soak up the sauce.

QUICK MEATBALLS

Some minced beef, a frying pan, and a few other ingredients make a quick and easy meal

Meatballs are a quick and easy dinner choice, and they are so versatile, too. Your own homemade meatballs are a great shortcut ingredient.

To make ahead of time, make the meatballs and cook them completely. Leave to cool for 30 minutes, then refrigerate until cold. Freeze meatballs in a single layer on a baking sheet, pack into rigid containers, label and freeze for up to three months. To thaw, leave in the fridge overnight. You can also add them frozen to recipes and simmer until hot.

Flavour your meatballs according to your favourite cuisine. Caribbean meatballs, for example, could be made with a bit of crushed pineapple and minced jalapeño peppers.

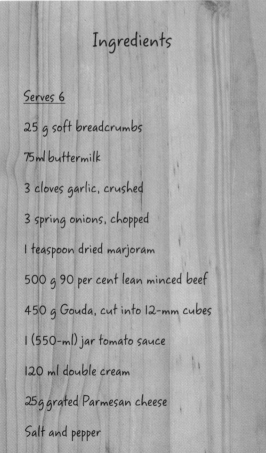

Ingredients

Serves 6

25 g soft breadcrumbs

75 ml buttermilk

3 cloves garlic, crushed

3 spring onions, chopped

1 teaspoon dried marjoram

500 g 90 per cent lean minced beef

450 g Gouda, cut into 12-mm cubes

1 (550-ml) jar tomato sauce

120 ml double cream

25 g grated Parmesan cheese

Salt and pepper

Cheese-Stuffed Meatballs

- In large bowl, combine breadcrumbs, buttermilk, garlic, onion, marjoram, salt and pepper, and mix.

- Add beef; mix just until combined. Form 2 tablespoons beef mixture into a ball; press a cheese cube into the centre; mould meat around cheese. Repeat.

- Chill meatballs for 2 hours.

- In large saucepan, bring pasta sauce to a simmer. Add meatballs and bring back to a simmer.

- Cover and simmer for 20 minutes without stirring. Gently stir in cream, sprinkle with Parmesan, and serve.

Garden Meatballs

Use same meatball recipe; don't stuff with cheese. Brown meatballs in 2 tablespoons olive oil. Remove meatballs from pan; add 1 chopped onion, 3 chopped carrots, 65 g sliced mushrooms; cook until tender. Sprinkle with 2 tablespoons flour, salt and pepper. Add 400 ml beef stock, meatballs, and 400-g can chopped tomatoes. Simmer until meatballs are cooked and sauce is thickened.

Spicy Meatballs and Rice

Use the same meatball recipe; add 1 chopped jalapeño pepper; omit cheese. Brown meatballs in 2 tablespoons oil. Remove meatballs. Add 1 chopped onion; cook until tender. Add 275 g rice; sauté. Add 1 litre beef stock and 1 tablespoon chilli powder. Return meatballs to pan. Cover and simmer for 25 minutes; add 225 g frozen peas; simmer until hot.

Fill Meatballs with Cheese

- Chop the ingredients included in the meatballs to a fine dice and make them all about the same size.

- Handle the beef mixture gently; don't compress it too much around the cheese or the meatballs will be tough.

- Be sure that the cheese is fully covered and in the centre of the meatballs or it may leak out during cooking.

- You can make and stuff the meatballs ahead of time; refrigerate for up to 8 hours.

Add Meatballs to Sauce

- Because the fat content of the meat is so low, you can cook the meatballs directly in the sauce.

- The meatballs will be very tender because they aren't browned first, and the sauce will have more meaty flavour.

- If you use a minced meat with more fat, you can brown the meatballs first, then drain off the fat and proceed with the recipe.

- You can serve this or any meatball recipe with cooked pasta or rice.

LOW-FAT CHICKEN STIR-FRY

Chicken is perfect for stir-fry recipes, especially when cooked with these flavourful ingredients

Stir-fried chicken is a wonderful choice for a quick and easy meal. You don't need a lot of oil to stir-fry food. Just 1–2 tablespoons will work well, especially if the food has been marinated. Stir-fried meals are automatically low in fat.

The chicken is almost always marinated in a mixture of cornflour, soy sauce and other ingredients to make it tender.

All tender vegetables, such as onions, peppers, courgettes and mushrooms, stir-fry beautifully and don't need much advance preparation.

Marinate the chicken for up to 8 hours. Any longer, and the marinade will start to toughen the fibres in the meat.

Ingredients

Serves 4

2 tablespoons cornflour

3 tablespoons soy sauce

1 tablespoon grated fresh ginger

1 tablespoon brown sugar

Pinch of pepper

3 cloves garlic, crushed

120 ml chicken stock

4 boneless, skinless chicken breasts

2 tablespoons groundnut oil

1 onion, chopped

225 g mushrooms, sliced

1 red pepper, chopped

350 g frozen edamame beans, thawed

Chicken Edamame Stir-Fry

- Combine cornflour, soy sauce, ginger, brown sugar, pepper, garlic and chicken stock.

- Cut chicken into 2.5-cm pieces and add to stock mixture; chill 20 minutes.

- Heat oil in wok or large frying pan. Drain chicken and add; stir-fry until almost cooked, about 4 minutes. Remove chicken from pan.

- Add onion and mushrooms; stir-fry for 3–4 minutes. Add pepper, edamame beans, and chicken; stir-fry for 2 minutes. Stir stock mixture and add; stir-fry for 3–4 minutes. Serve with rice.

Spicy Chicken Stir-Fry

Combine 250 ml chicken stock, 3 tablespoons each soy sauce, cornflour and lime juice, 2 chopped jalapeños, and 4 cubed chicken breasts. Refrigerate for 4 hours. Drain; stir-fry chicken in 2 tablespoons oil. Remove; add 1 sliced yellow courgette, 1 sliced red pepper, and 150 g sliced mushrooms. Stir-fry; add chicken and marinade; stir-fry.

Classic Chicken Stir-Fry

Combine 3 tablespoons each cornflour and soy sauce, 1 tablespoon each grated fresh ginger and brown sugar, 3 cloves garlic, and 250 ml chicken stock. Add 4 cubed chicken breasts; refrigerate for 4 hours. Drain; stir-fry chicken in 2 tablespoons oil. Remove; add 1 chopped onion, 175 g sliced carrots, 150 g sliced mushrooms; stir-fry. Stir marinade and add with chicken; stir-fry.

Prepare Ingredients

- Place ingredients in separate bowls after preparation so you can add them all at once to the wok or pan.

- To cut an onion, cut it in half and pull off the skin. Place cut side down on board. Cut horizontally, then vertically, then across.

- Prepare peppers by cutting in half. Pull out the seeds and membranes and discard. Place skin side down and cut.

- Trim off the bottoms of mushrooms and place cap side down; slice through the stem.

Marinate Chicken

- Instead of soy sauce you can add other flavourings to the chicken marinade. Think about using honey, mustard, sweet and sour or Tex-Mex flavours.

- For sweet and sour, combine equal amounts of cider or rice wine vinegar and

sugar; add cornflour and chicken stock.

- Tex-Mex flavours would use chilli powder, cumin, lime juice and salt and pepper along with the cornflour and stock.

PAN-FRIED CHICKEN ESCALOPES

Quick-to-cook chicken fillets will become one of your basics with these easy recipes

Escalopes are very thin pieces of lean, tender meat, either cut thinly or pounded before cooking. They cook in just a few minutes, so have to be very well flavoured.

Pan-frying is the best way to cook escalopes because they won't dry out. You can make a sauce for the dish to add flavour and moisture. The sauce is made in the pan after the escalopes

are cooked, using the pan juices, and then poured over them.

If you're going to cut the meat into thin slices, it will be easier if it is partially frozen first. Place in the freezer for 30–40 minutes, remove and quickly slice.

This is one of the most versatile recipes; use your favourite vegetables and flavours.

Tex-Mex Chicken Escalopes

Ingredients

Serves 6

6 boneless, skinless chicken breasts

1 tablespoon chilli powder

½ teaspoon ground cumin

40 g plain flour

3 tablespoons olive oil

1 onion, chopped

4 cloves garlic, crushed

2 jalapeño peppers, finely chopped

250 ml chicken stock

2 tablespoons lime juice

225 g cherry tomatoes

2 tablespoons butter

20 g chopped coriander

Salt and pepper

- Place chicken in a plastic bag; gently pound until about 6 mm thick. Season with salt, pepper, chilli powder and cumin, then dredge with flour.

- Heat olive oil over medium heat in large frying pan; sauté chicken for about 4–5 minutes, turning once, until

golden brown, and remove.

- Add onion, garlic and jalapeños to pan; sauté for 5 minutes. Add stock, juice, and tomatoes and simmer.

- Return chicken to pan and cook for 1–2 minutes until hot. Swirl in butter and sprinkle with coriander.

Honey Mustard Escalopes

Butterfly 4 small chicken breasts: with knife parallel to work surface, cut almost through chicken and open up. Pound to 6 mm thick; dredge in 25 g plain flour, salt, pepper, and ½ teaspoon dry mustard. Cook chicken 1–2 minutes on each side in 2 tablespoons butter; remove. Add 120 ml chicken stock, 2 tablespoons honey mustard, and 2 tablespoons honey; swirl and pour over meat.

Lemon Pesto Escalopes

Pound 4 chicken breasts, and dredge in 25 g plain flour, 1 teaspoon lemon zest, salt and pepper. Cook in 2 tablespoons butter for 1–2 minutes on each side. Remove chicken to plate and keep warm. Add 120 ml pesto, 2 tablespoons lemon juice, and 120 ml chicken stock to pan; stir over heat and when blended and bubbling pour over chicken.

Pound Chicken

- To pound the meat, place in a heavy-duty plastic bag. (Don't use cling film, baking parchment or greaseproof paper as they may tear.)

- Start pounding from the centre of the meat, working to the outside edges. Check the thickness frequently.

- Pound firmly but gently so you don't tear or rip the meat. If there are holes, the chicken will easily overcook and will not look as nice.

- Coat the chicken with flour to help protect it from the heat and thicken the sauce.

Finish Sauce

- If you use about the same amount of sauce mixture, the recipe will turn out right every time.

- For liquid, you can use chicken stock, sweet and sour sauce, or any other Asian marinade.

- Swirl in butter at the very end of cooking time to finish the dish. This adds a silky texture and a rich taste to the simple pan sauce.

- Add fresh chopped herbs at the very end so they keep their colour and flavour.

SAUTÉED CHICKEN COATINGS

Boneless, skinless chicken breasts can be coated with everything from crushed cornflakes to chopped nuts

Chicken is the perfect last-minute recipe for dinner, especially when it's coated with a crisp and flavourful mixture.

You can use almost anything you like for the coating mixture. Crushed cereal, ground nuts, fresh or dried breadcrumbs and cheeses are good bases for coatings. Flavour them with anything from dried herbs and spices to herbs and citrus zests. The meat will cook more evenly and the coating will be perfectly browned if you flatten the chicken before coating and cooking it. A rolling pin or meat mallet can be used to flatten the chicken.

Make a quick pan sauce from the meat juices, pour over the chicken, and serve in minutes.

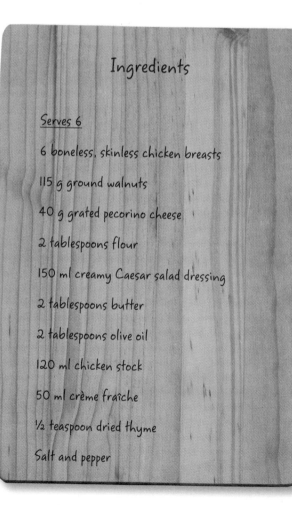

Ingredients

Serves 6

6 boneless, skinless chicken breasts

115 g ground walnuts

40 g grated pecorino cheese

2 tablespoons flour

150 ml creamy Caesar salad dressing

2 tablespoons butter

2 tablespoons olive oil

120 ml chicken stock

50 ml crème fraîche

½ teaspoon dried thyme

Salt and pepper

Crisp Walnut Caesar Chicken

- Place chicken in plastic bag; pound until 6 mm thick.

- In a shallow bowl, combine walnuts, cheese and flour, and season with salt and pepper. Coat chicken in salad dressing, then press into walnut mixture to coat evenly; leave to stand for 5 minutes.

- In large pan, melt butter and olive oil over medium heat. Add chicken, 3 pieces at a time, and sauté for 2–4 minutes on each side.

- Remove chicken and keep warm. Add stock, crème fraîche and thyme to pan, bring to the boil and pour over chicken to serve.

Brown Sugar Pecan Chicken
Pound 6 chicken breasts to 6 mm thick. On plate, combine 75 g ground pecans, 20 g dry breadcrumbs, 3 tablespoons brown sugar, salt and pepper. Dip chicken in 120 ml honey mustard, then press into pecan mixture to coat. Cook in 3 tablespoons butter for 4–6 minutes. Remove, add 250 ml chicken stock to pan, boil, and pour over chicken.

Chicken Parmesan
Pound 6 chicken breasts. Combine 50 g dried Italian breadcrumbs, 25 g grated Parmesan cheese, ½ teaspoon oregano, and ½ teaspoon salt. Dip chicken into 2 beaten eggs, then into breadcrumb mixture. Cook in 3 tablespoons butter until golden brown. Meanwhile, heat 750 ml pasta sauce in pan. Pour sauce over chicken; top with 115 g grated Mozzarella cheese.

Mix Coating Ingredients

- The coating mixture should be well mixed so each piece of chicken gets an equal amount of seasoning.

- You don't have to pound the chicken before coating. If you don't, cook for 4–6 minutes on each side over medium-low heat until cooked through.

- The amount of coating needed will depend on the size of the breasts. Add more if necessary.

- You could substitute ground pecans, cashews or pine nuts for the walnuts in this recipe if you like.

Coat Chicken

- Dip the chicken into the dressing until completely coated, then gently shake off the excess. Use more dressing if you run short.

- Drop the chicken into the coating mixture, scoop more of the coating mixture on top of the chicken, and press it on.

- The chicken should be evenly and completely coated, with no bare spots.

- Let the chicken dry on a wire rack for 5–7 minutes before sautéing so the coating stays on the chicken.

CHICKEN ENTRÉES

BAKED CHICKEN

Chicken cooks to juicy perfection in the oven, and can be flavoured in so many ways

Baked chicken will always come out tender and juicy because this cooking method is gentler than grilling or sautéing.

You can bake plain chicken breasts or thighs, coat them with flour or envelop them in a sauce, stuff boneless chicken breasts, or bake a jointed whole chicken. The baking times will be different, but the method is the same.

At 180°C boneless, skinless chicken breasts are cooked in 20 minutes. Boneless, skinless chicken thighs need 40–50 minutes. A whole jointed chicken will take 1¼ hours. Bone-in, skin-on chicken breasts need 35–45 minutes. Test by piercing the thickest part of the meat with a sharp knife or skewer: the juices should run clear, and there should be no pink meat..

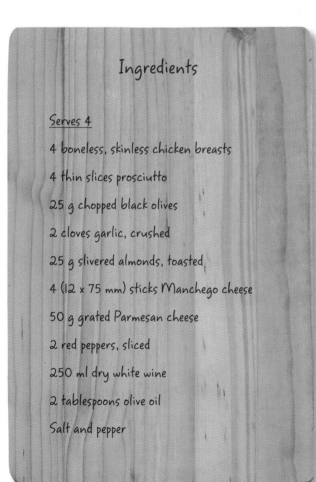

Ingredients

Serves 4

4 boneless, skinless chicken breasts

4 thin slices prosciutto

25 g chopped black olives

2 cloves garlic, crushed

25 g slivered almonds, toasted

4 (12 x 75 mm) sticks Manchego cheese

50 g grated Parmesan cheese

2 red peppers, sliced

250 ml dry white wine

2 tablespoons olive oil

Salt and pepper

Spanish Chicken Rolls

- Preheat oven to 170°C. Pound chicken until 6 mm thick and place flat on work surface. Season with salt and pepper.

- Top each breast with 1 slice prosciutto, olives, garlic, almonds and a stick of Manchego cheese. Roll up; fold in ends around filling.

- Press chicken rolls in Parmesan cheese to coat. Place in glass baking dish and add peppers. Pour wine and olive oil into dish.

- Cover and bake for 30–40 minutes, until chicken is thoroughly cooked. Serve with the sliced peppers.

Crispy Herb Chicken
Combine 50 g crushed cornflakes, 1 tablespoon dried parsley, 40 g grated Pecorino cheese, 1 teaspoon salt and 1 teaspoon each dried basil and thyme. Dip 12 boneless, skinless chicken thighs in 2 beaten eggs, then coat with cornflake mixture. Place in baking dish, drizzle with 2 tablespoons melted butter, and bake at 180°C for 30–40 minutes until done.

Sticky Baked Chicken
In medium saucepan, cook 1 chopped onion in 2 tablespoons olive oil. Add 50 ml soy sauce, 120 ml seafood cocktail sauce, 120 ml honey, 4 cloves crushed garlic, salt and pepper; simmer for 5 minutes. Arrange the joints from a whole chicken in baking dish; pour sauce over. Bake at 190°C for 1 hour until done.

Prepare Filling

- You could chop the prosciutto and cheese and combine all the ingredients before filling the chicken.

- Or just layer the ingredients on the chicken before rolling it up. Tuck in the sides to enclose the filling.

- Don't overfill the chicken breasts. If there's too much filling, it will just leak out of the chicken and burn on the pan.

- The filling should be well seasoned and complete in itself, since the chicken won't flavour it while it's cooking.

Roll to Enclose Filling

- Be sure that there is enough chicken around the filling to enclose it completely.

- Secure the chicken bundles with cocktail sticks or short metal skewers.

- You could add other quick-baking vegetables to the pan with the chicken. Be

sure they will cook in the time specified.

- Mushrooms, chopped onions or courgettes would be good choices for chicken breasts. For whole chicken, choose cubed potatoes or carrots.

CHICKEN ENTRÉES

BARBECUED CHICKEN BREASTS

Chicken on the barbecue is perfect and gorgeous, especially when marinated in a savoury dressing

Chargrilling chicken adds another layer of flavour to this tender, mild meat. The barbecue automatically caramelizes the chicken skin or coating because of the very high heat.

You can add smoke flavour with wood chips or fruit vines. Put these additions directly on a charcoal fire, or in a small pan placed under the rack on a gas barbecue. Wood chips

should be soaked for 1 hour before adding to the barbecue; herbs and vines do not need to be soaked.

Build a two-level fire when barbecuing chicken. Boneless, skinless thighs and breasts can be grilled completely over direct heat. Brown whole chickens and bone-in joints over direct heat, then finish over indirect heat.

Curried Honey Chicken Breasts

Ingredients

Serves 4

1 tablespoon olive oil

2 cloves garlic, crushed

1 tablespoon curry powder

50 ml honey

2 tablespoons mayonnaise

50 ml grainy Dijon mustard

Pinch of pepper

4 boneless, skinless chicken breasts

- In small microwave-safe dish, combine oil, garlic and curry powder. Microwave on high for 1–2 minutes until garlic is fragrant. Remove and stir in remaining ingredients except chicken. Place chicken in glass baking dish; marinate in refrigerator 30 minutes or up to 24 hours.

- Prepare barbecue for direct medium heat. Remove chicken from marinade, reserving marinade.

- Barbecue for 5–7 minutes on each side, turning once and basting with reserved marinade, until cooked.

Chargrilled Citrus Chicken
Combine 3 tablespoons each lime juice, lemon juice, and brown sugar, 50 ml Dijon mustard, 1 teaspoon grated lemon zest, 3 cloves crushed garlic, salt and pepper. Add 6 boneless, skinless chicken breasts and marinate for 30 minutes at room temperature or 12–24 hours in the fridge. Grill over direct medium heat for 5–6 minutes per side until done. Discard marinade.

Chargrilled Teriyaki Chicken
In plastic bag, combine 75 ml teriyaki sauce, 50 ml lemon juice, 4 cloves crushed garlic, 2 tablespoons soy sauce, 2 tablespoons honey and a pinch of cayenne pepper. Add 5 boneless, skinless chicken breasts; marinate for 30 minutes at room temperature or 12–24 hours in the fridge. Drain, discarding marinade. Grill for 6–8 minutes per side until chicken is thoroughly cooked.

Microwave Garlic and Curry Powder

Chargrill Chicken

CHICKEN ENTRÉES

- Curry powder is heated along with the garlic because the heat deepens and develops the flavours.

- Watch the mixture in the microwave carefully so it doesn't burn. If the garlic does burn, discard it and start again.

- The honey in the marinade flavours the chicken and adds moisture. It will also caramelize beautifully.

- Discard any remaining marinade after you've brushed the chicken with it once. There isn't enough to serve as a sauce for the chicken.

- Barbecue the chicken until it is cooked through (an instant-read meat thermometer should register 75°C).

- The chicken should stand for 5–6 minutes after grilling before you serve it: the temperature will continue to rise a little.

- You can cook this chicken on a dual-contact grill. Grill for half the time, as the chicken cooks on both sides at once.

- If you grill the chicken indoors, have your extractor fan on at full power, as the marinade will smoke while the chicken cooks.

QUICK WAYS WITH COOKED CHICKEN

Start with a ready-roasted chicken and you'll have dinner on the table in minutes

You can buy ready-roasted chickens in most supermarkets, either chilled or straight off the rotisserie. These fully cooked chickens are tender and juicy and offer a wealth of possibilities for quick and easy meals. A rotisserie chicken should be very hot when you purchase it. Take it home immediately and use it or refrigerate it as soon as you get home.

You can serve the chicken in large joints, or remove each section of light and dark meat and shred or cut it into small pieces. Use the chicken within two days. Leftovers, including the bones and skin, can be used to make stock.

Use these ideas for leftover cooked chicken from your own home-roasted birds too.

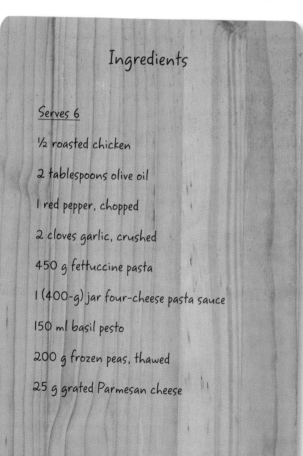

Ingredients

Serves 6

½ roasted chicken

2 tablespoons olive oil

1 red pepper, chopped

2 cloves garlic, crushed

450 g fettuccine pasta

1 (400-g) jar four-cheese pasta sauce

150 ml basil pesto

200 g frozen peas, thawed

25 g grated Parmesan cheese

Pesto Chicken with Fettuccine

- Remove chicken from bones and skin and shred; set aside. Bring a large pan of salted water to a boil.

- In large frying pan, heat oil over medium heat. Add pepper and garlic; cook and stir for 3 minutes.

- Cook fettuccine until almost al dente. Meanwhile, add pasta sauce, pesto and chicken to pan; bring to a simmer.

- When fettuccine is cooked, drain and add to pan with peas. Cook and stir over medium heat until mixture is blended and hot. Top with cheese and serve.

90

Chicken Cordon Bleu

Cut 450 g cooked chicken into bite-size pieces and set aside. Cook 1 chopped onion and 3 cloves garlic in 2 tablespoons olive oil. Add 150 g chopped ham and the chicken; cook until hot. Add 1 (400-g) jar four-cheese pasta sauce and simmer. Add 115 g grated Emmental cheese and 115 g frozen peas; cook until hot. Serve with pasta.

Chicken Cacciatore

Cut 450 g chicken into bite-size pieces and set aside. Cook 1 chopped onion and 2 cloves garlic in 3 tablespoons olive oil. Add 1 chopped green pepper, 225 g sliced mushrooms and 1 teaspoon Italian seasoning. Add 1 (400-g) can chopped tomatoes, 50 ml tomato purée, and 120 ml chicken stock. Simmer for 10 minutes, add chicken; simmer until hot. Sprinkle with chopped parsley.

Remove Meat from Chicken

- It's not difficult to remove the meat from a cooked chicken. Just use a sharp knife and work slowly around all the bones.

- Place the chicken on the work surface and cut along the backbone on each side.

- Cut along the bottom of each breast to remove it. Shred, slice or chop meat.

- Turn the chicken over and cut the meat from the drumsticks, wings and thighs. Freeze the bones to make into stock or soup.

Cook Pasta and Sauce

- Undercook the fettucine slightly, as it will finish cooking in the sauce.

- If the pasta is a little under-cooked when it's added to the dish, it will absorb some flavour from the sauce.

- You don't need to cook the mixture much once the pesto and pasta have been added. Keep the mixture moving by gently manipulating it with tongs.

CHICKEN ENTRÉES

CHICKEN BURGERS

Add a few ingredients to minced chicken for a delicious, fresh burger

Chicken burgers are a nice change from the traditional beef burger. They're lower in fat, and since the meat is milder than beef, can be flavoured in an infinite number of ways.

Minced chicken can sometimes be difficult to find at the supermarket. You can ask your butcher to mince some for you, or you can do it yourself at home.

Just cut up some raw, boneless, skinless chicken breasts and/or thighs and place the pieces in a food processor. Pulse the meat until it's coarsely minced. Don't go overboard: if you process too much the burgers will be mushy.

Minced chicken should be used or frozen within one day for food safety reasons. Enjoy these easy recipes.

Ingredients

Serves 4

1 tablespoon olive oil

1 onion, chopped

1 medium carrot, grated

20g soft breadcrumbs

1 egg

½ teaspoon barbecue seasoning

500 g minced chicken

4 burger buns, split

4 slices Emmental cheese

2 avocados, sliced

Avocado Chicken Burgers

- Heat olive oil over medium heat. Add onion and carrots; cook, stirring, until softened, about 5 minutes.

- Remove to large bowl; leave to cool. Stir in breadcrumbs, egg and seasoning. Add chicken; mix gently. Form into 4 patties and chill for 2–3 hours.

- Grill burgers on direct medium heat for 5–6 minutes per side until thoroughly cooked.

- Grill buns, add cheese to chicken, and cook for 1–2 minutes. Top burgers with avocado; serve on buns.

Blue Cheese Chicken Burgers

Cook 1 finely chopped stick of celery in oil. Add bread-crumbs, ½ teaspoon Tabasco, 25 g blue cheese, and 2 tablespoons chicken stock. Omit onion and carrot, Emmental and avocado. Top with blue cheese dressing and serve on toasted, buttered sourdough buns with crème fraîche, tomato and lettuce.

Thai Chicken Burgers

Combine 40 g dry breadcrumbs, 2 tablespoons soy sauce, 2 cloves crushed garlic, 1 tablespoon curry paste, 1 finely chopped red onion, 1 tablespoon lime juice, 2 tablespoons peanut butter and 2 tablespoons finely chopped mint. Add 450 g minced chicken. Form into 4 patties and grill until done. Serve in pitta breads with a mixture of mayonnaise, lime juice and hot pepper sauce.

Mix Burger Ingredients

- Ingredients such as onion, garlic and carrots must be cooked before the minced chicken is added.

- The cooking time on the barbecue isn't long enough to cook these vegetables. They will be tough if not cooked first.

- Work with minced chicken just as you do with minced beef: mix all other ingredients first, then add chicken and mix gently.

- Don't overwork the chicken mixture, and don't press the burgers together too hard or they will be tough.

Grill Burgers

- Chicken burgers are more delicate and fragile than beef burgers, so handle with care.

- The chilling time is important, so don't skip it. It gives the chicken mixture time to amalgamate and the breadcrumbs time to absorb liquid.

- If you are barbecuing the chicken burgers, you may want to cook them on a grill basket instead of directly on the rack.

- Don't press down on the burgers when they are cooking, or you'll press out liquid and lots of flavour.

MINCED POULTRY

93

DELUXE TURKEY BURGERS

Brie cheese is a fabulous addition to tender, juicy turkey burgers

Like chicken burgers, turkey burgers are a great change of pace. Minced turkey is usually easier to find in the supermarket than minced chicken, but you can also make your own in a food processor.

Minced turkey may be all white meat or a mix of white and dark meat. Either one works well for turkey burgers. If you use all white meat the burgers will be lower in fat, but a mixture of white and dark will have more flavour. All-white-meat burgers will need more additions because the meat is so low in fat. Sauté some onion in a little olive oil, or add some crème fraîche or grated cheese for moisture.

Flavour your turkey burgers with any combination of herbs, spices, cheeses and vegetables.

Ingredients

Serves 4

3 tablespoons butter

1 onion, finely chopped

3 cloves garlic, crushed

15 g dry breadcrumbs

1 teaspoon dried basil

1 teaspoon seasoning salt

1 egg

500 g minced turkey

25 g plain flour

1 wedge Brie cheese, sliced

4 burger buns, split

75 ml honey mustard salad dressing

4 lettuce leaves

French Brie Turkey Burgers

- Heat 1 tablespoon of the butter in a large pan and soften the onion and garlic. Remove to large bowl; cool.

- Add breadcrumbs, basil, salt and egg; mix. Add turkey; mix gently with hands. Form into 4 patties; make indentation in centre; chill for 2–3 hours.

- In the same pan, melt the remaining butter. Coat patties with flour; cook in butter, turning once, for 9–11 minutes.

- Remove burgers from heat, add Brie; cover. Toast buns. Spread with honey mustard dressing and fill with lettuce and burgers.

Tex-Mex Turkey Burgers

Finely chop 1 onion and 1 red pepper, and cook with 2 crushed garlic cloves and 2 jalapeño peppers until soft. Remove from heat; add 25 g crumbled tortilla chips; leave to stand for 5 minutes. Add 500 g minced turkey. Form into patties and cook as directed. Serve on toasted hamburger buns with Cheddar cheese, mayonnaise, salsa, tomatoes and sliced avocado.

Greek Turkey Burgers

Combine 20 g dried breadcrumbs, 1 egg, 50 g crumbled feta cheese, ½ teaspoon each dried oregano, basil and dill, and 25 g chopped olives. Add 500 g minced turkey and mix; form into patties. Cook as directed. Serve on toasted sesame buns with lettuce, tomato, mayonnaise and mustard.

Shape Patties

Melt Cheese on Top

- The turkey mixture will be more delicate than a minced beef mixture, so handle gently. Too much handling will make the burgers tough.

- It's always a good idea to chill poultry burgers before cooking, especially before barbecuing.

- You can use a grill basket if you want, which will help to stop the burgers from falling apart.

- If it's hard to shape the burgers, refrigerate the mixture before you shape it into patties.

- Brie is a delicate and rich cheese. For easier slicing, try putting it in the freezer for about 10 minutes before you slice.

- The rind on Brie cheese is edible, but the texture is very different from the cheese itself.

- You can remove the rind if you like for a more consistent topping on the burgers.

- For even more indulgent flavour, add some sliced avocados to the burgers along with the lettuce and dressing.

MINCED POULTRY

95

SALSA MEATBALLS

Mexican ingredients such as salsa and cumin add a spark of flavour to chicken meatballs

Making meatballs is the same as making meatloaf or burgers. Combine all the added ingredients first, then add the minced chicken or turkey and mix just until combined.

The chicken mixture, again, will be quite delicate. So baking or grilling the meatballs is a better option than trying to cook them in a frying pan.

An easy way to make meatballs, as well as meatloaf, is to cook a sauce, then use part of that sauce as an addition to the minced meat. The meatballs are then flavoured very well from the inside out.

You can serve the meatballs and sauce with rice, cooked pasta, or mashed potatoes or sweet potatoes.

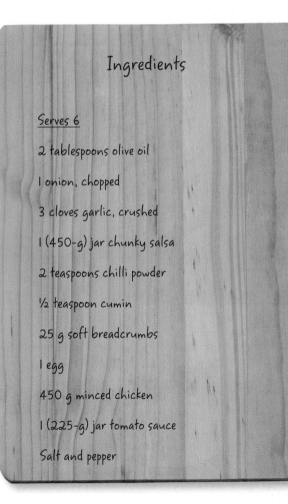

Ingredients

<u>Serves 6</u>

2 tablespoons olive oil

1 onion, chopped

3 cloves garlic, crushed

1 (450-g) jar chunky salsa

2 teaspoons chilli powder

½ teaspoon cumin

25 g soft breadcrumbs

1 egg

450 g minced chicken

1 (225-g) jar tomato sauce

Salt and pepper

Mexican Spicy Chicken Meatballs

- In large pan, heat olive oil over medium heat. Add onion and garlic; cook and stir until softened.

- Add salsa, chilli powder, cumin, salt and pepper; remove from heat. Combine 5 tablespoons of this mixture with breadcrumbs and egg in large bowl.

- Add chicken; mix well. Form into 18 meatballs. Place on greased grill rack; grill meatballs until light brown, turning once.

- Add meatballs to salsa mixture along with tomato sauce; simmer for 9–12 minutes until chicken is thoroughly cooked.

Parmesan Chicken Meatballs

Combine 1 egg, 25 g grated Parmesan cheese, 25 g dried breadcrumbs, 1 small red onion, finely chopped, 2 cloves crushed garlic, salt and pepper. Add 450 g minced chicken. Form into 2.5-mm balls. Bring 1 (800-g) jar tomato pasta sauce to the boil; add meatballs. Simmer for 15–25 minutes until meatballs are cooked. Serve with pasta.

Spicy Chicken Meatballs

Cook 1 small chopped onion and 2 crushed cloves garlic in 2 tablespoons butter. Place in bowl; add 2 tablespoons hot sauce, 50 ml four-cheese pasta sauce and 25 g breadcrumbs. Add 450 minced chicken; form into meatballs. Brown in 2 tablespoons olive oil; drain. Add 400 ml four-cheese sauce, 115 g chopped celery; simmer for 20–25 minutes. Add 115 g blue cheese; serve with pasta.

Prepare Ingredients

- Let the sautéed mixture cool for a while before you add the chicken. It doesn't have to be completely cold.

- If you like it spicy, add a lot more chilli powder. You could also add some chopped jalapeño or serrano peppers.

- The heat level of the salsa you choose will also affect the flavour. Remember that the chicken is very mild.

- If your family isn't used to hot foods, choose a mild salsa with green chillis instead of jalapeño peppers.

Grill Meatballs

- Watch the meatballs carefully under the grill. You may need to turn them several times, moving the meatballs slightly each time.

- Turn the meatballs with a pair of tongs, and handle gently. Lightly oil the grill pan before putting the meatballs on it.

- Because the meatballs don't cook completely under the grill, you can't stop at this point and refrigerate them.

- As soon as the meatballs are browned, add them to the pasta sauce and finish the cooking.

MINCED POULTRY

MICROWAVE CHICKEN QUICHE

Yes, you can make quiche in the microwave; just a few tricks make it perfect

Quiches used to be considered difficult to make, but nothing could be further from the truth. A quiche is simply a flan with a filling based on beaten eggs and cheese. That's it.

Quiches are conventionally baked in the oven, to brown the pastry and set the egg custard. But it is also possible to make a quiche in a microwave oven.

There are a few tricks to microwave quiche cooking. Because the pastry won't brown, you'll need to colour it somehow. Use spices like chilli powder or cinnamon, or dark liquids like soy sauce or Worcestershire sauce. And follow cooking, rotating and standing times to the letter.

Now invent your own microwave quiche!

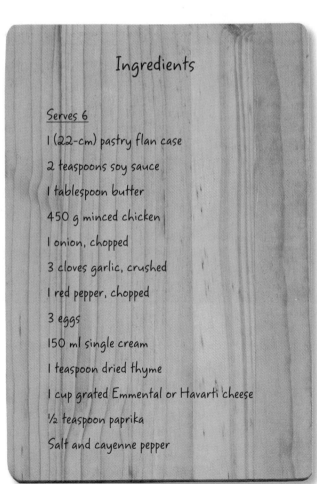

Ingredients

Serves 6

1 (22-cm) pastry flan case

2 teaspoons soy sauce

1 tablespoon butter

450 g minced chicken

1 onion, chopped

3 cloves garlic, crushed

1 red pepper, chopped

3 eggs

150 ml single cream

1 teaspoon dried thyme

1 cup grated Emmental or Havarti cheese

½ teaspoon paprika

Salt and cayenne pepper

Chicken and Onion Quiche

- Rub edge of pastry case with soy sauce; prick with fork. Microwave on high 5–7 minutes, until surface looks flaky.

- In a pan, melt butter; add chicken, onion and garlic; cook until meat browns. Add pepper, cook 2 minutes longer. Drain and spoon into flan case.

- In bowl, beat eggs, cream and thyme; add salt and cayenne pepper. Add cheese; pour into flan case. Sprinkle with paprika.

- Microwave on medium-high power for 19–25 minutes until knife inserted comes out clean. Leave to stand for 10 minutes before serving.

Havarti Dill Chicken Quiche

Prepare flan case as directed. Cook 450 g minced chicken, 1 chopped onion and 3 cloves garlic in 2 tablespoons butter in microwave. Add 150 ml milk, 3 eggs, 1 teaspoon dried dill and ½ teaspoon salt. Place 175 g grated Havarti cheese in pastry case; pour chicken mixture over. Sprinkle with 25 g grated Parmesan cheese. Cook as directed.

Chicken Divan Quiche

Prepare flan case as directed. Cook 450 g minced chicken and 1 chopped onion in 2 tablespoons butter in microwave. Add 150 g frozen broccoli florets, thawed and drained, 3 eggs, 250 ml single cream, 25 g Parmesan cheese and 2 tablespoons flour. Place 115 g grated Cheddar cheese in flan case, top with chicken mixture; sprinkle with 1 teaspoon paprika. Cook as directed.

Cook Filling Ingredients

- You can cook the filling ingredients in a pan or in the microwave oven.

- To cook in the microwave, place in microwave-safe dish. Microwave for 4 minutes on high power; remove and stir.

- Continue microwaving for 1-minute intervals until chicken and vegetables are tender. Place in flan case and proceed with recipe.

- The filling ingredients can be hot when you put them in the flan case, and when pouring the egg mixture over them.

Precook Flan Case

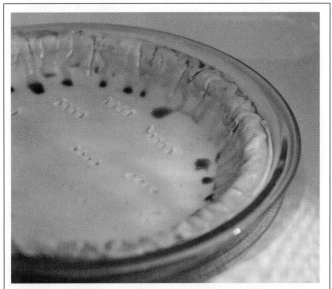

- Cooking the flan case in the microwave is easy, but you need to know a few rules.

- The pastry will cook in the microwave but it won't brown. You can use soy sauce or gravy browning, or a spice like curry powder.

- Make sure that you let the flan case, then the filled cooked quiche, stand on a solid surface after cooking.

- The solid surface keeps the heat in the pie, where it will redistribute, finishing the quiche to perfection.

MINCED POULTRY

TURKEY PASTA SAUCE

Minced turkey is the perfect addition to a classic pasta sauce; serve with spaghetti or other pasta shapes

Pasta with a rich tomato sauce is a classic quick recipe. All you really need is a jar of ready-made pasta sauce, some seasonings, cheese and pasta.

But that basic recipe can be varied in many ways. Adding minced turkey is an excellent way to add protein, flavour and texture to tomato sauce.

These sauces don't need to cook for a long time. Just a few minutes of simmering will blend flavours.

Make a Tex-Mex turkey pasta sauce by adding jalapeño peppers and salsa to the recipe, or add dried herbes de Provence and roasted red peppers for a French turkey pasta sauce. Enjoy experimenting!

Spaghetti with Tomato and Turkey Sauce

Ingredients

Serves 6

1 tablespoon olive oil

450 g minced turkey

1 onion, chopped

4 cloves garlic, crushed

1 (175 g) can tomato purée

2 (400-g) cans chopped tomatoes

250 ml tomato juice

2 teaspoons sugar

2 tablespoons chopped fresh basil

½ teaspoon dried oregano

450 g spaghetti

50 g grated pecorino cheese

Salt and pepper

- In large saucepan, heat olive oil; add turkey, onion and garlic. Cook and stir until turkey is tender; drain.

- Add tomato purée; allow to brown a little, then add tomatoes, juice, sugar and herbs; season with salt and pepper. Leave to simmer, stirring occasionally.

- Bring a large pan of salted water to the boil. Cook pasta until al dente.

- Drain pasta, reserving 3 tablespoons cooking water. Turn pasta in sauce, adding water if necessary; cook 2 minutes. Sprinkle with cheese; serve.

Homemade tomato sauce is an excellent standby ingredient to have in your freezer. It's worth making a large quantity in summer when tomatoes are well-flavoured and abundant, but at other times a few cans of tomatoes, with a little olive oil, some chopped onion, garlic, fresh or dried herbs, sugar, salt and pepper, simmered for 60–90 minutes in a large pan, make a very good sauce.

Turkey Sausage Marinara: Cook 450 g turkey sausage, skinned and crumbled, 1 chopped onion, 3 cloves garlic, and 1 green pepper in a little oil. Add 1 (660-g) jar tomato and basil pasta sauce, ½ teaspoon each dried oregano and basil, and 120 ml white wine. Simmer 15–20 minutes; serve with spaghetti and grated pecorino cheese.

Cook Sauce

- Because minced turkey is so mild, you can use any type of flavouring or seasoning in your pasta sauce recipe.

- You could substitute a large jar of ready-made tomato sauce for the tomato purée, tomatoes, juice, sugar, salt and seasonings.

- Minced chicken can be substituted for the minced turkey. The remaining ingredients stay the same.

- Stir the sauce frequently, scraping along the bottom so it doesn't burn and all the ingredients blend together.

Cook Spaghetti

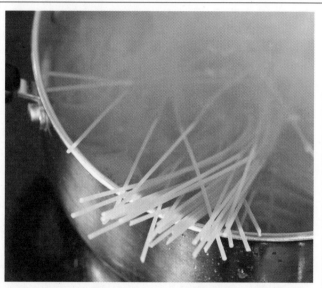

- Stir the spaghetti frequently while it's cooking so it doesn't stick together.

- The water has to be at a full boil all the time to get the pasta to absorb the water and soften.

- When the pasta is cooked al dente, there will still be a slight bit of firmness and a small white line in the centre of each strand.

- Take a bite and see what you think. If the pasta tastes good to you, it's done.

ONE-PAN CHICKEN

Shredded broccoli and other vegetables add great flavour and texture to minced chicken

Minced chicken is perfect for a one-pan meal. It cooks quickly and stays tender, and it's an excellent foil for other strongly flavoured ingredients.

You can use this idea as the base for other recipes; it is also a great way to use leftovers. Top some shredded lettuce or spinach with the hot chicken mixture for a delicious salad.

Use the mixture to fill enchiladas or tacos, or serve it as a sauce on pasta.

Because these meals cook quickly, have all of the ingredients prepared before you start cooking. A meal in a pan isn't very different from a stir-fried meal; the cooking time is just a bit longer. Use your favourite flavours and vegetables.

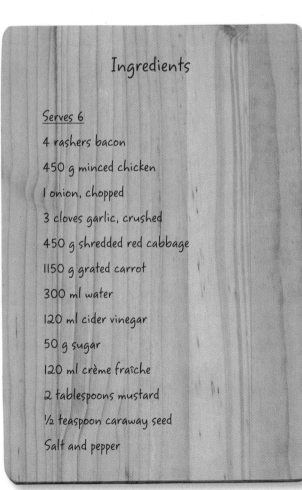

Ingredients

Serves 6

4 rashers bacon

450 g minced chicken

1 onion, chopped

3 cloves garlic, crushed

450 g shredded red cabbage

1150 g grated carrot

300 ml water

120 ml cider vinegar

50 g sugar

120 ml crème fraîche

2 tablespoons mustard

½ teaspoon caraway seed

Salt and pepper

German Chicken with Cabbage

- In a large frying pan, cook bacon until crisp; crumble and set aside. Drain all but 2 tablespoons bacon fat.

- Add chicken, onion and garlic; cook and stir until chicken is almost done. Remove from pan.

- Add cabbage and carrots to pan with 50 ml of the water; cover and simmer until cabbage is almost tender.

- In small bowl, combine remaining ingredients. Add to pan with chicken mixture; cook and stir for 3–4 minutes until sauce thickens and vegetables are tender. Top with crumbled bacon.

Chicken Taco Salad

Cook 450 g minced chicken with 1 chopped onion, 2 cloves garlic and 2 jalapeño peppers. Add 1 (425-g) can black beans, drained, 250 ml tomato sauce and 250 ml salsa; simmer. Serve on shredded lettuce with tortilla chips, grated Cheddar cheese, chopped tomatoes and a bowl of crème fraîche.

Thai Chicken

Cook 450 g minced chicken with 2 chopped red peppers, 1 chopped onion, 2 garlic cloves and 1 tablespoon finely chopped fresh ginger. Add 50 g peanut butter, 250 ml chicken stock, 120 ml coconut milk, 2 tablespoons soy sauce, 1 tablespoon lime juice and 2 teaspoons curry powder; simmer until thickened. Serve with rice.

Chop or Shred Cabbage

- To chop cabbage, first remove any outer wilted leaves. Cut the cabbage in half and cut out the core.

- Place the cabbage, cut side down, on work surface. Cut several times parallel to the work surface.

- Then cut cabbage from the rounded side to the flat side, forming strips. Finally, cut against those cuts to form cubes.

- Or you could shred the cabbage using a food processor. Follow directions for the appliance.

Add Sauce to Pan

- Depending on what you're cooking with the chicken, you may want to remove the meat from the pan when it's done.

- If you're using longer-cooking foods such as potatoes, remove the chicken while they cook.

- The best way to cook cabbage so it doesn't waft aromas through the house is to cook it quickly.

- You could replace the cabbage and carrot in the recipe with coarsely grated courgettes or chopped mushrooms.

MINCED POULTRY

PORK STIR-FRY

Stir-fry pork with some fresh fruits for a nice twist on a classic recipe

Pork isn't commonly stir-fried in Asian cuisines. But it's a great addition to this super quick meal. You can use pork chops cut into pieces, cubed pork tenderloin or strips of boneless pork loin. Or use cubes of cooked ham. If you do use ham, don't marinate it and add it at the end of stir-frying, when you add the sauce.

Using fruit in stir-fries is a bit different from using vegetables. The fruit doesn't need to cook for so long, but you still want it to heat through and release some juice. A light hand with the spatula is necessary, as it is done very quickly.

Other good fruits for this recipe include plums, nectarines and mangos.

Fruited Sweet and Sour Pork

Ingredients

Serves 6

2 tablespoons cornflour

2 tablespoons sugar

50 ml cider vinegar

120 ml pineapple juice

120 ml chicken stock

450 g pork tenderloin, cubed

2 tablespoons groundnut oil

1 red onion, chopped

3 cloves garlic, crushed

2 peaches, peeled and sliced

115 g stoned cherries

Salt and cayenne pepper

- In medium bowl, combine cornflour, sugar, vinegar, pineapple juice and stock; season with salt and pepper. Add pork and leave to stand for 10 minutes.

- Drain pork, reserving marinade. Heat oil in large pan or wok. Stir-fry pork until browned; remove from pan with slotted spoon. Add onion and garlic; stir-fry until tender, 5 minutes.

- Return pork to pan with marinade and fruit.

- Bring to a simmer; stir-fry gently until pork is cooked and sauce is thickened. Serve with rice.

You can skin soft fruits such as peaches with a knife, but it's easier if you blanch them before peeling, especially if they are slightly underripe. Bring a saucepan of water to the boil, remove from the heat and drop in the fruit for 15–30 seconds. Lift out the peaches and drain on paper towels. The skins will slip off easily.

Apple Pear Pork Stir-Fry: Make the marinade in the recipe, but substitute apple juice for pineapple juice. Marinate the pork for 10 minutes, then drain and stir-fry in 2 tablespoons groundnut oil; remove. Add 1 chopped onion, 2 sliced apples and 1 sliced pear. Stir-fry until crisp-tender. Return pork to pan along with marinade; stir-fry until thickened.

Prepare Sauce

Stir-Fry

- A wire whisk is the best tool to combine sauces made with cornflour. The wires mix the cornflour in with the liquids so there are no lumps.

- Be sure to whisk the marinade again when you add it to the wok to finish the dish so the cornflour is redistributed.

- You can use any fruit juice in the marinade. Try pear or mango nectar or cherry or orange juice.

- You could substitute honey or brown sugar for the granulated sugar in the marinade.

- Make sure that all of the ingredients are prepared and waiting before you start cooking.

- The onion and garlic, stir-fried after the pork, add moisture to the dish and help to deglaze the pan.

- Stone the cherries over a sink or a bowl so you hear every stone come out of the cherry. You don't want to bite down on a stone.

- Stir the mixture gently, but be sure to scrape the surface of the wok so the sauce doesn't burn.

PORK ENTRÉES

FIVE-INGREDIENT PORK PARCELS

Pesto and tender vegetables make these barbecued parcels a breeze

Make a meal with a combination of food wrapped in heavy-duty foil, then cooked to perfection. These delicious and super-easy one-dish meals are the ultimate quick dinner: no washing up and excellent flavour. If you're not lighting the barbecue, you can bake the parcels in the oven.

Because the food cooks all together in a sealed parcel, it steams. This means that the flavours of the foods mingle as they cook. As a bonus, steaming is one of the healthiest ways

to cook. You need little or no added fat, and vitamins aren't lost as the food cooks.

When you are using just five ingredients, everything has to be the best quality possible. Don't skimp, or try to use food that is not at peak quality. Every ingredient and every flavour is important.

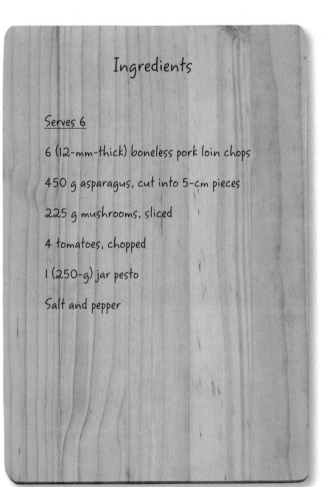

Ingredients

Serves 6

6 (12-mm-thick) boneless pork loin chops

450 g asparagus, cut into 5-cm pieces

225 g mushrooms, sliced

4 tomatoes, chopped

1 (250-g) jar pesto

Salt and pepper

Pork Pesto Parcels

- Prepare barbecue. Tear off 6 sheets of heavy-duty aluminium foil 45 x 30 cm.

- Place chops on foil; sprinkle with salt and pepper. Divide asparagus, mushrooms and tomatoes among chops.

- Spoon pesto on top. Fold foil over and secure with

double folds, allowing some room for expansion during cooking.

- Grill parcels over direct medium heat, turning and moving around frequently, for 20–25 minutes, until pork is thoroughly cooked and vegetables are tender.

Pork Rice Parcels

Cook 350 g parboiled wholegrain rice in 350 ml chicken stock for 10 minutes. Divide among four foil parcels and sprinkle each portion with ½ teaspoon chilli powder. Top with 4 boneless pork chops, 225 g thawed frozen corn, 250 ml salsa, and 75 g grated Cheddar cheese. Fold foil using a double fold and barbecue as directed.

Italian Pork Parcels

Place 4 boneless pork loin chops, about 12 mm thick, on 4 sheets of heavy-duty foil. Add 225 g frozen stir-fry vegetables, thawed, and 1 chopped red onion. Drizzle with 120 ml Italian salad dressing and top with 4 chopped tomatoes. Fold parcels and barbecue as directed.

Place Food on Foil

- You can make these parcels ahead of time if you wish. They will keep in the fridge until it's time to cook.

- Parcels are also an excellent way to entertain. Set out a selection of foods and let your guests assemble their own combinations.

- Keep the food in a fairly small area on the foil. You should be able to fit 6 parcels on an average-sized grill rack.

- Individual parcels will look the same on the barbecue, so imprint the foil with identifiable marks.

Make a Double Fold

- To make a double fold, first make sure that your foil sheet is large enough.

- It should be at least 45 cm long. Place the food in the centre, then bring the long sides together. Fold the edges over once, then twice, to seal securely.

- Then make a double fold on the short ends of the parcel, fastening securely.

- Leave some air space in the parcel to allow for heat expansion as the food cooks. And tell your guests to be careful of steam when they open the foil.

PORK ENTRÉES

PAN-FRIED PORK CHOPS

Apple and pork are natural partners in this simple and quick recipe

Pan-frying is an excellent way to cook tender pork chops. The trick is first to sear the chops to develop a good brown colour and caramelization, then finish cooking them in a sauce so they stay tender and juicy.

The thickest chops you can use for this method are about 2.5 cm thick. Thinner chops work well too; they just cook for a shorter period of time. If you have thicker chops, try pounding them so they cook through in the time specified.

You can cook everything in one pan if that's most convenient. Just cook the chops first and leave them in a warm dish, covered, to keep warm; then make the sauce. Return the chops to the pan and cook gently for a few minutes until the sauce is slightly thickened and the chops piping hot.

Ingredients

Serves 6

120 ml cider

2 tablespoons soy sauce

6 pork loin chops, 2.5 cm thick

5 tablespoons butter

175 g pecan pieces

1 onion, chopped

50 g brown sugar

2 tablespoons honey

Pinch each nutmeg and ground cardamom

2 Granny Smith apples, peeled and sliced

Apple Pecan Pork Chops

- In plastic bag, combine cider and soy sauce; add chops. Marinate for 15 minutes.

- Drain pork chops, reserving marinade. Melt 3 tablespoons butter in large pan and brown pecans; remove.

- Add onion; cook 5 minutes, then add remaining ingredients, including marinade, except pork and pecans; simmer.

- Meanwhile, in another pan heat remaining butter and sauté pork chops until done, about 5–8 minutes on each side. Add to first pan and simmer for 3–4 minutes. Sprinkle with pecans.

Creamy Mushroom Pork Chops

Season 6 boneless pork chops with salt and pepper. Heat 2 tablespoons olive oil in large frying pan. Add chops and brown over medium-high heat. Add 1 chopped onion and 150 g sliced chestnut mushrooms; cook for 2 minutes. Add 1 (450-g) jar Carbonara sauce and 1 (100-g) jar sliced preserved mushrooms, undrained. Simmer for 20 minutes.

Blue Cheese Chops

Season 6 pork chops with salt and pepper; dredge in 40 g flour. Brown chops in 3 tablespoons butter in large pan. Add 2 chopped onions and 4 crushed garlic cloves. Cook until chops are done, about 15–20 minutes longer. Remove pork. Add 120 ml each chicken stock and cream; boil for 2 minutes. Return chops to pan; sprinkle with 50 g crumbled blue cheese; cook for 2–3 minutes.

Brown Pork Chops

- When browning the chops, be sure to leave them alone until they easily release from the pan. Turn with tongs instead of a spatula to be sure.

- By the time the meat releases from the pan, the outside is seared and will have developed lots of flavour through caramelization.

- Repeat to sear the other side of the chops.

- Push the point of a sharp knife into the thickest part of the chop to check that the meat is cooked.

Add Sauce

- The sauce will become thicker as it simmers while the pork chops cook in the other pan.

- Stir the sauce occasionally as it cooks, making sure to scrape the bottom of the pan with the spoon or spatula so it doesn't burn.

- The pork simmers in the sauce just long enough to finish cooking and to absorb some liquid.

- You could substitute sliced pears for the apples in this recipe. Use pears that are just barely ripe.

PORK ENTRÉES

SAUSAGE KEBABS

Kebabs can be flavoured in many different ways; this Asian-influenced recipe is delicious

Threading meat on to skewers and cooking on the barbecue, in a pan or under the grill is a quick and easy cooking method.

Use precooked sausage for this type of recipe. The time on the grill isn't long enough to thoroughly cook raw sausages.

Metal skewers are better than bamboo when you're cooking this much food. The sausages are heavy, and you don't want the skewers to burn and fall apart while the food is cooking.

Tender vegetables like peppers and mushrooms can be grilled without precooking. If you want to use harder vegetables like potatoes or carrots, precook them in boiling water until almost tender, then thread on to the skewers and grill to perfection.

Ingredients

Serves 6

75 ml teriyaki sauce

2 tablespoons soy sauce

3 tablespoons honey

2 teaspoons sesame oil

3 cloves garlic, crushed

2 tablespoons finely chopped fresh ginger

2 tablespoons rice wine vinegar

Pinch of cayenne pepper

1 yellow and 2 red peppers, sliced

225 g chestnut mushrooms

4 spring onions, cut into 5-cm pieces

675 g cooked Polish sausage

Asian Sausage Kebabs

- In bowl, combine teriyaki sauce, soy sauce, honey, sesame oil, garlic, ginger, vinegar and cayenne pepper. Add vegetables; marinate for 15 minutes.

- Drain vegetables, reserving marinade. Slice sausage into 4-cm chunks. Prepare and preheat barbecue.

- Thread ingredients on to 6 metal skewers, alternating pieces of sausage with vegetables.

- Grill kebabs over direct medium heat, turning frequently and brushing with marinade, until sausage is hot and vegetables are tender.

There are several types of precooked sausages, including cooked, smoked and dried. Sausages that are cooked and smoked include kielbasa, also known as Polish sausage, and chorizo. Fresh sausages that are dried, such as salami, are usually eaten cold. Sausages that are cooked but not smoked include cooked knackwurst and Braunschweiger; just reheat these, and don't overcook them.

Italian Potato and Sausage Kebabs: Precook 8 small red potatoes, halved, and 4 carrots, cut into chunks, in boiling water for 6–8 minutes. Combine 120 ml Italian salad dressing and 50 ml crème fraîche for marinade. Thread skewers with 675 g Polish sausage, 225 g mushrooms, potatoes, and carrots. Grill as directed, brushing with reserved marinade.

Mix the Glaze

- Teriyaki sauce is made from soy sauce, ginger, garlic, and a sweetener such as brown sugar or honey.

- You can find low-sodium versions of the sauce. Hoisin sauce makes a good substitute, for a slightly more complex flavour.

- Sesame oil has a very strong flavour, which is why it's used in such small quantities.

- Prepare fresh ginger by first peeling with a vegetable peeler, then finely chopping or grating the flesh.

Thread Food on Skewer

- When you thread the food on the skewer, be sure to pierce the thickest part.

- You can put the food on the skewer ahead of time; just cover the assembled skewers and refrigerate until it's time to grill.

- Grill over direct medium heat, turning the skewers occasionally as the food browns.

- You can purchase skewer racks or holders, which hold the skewers in position and make them easier to turn.

PORK MEDALLIONS
Tender pork is quickly pan-fried and topped with a creamy sauce

Medallions are pieces of meat cut thin and pounded thinner to cook very quickly. A sauce is added to work the flavourful pan juices into the recipe and help keep the meat moist.

You can use pork tenderloin or pork chops to make medallions. Pork tenderloin is easier to work with and is naturally more tender than chops, so it's a better choice.

Pound the meat gently but firmly. Do not use the spiked side of a meat tenderizer. The bottom of a heavy saucepan, a rolling pin or the smooth side of a tenderizer can be used to flatten the meat.

Flavour these medallions any way you like. The delicately flavoured meat is complemented by any herb, spice, vegetable or fruit.

Ingredients

Serves 8

900 g pork tenderloin

40 g plain flour

1 teaspoon dried basil

2 tablespoons butter

2 tablespoons olive oil

1 onion, finely chopped

3 cloves garlic, crushed

75 ml lemon juice

120 ml chicken stock

75 ml double cream

Salt and pepper

Pork Medallions with Lemon

- Slice pork into 2.5-cm pieces, but slice the thin ends into 5-cm pieces.

- Combine flour, salt, pepper and basil on plate. Dredge pork in flour; place on greaseproof paper and pound until 1 cm thick.

- Melt butter and oil in pan on medium heat. Brown pork on both sides, 2–3 minutes; remove from heat.

- Add onion and garlic to pan and cook until softened. Add lemon juice, stock and cream; boil, stirring, until sauce is reduced. Return pork to pan and heat for 2 minutes; serve.

Pork Medallions with Mushrooms

Pound pork as directed, using dried thyme in place of basil. Sauté pork as directed. Remove pork from pan and add 1 chopped onion, 150 g sliced mushrooms and 2 cloves crushed garlic to pan; sauté. Stir in 250 ml chicken stock and 2 tablespoons lemon juice and deglaze pan; boil until reduced. Add medallions; simmer 2 minutes.

Mustard Pork Medallions

Pound pork as directed, using 1 teaspoon dried tarragon instead of basil. Sauté pork as directed. Remove pork from pan and add 1 chopped onion and 2 cloves crushed garlic; sauté. Add 75 ml white wine and 75 ml chicken stock and deglaze pan. Stir in 50 ml cream and 2 tablespoons Dijon mustard. Add medallions, simmer and serve.

Pound Medallions

- You can use greaseproof paper or heavy-duty plastic bags to hold the pork while you pound it.

- The flour is pounded into the meat so it forms a nice crust when the medallions are sautéed.

- The pounding action also pushes the seasonings into the meat.

- Don't pound so hard that the meat rips. Evenly pounded meat cooks more uniformly and looks good when served.

Finish Sauce

- Lemon and basil are natural partners, and they add a delicious brightness to tender pork medallions.

- When you add the liquid to the hot pan, a lot of steam will rise; be careful and stand back so you don't get scalded.

- You can substitute single cream or half-fat crème fraîche for the cream to make the dish lower in fat.

- Garnish the finished dish with some thinly sliced lemons and a few sprigs of fresh basil.

SLOW-COOKER PORK AND RICE

Wild rice and pork make a delicious casserole that you can leave to cook all day while you're out

The slow cooker is a great appliance for quick and easy cooking techniques. The long, slow cooking transforms even tougher cuts of meat into butter-like tenderness. And the actual hands-on work time for you is usually under 20 minutes.

It's important to layer food in the slow cooker in a specific way. Vegetables cook more slowly than meats; therefore they are placed in the bottom of the dish so they are closer to the heat source. Grains have to be covered by liquid, so they're placed in the bottom too.

Brown rice, wild rice, barley and quinoa are all good choices for cooking in the slow cooker. White rice tends to overcook.

Ingredients

Serves 6

4 rashers bacon

6 thin boneless pork chops

25 g plain flour

1 teaspoon dried marjoram

1 onion, chopped

2 cloves garlic, crushed

1 litre chicken stock

400 g wild rice

1 (400-g) jar four-cheese pasta sauce

Salt and pepper

Wild Rice Pork Casserole

- In large pan, cook bacon until crisp; drain, crumble and set aside.

- Dredge pork in mixture of flour, salt, pepper and marjoram. Add to pan and brown in bacon fat on both sides; remove from pan.

- Cook onion and garlic in pan until tender, about 5 minutes. Add stock and bring to a simmer.

- Place wild rice in 4-5-litre slow cooker. Pour in stock mixture; layer pork chops, bacon, and pasta sauce on top. Cover and cook for 7–8 hours until rice is tender and pork is cooked.

Pork Chops with Brown Rice

Brown chops as directed in 2 tablespoons butter. In slow cooker, layer 400 g long-grain brown rice, 450 g baby carrots, and 2 chopped onions, then chops. To pan, add 1 litre chicken stock, 2 tablespoons sugar, 3 tablespoons cider vinegar, 2 tablespoons soy sauce, 120 ml chilli sauce. Boil; pour over chops. Cook on low for 8–9 hours.

Pork with Wild and Brown Rice

Cube 6 boneless pork chops; toss with seasonings as directed. Place 200 g brown rice and 200 g wild rice in slow cooker. Top with 1 litre vegetable or chicken stock. Add 2 chopped onions, 3 cloves crushed garlic, and 150 g sliced mushrooms. Top with pork. Cover and cook on low for 8–9 hours, stirring once during cooking time.

Brown Pork in Frying Pan

- Make sure that the bacon is very crisply cooked so it doesn't get soggy or limp in the slow cooker.

- The bacon will soften a bit, but will retain a nice, slightly chewy texture after long hours of cooking.

- Only cook the chops until they brown. This shouldn't take longer than 4–5 minutes.

- The stock is added to the pan to deglaze it and incorporate all the pan juices from cooking the meat, onion and garlic.

Layer Food in Slow Cooker

- The pan juices contribute much of the flavour of this dish. The brown bits are caramelized, with lots of complex compounds.

- Make sure that the rice is covered with the stock before you add the chops, bacon and cheese sauce.

- Keep the cover on the slow cooker while it's cooking. The lid creates a seal that holds in the heat and moisture.

- Every time you lift the lid you need to add 20 minutes to the total cooking time.

PORK ENTRÉES

HAM STIR-FRY

Ham is the perfect stir-fry meat for one of the quickest meals ever

A stir-fry meal can be on the table in literally minutes, especially if you choose a precooked meat like ham. Ham shouldn't be marinated, as it is flavourful and tender enough, so skipping that step shaves at least 10 minutes off the preparation time.

You can sometimes find cubed or diced cooked ham in the supermarket, so you don't even have to do that work. And look in the produce section, too, for vegetables and fruits that

are already trimmed and cut ready for stir-frying. Everything from grated carrots to chopped pineapple to trimmed sugar snap peas is available, ready and waiting, and you can even buy ready-made stir-fry combinations.

Have fun creating your own quick and easy stir-fry recipes using ham.

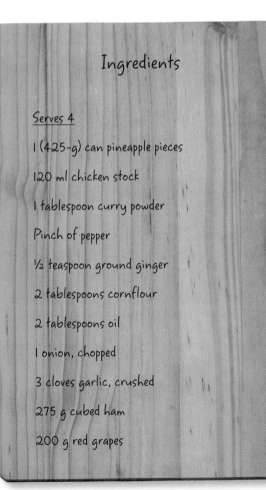

Ingredients

Serves 4

1 (425-g) can pineapple pieces

120 ml chicken stock

1 tablespoon curry powder

Pinch of pepper

½ teaspoon ground ginger

2 tablespoons cornflour

2 tablespoons oil

1 onion, chopped

3 cloves garlic, crushed

275 g cubed ham

200 g red grapes

Curried Ham and Fruit Stir-Fry

- Drain pineapple, reserving juice. In small bowl, combine reserved juice, chicken stock, curry powder, pepper, ginger and cornflour.

- In large pan, heat oil over medium-high heat. Add onion and garlic; stir-fry until tender, about 5 minutes.

- Add ham; stir-fry until ham starts to brown around edges, about 5–6 minutes. Add pineapple and grapes.

- Stir pineapple juice mixture and add to pan. Stir-fry until food is hot and sauce thickened, about 3–4 minutes. Serve with brown rice.

Think about the kinds of flavours that typically go with ham when you're inventing your own recipes for stir-fry sauces. Sweet and tart fruits such as pineapple, pear and peaches are naturals. Combine them with sharper flavours such as barbecue sauce, onion, garlic and mustard. Sugar or honey mellows the mixture, while herbs like basil or mint add fresh flavour.

• • • • RECIPE VARIATION • • • •

Ham and Pea Stir-Fry: For sauce, combine 250 ml chicken stock with 2 tablespoons each cornflour, soy sauce and mustard. Stir-fry 1 onion in 2 tablespoons oil; add 200 g sugar snap peas, 65 g sliced mushrooms, 1 red pepper, and 275 g cooked ham. Stir and add sauce along with 225 g frozen petits pois. Stir-fry until sauce bubbles and thickens. Serve with rice.

Prepare Ingredients

- Use a sharp knife to cut the fruit and onions into cubes of about the same size.

- If the grapes are large, cut them in half. Work slowly, because they have a tendency to roll around.

- Have all the ingredients ready to go and waiting before you heat the wok. There's no time to prepare ingredients after the cooking has started.

- Divide the ingredients into bowls according to when they are added to the wok.

Stir-Fry

- You'll develop your own method and rhythm of stir-frying after a few tries.

- Use a metal or heatproof spatula so you can cover the most surface area with each turn of the wok.

- Always stir the sauce or marinade before you add it to the wok, because the cornflour settles to the bottom.

- Cook your rice in a rice cooker, then it will be ready and waiting for you when the food is done.

HAM AND FRUIT PARCELS

Whether grilled or baked, these special parcels are perfect for last minute entertaining

These parcels can be cooked on the barbecue or baked in the oven. If you barbecue them, you need to use heavy-duty foil to stop the food from burning.

Don't overfill the parcels, whether you're grilling or baking them. There must be space inside to allow for steam and for expansion as the food heats.

If you are baking them in the oven, place the parcels on a baking sheet, even if you're using heavy-duty foil, in case any of the parcels leak. On the barbecue, any leaks won't matter, but pay attention. When you're removing the parcels from the grill, you don't want to spill hot liquid on yourself.

Ingredients

Serves 4

450 g cooked ham in a piece

1 (425-g) can sweet potatoes

3 peaches or nectarines

1 red onion, chopped

2 cloves garlic, crushed

120 ml peach nectar or juice

2 tablespoons honey

1 teaspoon ground ginger

Pinch of pepper

Ham and Peach Parcels

- Cut ham into 2.5 x 7.5-cm strips. Tear off 4 sheets of heavy-duty foil, 45 x 30 cm.

- Drain sweet potatoes, discarding liquid. Cut sweet potatoes into 2.5 cm pieces.

- Peel peaches and slice; just slice nectarines, if using.

- Divide ham, sweet potatoes, fruit, onion and garlic among foil sheets.

- Combine remaining ingredients and drizzle over food. Fold up and seal parcels; grill over direct medium heat for 17–23 minutes until food is hot.

~ VARIATIONS ~

Baked Ham Parcels

Cook 350 g parboiled wholegrain rice in 350 ml chicken stock for 10 minutes. Cut 4 pieces of baking parchment, 45 x 30 cm. Divide rice among sheets of parchment. Top with green pepper rings, 500 g chopped cooked ham, 1 chopped onion. Divide 1 (400-g) can chopped tomatoes among packets. Fold up. Bake at 200°C for 35–45 minutes.

Pesto Ham Parcels

Place 4 cooked ham steaks on 4 sheets of heavy-duty foil. Top with 2 sliced plum tomatoes, 1 chopped green pepper and 350 g frozen sweetcorn. Combine 175 ml green pesto with 175 ml crème fraîche; spoon over ingredients. Fold up parcels and grill over direct medium heat for 12–18 minutes until food is hot.

Place Food on Foil

- You can use canned or frozen peaches if fresh fruits aren't readily available or in season.

- Drain canned peaches well. Thaw frozen peaches and drain them thoroughly, too. Too much water will dilute the flavours.

- A finished parcel should be about a 15 x 20-cm rectangle, whether you are using foil or parchment.

- To fold parchment, start at one end and crimp the edges together; keep crimping all the way around to the other end.

Fold Foil Parcels

- Be careful pulling the parcels off the barbecue or out of the oven. They will be very hot.

- The baking parchment will start to brown and the edges may burn a little; that's OK.

- You can cut a large cross in the centre of the parcels to open them up, or unfold the foil or paper.

- And be sure to warn your guests about the steam that will billow out when they open the parcels.

BARBECUED HAM STEAKS

Cooked ham is one of the best cuts in the supermarket for super quick and easy meals

With cooked ham, all you're doing on the barbecue is reheating it and adding some caramelization and smoky flavour.

Since the time on the barbecue will be quick, you'll have to stagger how you cook other foods. Tender vegetables like peppers, mushrooms and tomatoes can be cooked at the same time as the ham, but others, including potatoes and

carrots, should either be precooked or put on the barbecue long before the ham.

There are so many ways to flavour ham. Try a sauce made with curry powder and chutney and serve it with chargrilled pineapple and peaches. Or use zesty Italian dressing and grill peppers and onions.

Ingredients

Serves 4

1 tablespoon olive oil

1 onion, chopped

2 cloves garlic, crushed

2 apples, chopped

250 ml apple juice

Pinch of nutmeg

2 tablespoons cider vinegar

1 tablespoon cornflour

450 g cooked ham in a piece

Salt and pepper

Ham Steak with Apples

- In medium pan, heat olive oil over medium heat. Add onion and garlic; cook and stir for about 5 minutes.

- Add apples and sauté for 3 minutes. Add apple juice, nutmeg, salt and pepper; bring to a simmer.

- Simmer sauce for 8–10 minutes until apples are tender. Stir in vinegar and cornflour; simmer until thickened, about 2 minutes.

- Barbecue ham on direct medium heat, turning once and brushing with apple mixture, until hot and glazed, 9–10 minutes. Serve ham with remaining sauce.

120

~ VARIATIONS ~

Cranberry Ham Steak
Cook 1 chopped onion and 2 cloves crushed garlic in 2 tablespoons olive oil. Add 75 ml prawn cocktail sauce, 2 tablespoons Dijon mustard, 250 ml cranberry sauce, and 50 g dried cranberries; simmer for 10 minutes. Grill a 450-g ham steak, brushing occasionally with sauce, until hot, about 10–15 minutes. Serve with sauce.

Peachy Ham Steak
Cook 2 finely chopped shallots in 1 tablespoon olive oil. Add 2 peaches, chopped, 120 ml peach nectar, 75 ml peach jam, 2 tablespoons lemon juice, and a pinch of pepper; simmer for 10 minutes. Grill a 450-g ham steak as described, brushing occasionally with sauce, until hot, about 10 minutes. Serve with sauce.

Prepare Sauce

- You can prepare the glaze or sauce ahead of time if you like. If the sauce uses perishable ingredients, refrigerate.

- Just cool it to room temperature, cover, and then reheat before you start barbecuing.

- Substitute other fruits and fruit juices in place of the apples and apple juice. Chopped pears and pear juice, or pineapple pieces would work.

- Because the ham is fully cooked, you don't have to worry about boiling the sauce after it's been in contact with the meat.

Grill Ham

- Using a silicone brush to baste the ham on the grill makes washing up easy, but you can also use an ordinary pastry brush.

- Or think about making a grill brush with bunches of herbs. For this recipe, tie sprigs of thyme together.

- Turn the ham with tongs. If you turn it with a spatula, you'll scrape off the sauce.

- Let the ham sit on the grill rack until it releases easily. Make sure the rack is clean and oiled before you begin.

HAM IN A PAN

Add a few ingredients and a sauce to ham for a delicious one-pan meal that's ready in minutes

This kind of meal is cooked entirely in one pan, leaving you with very little washing up to do. And when you start with fully cooked ham, the cooking process is even faster.

The difference between a stir-fry and a one-pan meal is that the pan usually involves a longer cooking time. The food doesn't have to be constantly manipulated with a spatula or spoon. And there are times when the pan is covered and the food left to simmer for a few minutes.

These dishes can be flavoured in many ways. A Tex-Mex-style meal would use jalapeño peppers, salsa, tomatoes, sweetcorn and chopped ham. An Italian ham dish could use basil, onions, red pepper and fusilli pasta.

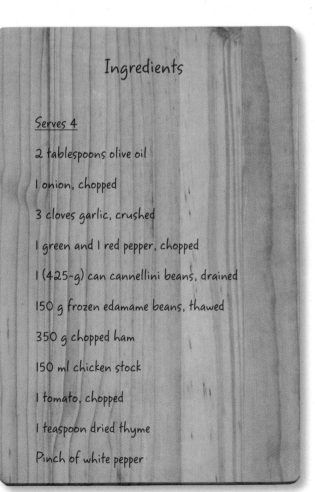

Ingredients

Serves 4

2 tablespoons olive oil

1 onion, chopped

3 cloves garlic, crushed

1 green and 1 red pepper, chopped

1 (425-g) can cannellini beans, drained

150 g frozen edamame beans, thawed

350 g chopped ham

150 ml chicken stock

1 tomato, chopped

1 teaspoon dried thyme

Pinch of white pepper

Fried Ham and Beans

- In large pan, heat olive oil over medium heat. Add onion and garlic; cook and stir until tender, about 5 minutes.

- Add peppers; cook and stir for 3 minutes longer. Add cannellini and edamame beans, ham and chicken stock; bring to a simmer.

- Add tomato, thyme and pepper and stir. Bring mixture back to a simmer; cover and simmer for 7–9 minutes until vegetables are tender.

- Serve this mixture with hot cooked couscous or rice; sprinkle with chopped parsley.

~ VARIATIONS ~

Italian Ham Pasta

Cook 225 g gemelli pasta in boiling water until al dente. Meanwhile, cook 1 chopped onion and 2 cloves garlic with 2 tablespoons olive oil. Add 1 chopped red pepper, 450 g cubed ham, and 1 teaspoon dried Italian seasoning. Stir in pasta and 350 ml chicken stock; simmer for 4 minutes. Sprinkle with 40 g grated pecorino cheese.

Tex-Mex Ham Rice

Cook 1 chopped onion and 2 chopped jalapeños in 2 tablespoons oil. Add 200 g long-grain rice, 450 g cubed ham, and 250 ml salsa. Cover and simmer for 20–25 minutes until rice is tender. Stir in 115 g grated cheese and 50 ml crème fraîche, and remove from heat. Leave to stand for 5 minutes before serving.

Add Peppers to Pan

- The onions and garlic are cooked first because they take longer to become sweet and tender.

- If you like peppers very crisp, add them when you add the tomato at the end of cooking time.

- Edamame beans are soya beans. You can find them, frozen, in most supermarkets.

- To make this dish even easier, use a frozen onion and pepper stir-fry mix, thawed and drained.

Finish Sauce

- The tomato will add more liquid to the pan. If you squeeze out the seeds and juice, it will add less.

- If the sauce isn't thick enough, add 1 tablespoon cornflour mixed with 2 tablespoons water; simmer 4–5 minutes.

- It's not a good idea to try to make this kind of dish ahead of time; it's best eaten immediately.

- You can reheat leftovers, however, and eat them as they are or as a filling for a wrap.

HAM IN FILO PASTRY

For those special breakfasts, or a late supper, a filo roll is beautiful and distinctive

Filo is the non-fat dough rolled into paper-thin sheets that is used in Greek cooking. You can find it in the frozen section of any supermarket.

The dough is layered with butter or other ingredients, including honey or flavoured oils, then baked until crisp. It's easy to work with, but you do have to follow a few rules.

Thaw according to package directions, usually overnight in the refrigerator. There are quick thawing options, too.

Cover the thawed dough as you work with individual sheets, because it dries out and becomes brittle very quickly.

Once you've learned how to work with this dough, you can fill it with any lightly sauced food.

Ingredients

Serves 6

125 g basmati rice

120 ml chicken stock

120 ml apple juice

2 tablespoons butter

1 Granny Smith apple, peeled and chopped

350 g cooked ham, diced

1 teaspoon dried marjoram

115 g ricotta cheese

115 g Cheddar cheese, grated

16 sheets frozen filo pastry, thawed

50 g butter, melted

Ham and Apple Filo Roll

- Preheat oven to 190°C. In saucepan, combine rice, chicken stock and apple juice; simmer for 20 minutes.

- In medium frying pan, melt butter; cook apple 2 minutes. Add ham and marjoram; remove from heat. Add rice; leave to cool for 15 minutes; stir in cheeses.

- Brush one sheet of filo with melted butter. Lay another sheet on top and repeat to make 8 layers; top with half of ham mixture. Roll, brush top with butter. Repeat.

- Place rolls on baking sheet. Bake 25–35 minutes until browned. Cut into thirds to serve.

····· RECIPE VARIATION ·····

Potato and Ham in Filo: In a pan, cook 1 chopped onion and 2 cloves garlic in 2 tablespoons butter. Add 1 chopped green pepper, 350 g diced cooked ham, 300 g frozen grated potatoes, and 300 ml bottled carbonara sauce. Add 100 g grated Emmental cheese. Roll up in filo and bake as directed in recipe.

Prepare Filling

Layer Filo Sheets

- The filling should have a sauce, but that sauce shouldn't overwhelm the food.

- The sauce also has to be thick so the filo dough, which is quite delicate, can contain it. A runny sauce will make the filo soggy.

- You can make the filling ahead of time and refrigerate it. Layer the filo and fill it when you want to eat.

- Other good fillings include ham mixed with chopped spinach in a creamy cheese sauce, or scrambled eggs with ham.

- The filo pastry rips easily, so handle it gently. If it does tear, just layer it on a solid sheet and brush with more melted butter.

- The butter will help repair rips, and the layering process automatically fixes them.

- Brush the butter mixture sparingly over the dough. Don't soak the dough; the butter should lightly coat most of it.

- Serve this recipe immediately so the dough is as crisp as possible. Reheat leftovers on a rimmed baking sheet.

SLOW-COOKER HAM CASSEROLE

Potato and ham in a rich, creamy sauce make perfect partners in the slow cooker

Cooked ham is a great ingredient for slow cooker dishes. As with other methods, you don't have to worry about whether it's completely cooked, but it won't overcook in the low, slow heat of this appliance.

Since all you're doing is reheating cooked ham, place it on top in the slow cooker. Other foods, such as root vegetables,

rice, and grains, should be on the bottom. Just pour a sauce or stock over everything, cover it, and let it start cooking. Dinner will be ready and waiting for you.

Cubed or sliced ham cooks best in the slow cooker, especially when combined with other ingredients. It will release some salty juices to flavour the entire dish to perfection.

Ingredients

Serves 6

2 tablespoons olive oil

1 onion, chopped

4 cloves garlic, crushed

1 (450-g) jar four-cheese pasta sauce

225 g grated Havarti cheese

250 ml crème fraîche

900 g frozen potato rosti, thawed

350 g cubed ham

2 green peppers, chopped

Creamy Potato and Ham Casserole

- In medium pan, heat olive oil over medium heat. Add onion and garlic; cook and stir for 5 minutes.

- Stir in cheese sauce, cheese and crème fraîche; cook and stir until melted. Grease a 4–5 litre slow cooker.

- Layer potatoes, ham, green pepper and cheese sauce in slow cooker, ending with cheese sauce.

- Cover and cook on low for 7–8 hours or until mixture browns around the edges and potatoes are tender.

~ VARIATIONS ~

Slow-Cooker Ham and Beans
Combine 1 chopped onion, 3 cloves crushed garlic, 6 (415-g) cans baked beans, drained, 1 (415-g) can black beans, drained, 120 ml tomato ketchup, 120 ml chilli sauce, 50 ml Dijon mustard, 50 g brown sugar, and 700 g diced, cooked ham in a 5-litre slow cooker. Cover and cook on low for 8–9 hours.

Slow-Cooker Ham and Potatoes
In 5-litre slow cooker, combine 2 chopped onions, 4 cloves crushed garlic, 900 g frozen potato rosti, thawed and drained, and 500 g diced, cooked ham. Combine 450 ml four-cheese pasta sauce, 120 ml crème fraîche, and 225 g grated Emmental cheese; stir into slow cooker. Cover and cook on low for 7–9 hours.

Prepare Ingredients

- Experts advise against cooking food from frozen in a slow cooker, for safety reasons.

- It can cool down the other ingredients and keep them in the danger zone of 5–60°C for too long.

- Make sure the frozen potatoes are thawed and well drained, as liquid doesn't evaporate from the slow cooker during cooking.

- You could use vacuum-packed rosti potatoes instead of the frozen ones.

Low-Fat Ingredients

- Look for low-fat creamy pasta sauces if you want to reduce the fat content of the dish.

- You could use low-fat crème fraîche and cheese as well, to dramatically reduce the fat content in this recipe.

- When cooking and baking, don't use all non-fat products, as the texture and flavour will be compromised.

- Use a mixture of low-fat and non-fat products for best results.

STIR-FRIED SALMON
Stir-frying isn't the most obvious way to prepare salmon, but it's quick and delicious

There aren't many recipes for stir-fried fish, with the exception of prawns and scallops. Most fish is too delicate to withstand the rough-and-tumble environment of the wok. But salmon is different.

Salmon and tuna are both good choices for a stir-fry recipe because they are sturdy. You still need to use a gentle hand, but the fish will keep its shape in the wok or frying pan. Salmon will cook in the wok in just a few minutes, so it's added at the very end of the cooking time.

Once cut into cubes, the salmon can be marinated for a few minutes. Never marinate for longer than 20 minutes, or the fish's texture may be compromised.

Ingredients

Serves 4

300 ml orange juice

2 tablespoons cornflour

50 ml orange marmalade

1 tablespoon soy sauce

3 tablespoons honey

450 g salmon fillet, skin removed

1 onion, chopped

2 green peppers, sliced

2 nectarines, sliced

2 tablespoons groundnut oil

Salt and pepper

Orange Stir-Fried Salmon

- In medium bowl, combine the first 5 ingredients. Cut salmon into 2.5-cm cubes and add to marinade.

- Meanwhile, prepare onion, peppers and nectarines. Heat oil in large pan or wok over medium-high heat.

- Add onion; stir-fry for 3 minutes. Drain salmon, reserving marinade. Add salmon with peppers to pan; stir-fry for 3 minutes.

- Stir marinade and add to pan with nectarines; stir-fry for 3–5 minutes until salmon is cooked and sauce has thickened. Serve with rice.

Salmon Nectarine Stir-Fry

Combine 120 ml each apple juice and chicken stock, and stir in 2 tablespoons each soy sauce, cornflour and mustard; season with pepper. Marinate 450 g cubed salmon for 15 minutes. Stir-fry 1 chopped red onion and 2 green peppers in 2 tablespoons oil. Add 2 sliced nectarines and drained salmon; stir-fry. Add sauce and stir-fry until bubbling.

Salmon Black Bean Stir-Fry

Combine 250 ml chicken stock, 2 tablespoons fermented black beans, rinsed and finely chopped, and 2 tablespoons each cornflour, soy sauce and cider vinegar. Marinate 450 g cubed salmon for 10 minutes. Stir-fry 1 red onion, 2 cloves garlic, and 200 g green beans in 2 tablespoons oil. Add salmon; stir-fry, then add sauce with 1 can black beans, drained.

Marinate Salmon

- When buying salmon, look for firm, shiny flesh that's a bright pink colour, with a fresh sea smell.

- Remove skin from the salmon before marinating for best results. This will make the salmon more delicate.

- There may be some pin bones in the salmon. Feel for them with your fingers and pull out with tweezers.

- Toss the salmon with the marinade until it's coated, then let it stand while you prepare the other ingredients.

Stir-Fry

- After the sauce has been added to the wok or pan, let it stand for 1 minute to start heating.

- Then carefully stir, using the spatula to scrape the bottom of the wok or pan to move the food around.

- The stir-fry is ready when the sauce becomes clear, bubbles and thickens.

- Have the rice perfectly cooked, hot, and ready and waiting for you in a rice cooker. Serve the stir-fry immediately.

LOW-FAT STEAMED FISH

Steaming is a quick and healthy way to cook, and the presentation is spectacular

Steaming is a wonderful and healthy way to cook fish. It's also a very quick method of cooking. The food is usually put into one or more steamer baskets – metal or bamboo contraptions that have holes in the bottom to let steam through.

The steamer baskets should be tightly covered to keep the steam moving around the food. And the food has to be carefully arranged in the baskets. Make sure that the food is placed in a single layer in the baskets, unless the recipe specifies otherwise.

The baskets should be rearranged every 2–3 minutes when cooking, so all the food cooks evenly. Move the bottom basket to the top.

Ingredients

Serves 4

450 g chard or spinach

2 tablespoons olive oil

I onion, chopped

4 cloves garlic, crushed

2 jalapeño peppers, finely chopped

1¼ teaspoons dried chilli flakes

50 ml lemon juice

4 (175-g) halibut fillets

Salt and pepper

Steamed Fish with Spicy Greens

- Immerse chard leaves in cold water, then shake off water. Dry and coarsely chop.

- In large pan, heat oil over medium heat. Add onion, garlic and jalapeño; cook and stir for 3 minutes.

- Add greens, salt, pepper, chilli flakes and lemon juice; cover and steam for 2 minutes until greens start to wilt.

- Line 4 steamer baskets with greens, top with fish, and drizzle with mixture from pan. Steam over simmering water, rearranging baskets, until fish is cooked, about 10–12 minutes.

Place Food in Baskets

- You can use other liquids to add a bit of flavour to steamed foods.

- Stock, fruit juices, and wine are good choices for additions to the steaming water. You could also add aromatic ingredients like chopped onion, fresh ginger and herbs.

- You can add other ingredients to the baskets if you like, but they must be quick cooking, like mushrooms or sliced peppers.

- Leave some space around each piece of food so the steam can circulate and cook the food evenly.

Rearrange Baskets

- Make sure that the bottom of the steamer basket does not touch the simmering liquid.

- If it does touch, carefully remove some of the liquid. You don't want the bottom layer of food to overcook.

- Use oven mitts to protect your hands while you're rearranging the baskets, especially if they are made of metal.

- The same steam that gently cooks food can burn you in seconds. Be careful when rearranging the baskets.

FISH AND VEGETABLE PARCELS

Rice, fish and lemon pair up in these easy one-dish meal parcels cooked on the barbecue

Fish picks up great flavours from other foods when they are cooked all together in foil parcels on the barbecue. These parcels can also be baked in the oven. Heavy-duty foil works well for both methods.

If you're going to be cooking foods such as rice, potatoes or other long-cooking foods along with the fish, they need to be precooked. Cook rice, grains or pasta until they are almost done. They will finish cooking in the steam that builds up in the foil parcels.

Because the heat is so intense underneath these parcels when they are on the barbecue, it's best if there is a layer of food such as rice or pasta between the fish and the foil.

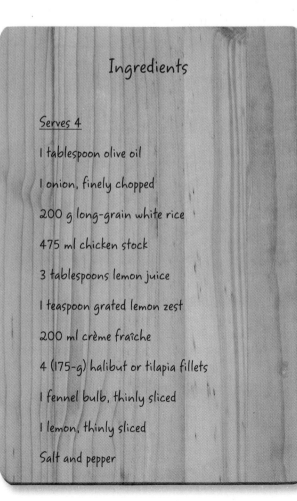

Ingredients

Serves 4

1 tablespoon olive oil

1 onion, finely chopped

200 g long-grain white rice

475 ml chicken stock

3 tablespoons lemon juice

1 teaspoon grated lemon zest

200 ml crème fraîche

4 (175-g) halibut or tilapia fillets

1 fennel bulb, thinly sliced

1 lemon, thinly sliced

Salt and pepper

Lemon Rice Fish Parcels

- In pan, heat olive oil over medium heat. Add onion; cook and stir for 5 minutes. Add rice; cook and stir for 2 minutes.

- Add stock; cover and simmer for 15–20 minutes until rice is almost cooked. Stir in lemon juice, zest and crème fraîche.

- Tear off 4 sheets of heavy-duty foil, 45 x 30 cm. Divide rice mixture among sheets; top with fish fillets; season with salt and pepper.

- Arrange fennel and lemon on fish; wrap parcels. Barbecue over direct medium heat for 18–23 minutes, until fish flakes.

Fish and Spinach Parcels

Divide 100 g baby spinach among 4 sheets of heavy-duty foil. Top with 1 chopped red onion, 4 chopped tomatoes, and 3 cloves garlic, crushed. Add 4 175-g cod fillets. Drizzle with mixture of 75 ml chilli sauce, 2 tablespoons lemon juice, salt, pepper, and 1 tablespoon brown sugar. Seal and barbecue as directed.

Thai Fish Parcels

Divide 275 g grated carrots among 4 sheets of foil. Top with 4 chopped spring onions, 2 cloves garlic, crushed, and 2 tablespoons finely chopped fresh ginger. Top with 4 fish fillets; sprinkle with mixture of 50 ml chicken stock, 2 tablespoons honey, 2 tablespoons fish sauce and ¼ teaspoon cayenne pepper. Bake at 200°C for 18–23 minutes.

Partially Cook Rice

- The rice should be soft on the outside with a firm centre to each grain when it is partially cooked.

- You can precook the rice ahead of time and chill it in the fridge. Reheat in the microwave before proceeding with the recipe.

- In the parcels, the rice will continue cooking and will absorb flavours from the fish, the lemon juice and the zest.

- You could substitute sliced peppers and mushrooms for the fennel if you like.

Arrange Food on Foil

- Arrange the food in a compact, stable pile in the centre of the foil, so that it keeps its shape when you wrap the parcel.

- Move the parcels around on the barbecue as they cook, to keep the food moving a bit and distribute the heat evenly.

- Use a spatula to move the parcels. You can find large spatulas at most kitchenware stores.

- Warn your guests that there will be hot steam billowing from the parcels when they're opened.

LOW-FAT GRILLED FISH FILLETS
Three kinds of mustard make a crisp and flavourful coating on simple grilled fish

Grilling is a dry-heat, quick and simple method of cooking. The food is placed 10–15 cm away from the heat source, which is turned to the highest temperature.

Because the food cooks so quickly, many fish fillets don't need to be turned. Fish usually needs to be cooked for 10 minutes per 2.5 cm of thickness.

The heat from the grill is quite intense, so a sauce or other coating is sometimes added to the fish to protect it from drying out. The sauce caramelizes in the heat, adding another layer of flavour to the dish.

Any fairly thick sauce, flavoured any way you like, can be used with the fish.

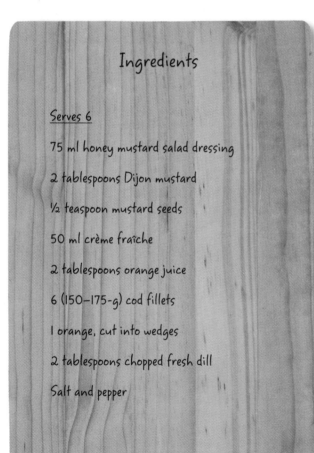

Ingredients

Serves 6

75 ml honey mustard salad dressing

2 tablespoons Dijon mustard

½ teaspoon mustard seeds

50 ml crème fraîche

2 tablespoons orange juice

6 (150–175-g) cod fillets

1 orange, cut into wedges

2 tablespoons chopped fresh dill

Salt and pepper

Three-Mustard Grilled Fish

- Preheat grill. In small bowl, combine dressing, mustard, mustard seeds, crème fraîche and orange juice.

- Place fish fillets in grill pan and season with salt and pepper. Grill fish 15 cm from heat for 3 minutes.

- Spoon mustard mixture over fish and grill for 4–6 minutes longer until fish flakes when tested with fork and mustard mixture has browned.

- Remove fish from heat and serve immediately, garnished with orange wedges and fresh dill.

Curried Monkfish

Combine 50 ml pineapple juice, 2 tablespoons olive oil, 1 tablespoon curry powder, 1 tablespoon grated fresh ginger, salt and pepper in small bowl. Place 4 portions monkfish fillet in glass baking dish and pour marinade over; marinate for 20 minutes. Grill 15 cm from heat for 10 minutes per 2.5 cm of thickness.

Bacon Halibut

Grill 8 rashers of bacon until partially cooked. Bacon will still be pliable. Sprinkle 4 halibut fillets with salt and pepper and wrap each with 2 rashers of bacon. Brush with mixture of 2 tablespoons honey, 2 tablespoons mustard and 2 tablespoons cider vinegar. Grill, turning once, until bacon is crisp and fish is cooked.

Mix the Glaze

Grill the Fish

- You can make the glaze ahead of time and refrigerate it until you're ready to cook. The thin layer will warm up quickly under the hot grill.

- The glaze can be varied easily by using more crème fraîche and omitting the mustard ingredients.

- Replace the mustard with ingredients such as honey, orange zest, chopped herbs like basil and tarragon, or cheeses.

- The same mustard mixture will taste very different if you add some grated cheese and different herbs.

- Be sure not to leave the grill while the fish is cooking. The glaze can go from perfectly browned to burned in seconds.

- If the fish is thicker than 12 mm, turn it over after the first 5 minutes, then apply the glaze mixture.

- The fish is done as soon as it flakes. That means that the fish parts between the natural muscle lines.

- The fish will also become opaque when it's perfectly cooked. These two tests are both reliable.

MICROWAVE SALMON

A quick fruit chutney, also made in the microwave, tops tender salmon in this fabulous recipe

The microwave is an excellent means of cooking fish. This appliance works by making molecules in the food move quickly, which generates heat. The heat moves throughout the food, cooking it. Follow directions for the amount of heat, cooking time, stirring and rearranging food carefully. And be sure that you understand how to test that food is cooked.

Microwave cooking also demands standing time. After cooking, the food must stand on a solid surface, not a wire rack, to let the heat redistribute and finish cooking the food.

You can also use the microwave to cook sauces and relishes to accompany the main dish.

Ingredients

Serves 6

350 g blueberries

1 onion, finely chopped

½ teaspoon ground ginger

75 ml cider vinegar

115 g brown sugar

2 tablespoons cornflour

6 (125–150-g) skinless salmon fillets

1 teaspoon dried thyme

50 ml orange juice

Salt and pepper

Microwave Salmon with Blueberry Chutney

- In medium microwave-safe bowl, combine blueberries, onion, ginger, vinegar and brown sugar.

- Cover and microwave on high for 2 minutes, remove and stir. Add cornflour, mix well, and microwave for another 2 minutes. Remove and cool.

- Place salmon in microwave-safe dish. Sprinkle with salt, pepper and thyme. Add orange juice.

- Cover and microwave on high for 8–12 minutes, re-arranging salmon once, until fish flakes. Leave to stand for 5 minutes, then serve with chutney.

Honey Mustard Salmon

Place 6 fillets of salmon in a microwave-safe dish. Sprinkle with salt, pepper and ½ teaspoon dried dill. Combine 50 ml honey mustard salad dressing with 2 tablespoons coarse brown mustard and 2 tablespoons honey. Spread over salmon. Pour 2 tablespoons orange juice into dish. Microwave on high for 8–12 minutes. Leave to stand for 5 minutes.

Microwave Parmesan Salmon

Place 6 salmon fillets in microwave-safe dish. Sprinkle with salt, pepper and 1 teaspoon dried thyme. In bowl, mix 200 ml crème fraîche with 40 g grated Parmesan cheese and 4 spring onions, chopped. Pour over fish and microwave as directed. Leave to stand for 5 minutes.

Make Blueberry Chutney

- This chutney can be made with other fruits. Substitute chopped peaches or nectarines, chopped strawberries or pears.

- You can make the chutney ahead of time. Refrigerate it for up to 2 days. It can be served cold with the fish, or reheated in the microwave.

- To reheat the chutney, microwave on medium power for 2–3 minutes, stirring once, then leave to stand.

- You can cook the salmon as directed and serve with another sauce, including mango chutney.

Cook Salmon

- You can ask your fishmonger or butcher to remove the salmon skin from the fillets. Or do it yourself with a very sharp knife.

- Feel carefully in the salmon flesh with your fingers for any pin bones, which are very tiny.

- Remove the bones, if there are any, with tweezers and discard. You can do this ahead of time.

- Salmon can be served slightly undercooked in the centre, but only if you're sure that your source is impeccable.

QUICK FISH SOUP

Greek seasonings are the perfect complement to tender, mild-flavoured fish in this simple soup

Fish and soup are natural partners. Because fish cooks quickly, it's added at the end of the cooking time.

Quick soups rely on ingredients such as fresh ready-made stocks. These products give a good depth of flavour with no work on your part. Look for low-sodium broths. Not only are they better for you, but they usually taste better because the manufacturer can't rely on salt. Flavour these soups any way you like. As long as you cook the ingredients for the appropriate time, you can make fish soups out of everything from potatoes and carrots to apples and pears.

Have fun inventing your own fish soups, using flavours from subtle French to spicy Creole.

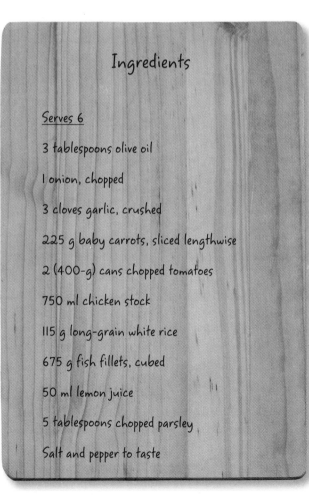

Ingredients

Serves 6

3 tablespoons olive oil

1 onion, chopped

3 cloves garlic, crushed

225 g baby carrots, sliced lengthwise

2 (400-g) cans chopped tomatoes

750 ml chicken stock

115 g long-grain white rice

675 g fish fillets, cubed

50 ml lemon juice

5 tablespoons chopped parsley

Salt and pepper to taste

Greek Fish Soup

- In large saucepan, heat olive oil over medium heat. Add onion, garlic and carrots; cook, stirring, for 5 minutes.

- Add tomatoes and chicken stock; bring to a simmer. Reduce heat to low and simmer for 15 minutes.

- Add rice; cover and simmer for 18 minutes until rice is partially cooked. Stir in fish and bring to a simmer.

- Cover and simmer for 7–8 minutes until fish flakes when tested with fork. Stir in lemon juice and parsley, season to taste, and serve.

Creole Fish Soup
Cook 1 onion and 2 cloves garlic in 2 tablespoons butter. Add 400-g can chopped tomatoes, 1 litre chicken stock, 2 bay leaves, 2 teaspoons chilli powder, and a pinch of cayenne pepper; simmer. Add 200 g frozen sweetcorn, 2 sticks celery, chopped, and 450 g cubed cod. Simmer for 8–10 minutes until fish flakes easily. Remove bay leaves.

Creamy Fish and Sweetcorn Soup
Cook 1 chopped onion and 3 cloves garlic in 2 tablespoons butter. Add 300 g frozen rosti potatoes; cook until thawed. Add 750 ml water, 1 (425-g) can creamed sweetcorn, and 1 (425-ml) jar four-cheese pasta sauce; simmer. Add 450 g cubed fish, 475 ml milk, 200 g sweetcorn, 1 teaspoon thyme, salt and pepper; simmer.

Prepare Ingredients

- You can prepare ingredients like onions, garlic and carrots ahead of time. Cover and refrigerate until you're ready to cook.

- The ingredients are first softened in oil to provide a good base for the soup.

- The size of pan you choose depends on the recipe. Choose one that won't be overfilled by the quantities you are using.

- For this quickly cooked soup, cut ingredients fairly small so they cook evenly in the short time frame.

Homemade Stock

- You could use brown or wild rice if you like. Just simmer for 30 minutes instead of 18, then add fish.

- A homemade stock is easy to make. Combine 1 kg chicken pieces with 3 litres water, onions, garlic and carrots.

- Add pepper and herbs like thyme and tarragon. Simmer the stock for 2–3 hours. Then cool, strain and freeze in 50 ml portions.

- Use homemade stock for soups and sauces. Light chicken stock works very well in fish dishes.

PRAWN STIR-FRY

Plump prawns are spicy and tender in this simple stir-fry recipe

Prawns are one of the best foods for stir-frying because they cook so quickly. They can be flavoured so many ways, and pair beautifully with almost any fruit or vegetable.

Prawns don't need to be marinated before they are stir-fried, because they don't readily absorb flavours. They're also perfectly tender if not overcooked, so don't need the marinade's tenderizing properties. You can use prawns as a substitute for the meat in any classic stir-fry recipe.

There's just one caveat when cooking prawns: don't over-cook them. They are done when they curl and turn pink. If prawns are overcooked, they will be tough and rubbery.

Flavour prawns with bold ingredients such as fermented black beans, or with sweet and gentle flavours like thyme and fruit. Enjoy these recipes.

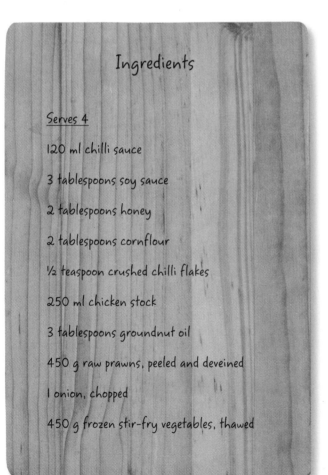

Ingredients

Serves 4

120 ml chilli sauce

3 tablespoons soy sauce

2 tablespoons honey

2 tablespoons cornflour

½ teaspoon crushed chilli flakes

250 ml chicken stock

3 tablespoons groundnut oil

450 g raw prawns, peeled and deveined

1 onion, chopped

450 g frozen stir-fry vegetables, thawed

Spicy Red Prawn Stir-Fry

- In small bowl, combine chilli sauce, soy sauce, honey, cornflour, chilli flakes and chicken stock.

- In large pan or wok, heat oil over medium-high heat. Add prawns; stir-fry for 2–3 minutes until they curl and turn pink. Remove prawns from wok.

- Add onion; stir-fry for 3 minutes. Add drained vegetables; stir-fry for 3–4 minutes until vegetables are hot.

- Stir chicken stock mixture and add to pan along with prawns. Stir-fry for 2–3 minutes until sauce bubbles and thickens. Serve with hot cooked rice.

Szechuan Prawns

Combine 120 ml chicken stock, 50 ml seafood cocktail sauce, 2 tablespoons soy sauce, 1 tablespoon cornflour, 1 tablespoon brown sugar, pinch of cayenne pepper, and ½ teaspoon ginger. Stir-fry 450 g raw prawns in 2 tablespoons oil; remove. Stir-fry 1 onion, chopped, 1 jalapeño pepper, and 2 cloves garlic, crushed. Add prawn and sauce; stir-fry.

Sesame Prawns

Combine 50 ml teriyaki sauce, 120 ml chicken stock, 1 tablespoon cornfloor, 2 teaspoons sesame oil, ½ teaspoon ginger, pinch of cayenne pepper and 2 cloves garlic, crushed. Stir-fry 450 g prawns in 2 tablespoons oil; remove. Add 1 chopped onion and 1 sliced red pepper. Add prawns and sauce; stir-fry. Sprinkle with 2 tablespoons toasted sesame seeds.

Make Sauce

- You could substitute tomato ketchup or seafood cocktail sauce for the chilli sauce for a milder recipe.

- If you like bolder flavours, add some finely chopped onion or garlic to the sauce, or add a chopped serrano pepper.

- Or add spices and herbs. Add a little curry powder for spice, or fresh herbs such as thyme or rosemary.

- The sauce can be made ahead of time; just cover it and keep it in the fridge until you're ready to cook.

Stir-Fry

- The prawns are stir-fried first to make sure they have good contact with the hot oil and cook very quickly.

- Remove the prawns to a clean plate and continue with the recipe. They will be reheated when the sauce is added.

- Make sure that you drain the thawed frozen vegetables very well; you want them to fry, not steam.

- If they are too wet, the oil will spatter when the vegetables are added, which is a safety hazard.

SEAFOOD

SEAFOOD PARCELS

Tender white fish can be flavoured in many ways, but this lemon sauce is superb and easy

Fish is one of the best foods to cook in parcels with other ingredients. Because it's so mild it can be paired with many other foods. And the food cooks in a parcel by steaming – the ideal way to cook delicate fish.

These parcels are one-dish meals that cook on the barbecue or in the oven. The presentation is really beautiful, and perfect for a celebration or party. You can make the parcels ahead of time, so you just need to cook them for a few minutes and you're ready to eat.

Flavour these parcels any way you like. You can use flavoured yogurt, your favourite salad dressing, or just slices of lemon with herbs, salt and pepper.

Ingredients

Serves 4

4 (150–175-g) cod or halibut fillets

120 ml plain yogurt

2 teaspoons grated lemon zest

2 tablespoons lemon juice

2 tablespoons honey

1 tablespoon chopped fresh dill

2 tomatoes, sliced

2 yellow courgettes, sliced

Salt and pepper

Lemon Dill Fish Parcels

- Tear off 4 sheets of heavy-duty aluminium foil, 45 x 30-cm. Lightly oil the centre of each sheet. Place fish fillets in centre of foil; season with salt and pepper.

- In bowl, combine all remaining ingredients except tomatoes and courgettes.

- Arrange tomatoes and courgettes on top of fish. Spoon on lemon sauce; add more salt and pepper.

- Fold up parcels using a double fold, leaving room for expansion. Grill on direct medium heat for 9–12 minutes until fish flakes when tested with fork.

Hawaiian Prawn Parcels

Slice 1 red onion thinly and divide among 4 sheets of baking parchment. Arrange 500 g raw prawns on the onion and top with 425 g can drained pineapple pieces. Add 1 chopped red pepper. Combine 50 ml pineapple juice with 50 ml teriyaki sauce and drizzle over food. Bake at 200°C for 20–25 minutes.

Fish and Pepper Parcels

Slice 1 red, 1 yellow, and 1 green pepper; divide among 6 pieces of heavy-duty foil. Lay 6 tilapia fillets on top of peppers. Top with 1 thinly sliced lemon. Combine 75 ml seafood cocktail sauce with 50 ml chicken stock; drizzle over food. Fold up parcels; barbecue over direct medium heat for 15–20 minutes.

Make Lemon Sauce

- Use whole-milk yogurt or Greek strained yogurt for a creamy texture.

- You could substitute half-fat crème fraîche for the yogurt for an even richer flavour and texture.

- Make the sauce ahead of time and keep it in the fridge up to 4 days.

- Then when you want to cook, just assemble the parcels, add the sauce and get ready to eat.

Layer Seafood with Vegetables

- If the fish fillets are quite thin and delicate, put some of the vegetables underneath them as well as on top.

- The vegetables will steam and act as a shield for the fish against the intense heat. They also add flavour to the fish.

- You could substitute other quick-cooking vegetables for the courgettes and tomatoes.

- Sliced mushrooms, peppers, whole baby corn, or sweetcorn cut off the cob would be delicious.

SEAFOOD

GRILLED PRAWN KEBABS

Grilling tender prawns for just a few minutes makes them smoky and sweet

Prawns, along with other seafood, grill to perfection in just a few minutes. The grill is a good choice for cooking seafood, especially if you'd like to eat barbecued food but the weather isn't being cooperative.

Threading prawns on skewers is a fun and easy way to prepare dinner and to entertain. Preparation is dictated by the types of foods you thread on the skewers with the prawns. Tender vegetables and fruits can be grilled along with the prawns because they cook in about the same amount of time. Potatoes, cauliflower and carrots should be parboiled or precooked in the microwave before they are added. Use your imagination and enjoy creating your own kebabs.

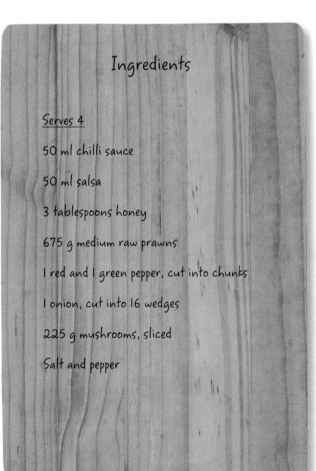

Ingredients

Serves 4

50 ml chilli sauce

50 ml salsa

3 tablespoons honey

675 g medium raw prawns

1 red and 1 green pepper, cut into chunks

1 onion, cut into 16 wedges

225 g mushrooms, sliced

Salt and pepper

Tex-Mex Prawn Kebabs

- In large bowl, combine chilli sauce, salsa, honey, salt and pepper. Add prawns, peppers, onion and mushrooms and toss to coat.

- Cover and refrigerate for 15–20 minutes. Drain prawns and vegetables, reserving marinade. Preheat grill.

- Thread prawns and vegetables on metal skewers. Lightly oil grill pan; place kebabs on pan.

- Grill 15 cm from heat for 5–7 minutes, turning once and brushing with reserved marinade, until prawns curl and turn pink and vegetables are crisp-tender.

Spicy Grilled Prawns
Combine 2 crushed garlic cloves, 1 onion, finely chopped, 50 ml olive oil, 50 ml seafood cocktail sauce, 1 tablespoon cider vinegar, ½ teaspoon salt and 1 teaspoon dried basil. Add 675 g raw peeled prawns; marinate for 30 minutes. Thread on skewers and grill prawns 15 cm from heat for 2–4 minutes per side until curled and pink.

Prawn and Nectarine Skewers
Combine 3 tablespoons lemon juice, 2 tablespoons honey, 2 crushed garlic cloves, 1 tablespoon tequila, 2 jalapeño peppers, finely chopped, and a pinch of cayenne pepper. Skewer 675 g raw jumbo prawns, 4 spring onions and 4 sliced nectarines. Barbecue over medium direct heat, brushing often with the sauce, until prawns turn pink.

Prepare Vegetables

- Don't marinate the vegetables and prawns for longer than the recipe specifies. The vegetables will be soggy and the prawns tough.

- You can make the marinade ahead of time and keep it in the fridge until you're ready to cook.

- The onions will probably fall into pieces when cut into small wedges. Thread them on cocktail sticks before skewering them.

- Remove the sticks before you put the skewers under the grill, because they're so small.

Thread Food on Skewers

- When you're using tender, quick-cooking vegetables, you can use bamboo skewers, soaked in water for 30 minutes.

- Metal skewers can be used over and over again and don't scorch under the grill.

- Be careful handling metal skewers, because they transmit heat. Use oven gloves.

- Arrange the food on the skewers with a little space between each piece, so the food cooks evenly.

MICROWAVE PRAWNS

Jumbo prawns are flavoured with garlic, butter and lemon; the microwave makes this dish super quick

Tender prawns cook very well in the microwave oven. You just have to be careful about stirring and standing times so they don't overcook.

Since prawns are fairly dense, standing times are important so the heat can move evenly through the flesh. Make sure that the dish stands on a solid surface when you remove it from the microwave, not on a wire rack, so heat doesn't escape from the bottom of the dish.

You can substitute prawns for the meat in any recipe. Just make sure that all the other ingredients are almost cooked before you add the prawns, as they cook in 3–5 minutes. Be adventurous pairing them with flavourings and ingredients.

Ingredients

Serves 4

50 g butter

3 tablespoons olive oil

1 onion, chopped

6 cloves garlic, crushed

75 ml white wine

50 ml lemon juice

1 teaspoon grated lemon zest

675 g raw jumbo prawns

115 g sugar snap peas

115 g frozen petits pois

Jumbo Prawns with Peas

- In 2-litre shallow microwave-safe baking dish, combine butter, olive oil, onion and garlic.

- Microwave on high for 2–3 minutes, stirring once during cooking time, until onion and garlic are crisp-tender.

- Add wine, lemon juice and zest; microwave for 1 minute until hot. Add prawns and sugar snap peas; stir to coat.

- Cover and microwave on high for 2 minutes. Add petits pois; microwave on high for 1–3 minutes until prawns curl. Leave to stand for 5 minutes.

Old Bay Prawns and Vegetables

Cook 2 finely chopped shallots in 2 tablespoons olive oil and 2 tablespoons butter for 4–5 minutes at high power. Add 200 g trimmed green beans and 2 chopped tomatoes; microwave for 4 minutes. Add 450 g raw jumbo prawns sprinkled with 2 teaspoons Old Bay Seasoning. Microwave for 2 minutes, stir, microwave for 2–4 minutes longer until done.

Zesty Prawns and Asparagus

Combine 450 g asparagus, cut into 5-cm pieces, 1 chopped red onion, 2 crushed garlic cloves, and 75 ml zesty Italian salad dressing. Microwave on high for 3 minutes and stir. Add 450 g raw jumbo prawns along with 2 tablespoons lemon juice; season with salt and cayenne pepper. Microwave for 2 minutes, stir, then microwave 2–4 minutes longer until done.

Prepare Prawns

- To prepare raw unpeeled prawns, first pull off the legs. Then cut off the head if it's still attached.

- Run a small, sharp knife along the back of the prawn and gently pull off the shell. Make sure you remove it completely.

- There may be a dark line running along the curved back of the prawn. Cut along it and rinse to remove.

- You can prepare the prawns well in advance of cooking time. Store, tightly covered, in the refrigerator.

Microwave Prawns

- All microwave ovens cook unevenly. They create hot spots and cool spots. This is why the food has to be moved around.

- Be sure that you stir the food and the sauce very well. Overcooking food may make it unpalatable, but undercooking can be dangerous.

- If some of the prawns seem to be cooking more slowly, arrange them around the outside of the dish.

- Similarly, if they are cooking too fast, put them in the centre of the dish.

SEAFOOD

BARBECUED SHELLFISH

Chargrilled clams and mussels make an easy and spectacular main dish, perfect for entertaining

Shellfish, including clams, mussels and oysters, cook beautifully on the barbecue, which adds a wonderful smoky flavour to these tender and delicious meats.

The shellfish can be cooked directly on the grill rack, or can be placed in an aluminium pan or roaster. Clams, mussels and oysters will cook at different times, so you have to pay attention when they're on the barbecue. Remove the shellfish as soon as their shells open; place in a warmed bowl and cover with foil or a lid to keep them warm.

Savoury and spicy flavours work best with these slightly salty and rich foods. Soy sauce, wine, cocktail sauces and hot peppers are delicious, so include them in your creations.

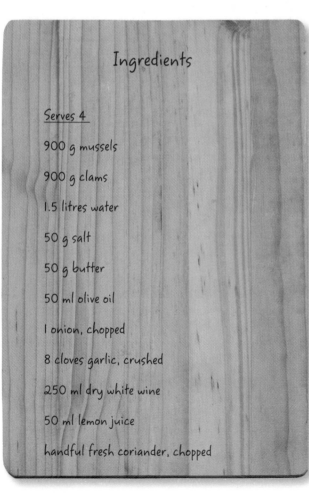

Ingredients

Serves 4

900 g mussels

900 g clams

1.5 litres water

50 g salt

50 g butter

50 ml olive oil

1 onion, chopped

8 cloves garlic, crushed

250 ml dry white wine

50 ml lemon juice

handful fresh coriander, chopped

Barbecued Clams and Mussels

- Scrub mussels and clams; remove beards from mussels. Discard open shellfish. Soak in mixture of water and salt for 10 minutes.

- Place roasting pan on barbecue over medium-high heat. Add butter and olive oil; heat for 2 minutes.

- Add onion and garlic; cook and stir for 4–5 minutes. Add wine and lemon juice and bring to a simmer.

- Put mussels and clams on rack. Cover and grill for 8–12 minutes until shellfish open. Add to roasting pan and stir; serve with dipping sauce.

Curried Mussels

Scrub 2 kg mussels and pull beards off using needle-nose pliers. Discard open or cracked mussels. In sauce-pan, combine 4 oz butter with 1 chopped onion and 4 crushed garlic cloves. Add 1 tablespoon curry powder, ½ teaspoon salt, and a pinch of cayenne pepper; cook for 3 minutes. Barbecue mussels until opened; discard unopened shells. Serve with flavoured butter.

Dipping Sauce

In small bowl, combine 115 g finely crumbled goat cheese, 3 tablespoons chopped coriander, 1 teaspoon grated lemon zest and a pinch of pepper; mix well. Chill until ready to serve. Serve with barbecued clams and mussels.

Soak Shellfish

Discard Bad Shellfish

- Pull the beards, which are the wiry threads, off the mussels using small needle-nose pliers.

- You can try soaking shellfish before cooking; soak in a mixture of water and salt or cornmeal. Neither is really proven to remove sand from the shells.

- There shouldn't be much sand in rope-grown shellfish. Just scrub the shells gently but thoroughly and rinse.

- Oysters can be barbecued just like clams and mussels; they may take a few more minutes on the heat.

- There's a strict rule about shellfish and food safety. When raw, clams and mussels should be tightly closed.

- Tap on an open shell; if it doesn't close, discard it along with any shellfish with cracks or chips.

- After cooking, the clams and mussels must be open. Discard any that are closed.

- If you're serving this as a main dish, you'll need about 450 g shellfish per person; as an appetizer, serve 150 g per person.

SEAFOOD

SCALLOPS WITH PASTA

Tender and mild scallops are the perfect partner with pasta and pesto

Scallops are sweet and delicate shellfish, with fan-shaped shells (which you can wash and save to make pretty containers for other seafood dishes). They have a delicate nugget of white flesh and a more strongly flavoured orange roe.

Scallops may be dredged or collected by hand; the hand-dived ones are the finest and are more expensive. There are many species. King scallops are large and can measure up to 15 cm across. Queen scallops are much smaller and are more suitable for mixed seafood dishes.

Use your nose when buying scallops. They should smell sweet and like seawater; not at all fishy or strong. Use them on the day you buy them.

KNACK QUICK & EASY COOKING

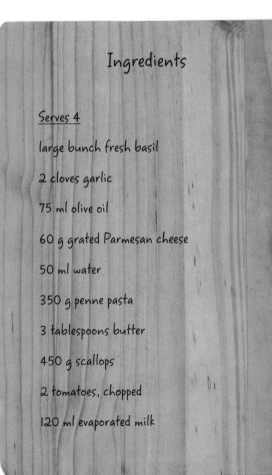

Ingredients

Serves 4

large bunch fresh basil

2 cloves garlic

75 ml olive oil

60 g grated Parmesan cheese

50 ml water

350 g penne pasta

3 tablespoons butter

450 g scallops

2 tomatoes, chopped

120 ml evaporated milk

Pesto Scallops with Pasta

- Bring a large saucepan of water to the boil. In blender or food processor, combine basil, garlic, olive oil, and Parmesan cheese.

- Cover and blend or process until mixed. Gradually add enough water to form a thick sauce. Set aside.

- Add pasta to boiling water. In large pan, melt butter over medium heat. Add scallops; cook, turning once, until browned.

- Drain pasta and add to pan along with sauce, tomatoes, and milk. Cook and stir until sauce blends and tomatoes are hot, about 3–5 minutes.

Scallops and Asparagus

Cook 300 g brown rice in 750 g chicken stock. Meanwhile, in large frying pan melt 3 tablespoons butter with 1 tablespoon olive oil. Add 450 g asparagus, trimmed and cut into 5-cm pieces, 3 crushed garlic cloves and 1 chopped onion; cook for 5 minutes. Add 450 g scallops, 2 tablespoons lemon juice, salt, pepper and basil; cook for 5–8 minutes. Serve with rice.

Scallops with Bacon

Cook 4 rashers bacon; drain and crumble. Pour off fat; add 2 tablespoons butter. Sear 450 g scallops, turning once, until surface is golden brown; remove. Add 225 g sugar snap peas and 2 crushed garlic cloves; cook for 3 minutes. Return scallops and bacon to pan with 50 ml honey mustard and 75 ml crème fraîche; cook for 2–3 minutes. Serve with pasta.

Prepare Pesto

- The pesto can be prepared in a blender or food processor, or mixed by hand with a mortar and pestle.

- You can substitute baby spinach leaves for some of the basil to reduce cost and add nutrition. Or try coriander leaves or parsley.

- Make the pesto ahead of time if it's convenient; cover and refrigerate until you are ready to cook.

- You can substitute 250 g prepared pesto for the homemade version; just add with the tomatoes.

Combine Ingredients

- Sometimes scallops come with a small, tough muscle attached to one side that should be removed. This muscle will be exposed if you run your fingers over the scallop. Just pull it off and discard.

- The pasta finishes cooking in the sauce along with the pesto, so be sure to undercook it slightly.

- The pasta will absorb flavours from the sauce, including the garlic and cheese in the pesto and the tomatoes.

PASTA WITH TOMATO SAUCE

White wine is the surprising ingredient in a creamy tomato sauce tossed with tender pasta

Pasta tossed with a simple tomato sauce is the classic Italian dish. Italians don't use a lot of sauce in their pasta recipes, because they believe it smothers the taste of the pasta.

Pasta has to be cooked in a lot of boiling salted water. Italians say that the water should taste like the sea. Stir the pasta several times as it is cooking so it doesn't stick together.

When you're going to finish the pasta in a sauce, undercook it slightly in the boiling water. As it finishes cooking in the sauce, it will absorb some of those flavours.

Have fun using different sauces and flavourings to make these simple recipes.

Ingredients

<u>Serves 6</u>

5 rashers bacon

2 tablespoons olive oil

3 cloves garlic, crushed

3 tablespoons tomato purée

50 ml dry white wine

1 (450-g) jar passata

450 g penne pasta

120 ml whipping cream

50 g grated pecorino cheese

Penne with Wine and Tomato Sauce

- Bring a large pot of salted water to the boil. Meanwhile, in large pan, cook bacon until crisp. Drain on paper towels, crumble, and set aside.

- Pour off bacon fat; do not wipe saucepan. Add olive oil and garlic; cook for 3 minutes.

- Add tomato purée; cook until paste begins to brown, about 4 minutes. Add white wine; cook and stir to deglaze pan.

- Add passata; simmer for 10–15 minutes. Cook penne. Add to sauce with bacon and cream. Top with cheese and serve.

Hearty Pasta Sauce

Cook 450 g pork sausagemeat with 1 chopped onion and 2 crushed garlic cloves until done; drain. Add 1 (400-g) can chopped tomatoes, 150 g tomato purée, 1 (225-g jar) passata, 1 teaspoon sugar, 1 teaspoon dried basil and ½ teaspoon fennel seed; season with pepper and simmer for 20 minutes. Serve with 450 g linguine.

Pasta Alfredo

Cook 1 chopped onion and 3 crushed garlic cloves in 2 tablespoons olive oil. Add 450-g jar four-cheese pasta sauce, 75 g cream cheese, 250 ml milk, and 25 g grated pecorino cheese; simmer for 5 minutes. Add 350 g cooked and drained penne pasta; cook for 3–4 minutes longer. Sprinkle with chopped parsley and grated Parmesan cheese and serve.

Simmer Sauce

- The bacon fat adds flavour you really can't get any other way. Just a little bit makes a big difference.

- The white wine deglazes the pan and incorporates the scrapings into the sauce. The alcohol will not completely burn off.

- Brown the tomato purée to add flavour to the sauce. The browned bits are caramelized. Don't let it burn.

- Because they're high in sugar, tomato sauces can burn fairly easily; stir frequently from the bottom.

Add Pasta

- Whenever you're cooking pasta with sauce, reserve some of the pasta cooking water.

- The water contains starch from the pasta, so it gives the sauce body even as it's diluting the texture.

- Any tomato sauce can be made smoother and richer with the addition of a dairy product.

- Cream, evaporated milk, yogurt, crème fraîche and cheese all take the sharp edge off tomato sauce.

PASTA

ORZO PASTA SALAD

Orzo pasta, which looks just like rice, is delicious tossed with a cheesy dressing in a main dish salad

Orzo is a delicious, tiny pasta that is shaped like grains of rice. It is a great addition to cold or hot salads.

Many recipes will tell you to rinse the hot cooked pasta in cold water before adding it to the salad dressing and other ingredients. This does rinse off surface starch, but then the pasta doesn't absorb the flavours of the dressing.

You can make a pasta salad out of just about anything. Vegetables, meats, cheeses and fruits all work well.

The amount of dressing looks like a lot, but the pasta will absorb it as it cools. You can add more of the dressing ingredients as needed if you think the salad needs it.

Ingredients

Serves 8

120 ml plain yogurt

150 ml creamy Italian salad dressing

40 g grated Parmesan cheese

200 g sugar snap peas

200 g frozen petits pois

200 g mangetout peas

450 g orzo pasta

3 spring onions, chopped

Three-Pea Parmesan Orzo Salad

- Bring a large pot of salted water to the boil over high heat. Meanwhile, combine yogurt, salad dressing and cheese in large bowl.

- Blanch sugar snap peas, petits pois and mangetout peas for 3 minutes in boiling water. Drain and add to dressing.

- Cook pasta according to package directions until al dente. Drain and add to dressing along with spring onions.

- Toss gently to coat ingredients with dressing. Cover and chill for 3–4 hours to allow flavours to blend.

Orzo Fruit Salad

Combine 175 ml plain yogurt, 175 ml mayonnaise, 3 tablespoons each mustard and milk, and ½ teaspoon dried thyme. Add 450 g orzo, cooked and drained, 175 g diced cooked ham, 3 nectarines, chopped, 1 (425-g) can drained mandarin oranges, 225 g red grapes, and 50 g toasted flaked almonds. Stir well and chill.

Orzo Prawn Salad

Combine 120 ml honey mustard salad dressing, 50 ml olive oil, 120 ml plain yogurt and ½ teaspoon dried dill. Add 450 g cooked medium prawns, 450 g orzo, cooked and drained, 1 each chopped green , red, and yellow peppers, 3 sticks celery, chopped, and 50 g crumbled blue cheese. Mix and chill.

Make Dressing

Cook Pasta

- The dressing should be smooth and well mixed before you add the salad ingredients.

- You can use any creamy salad dressing in this recipe: honey mustard, Caesar, Thousand Island, or blue cheese.

- Substitute ingredients such as chopped peppers, mushrooms, cherry tomatoes or cooked green beans for some or all of the peas.

- Be sure to stir the orzo pasta often as it cooks, as it has a tendency to stick to the bottom of the pan.

- Salt the water generously. A handful of salt is an appropriate amount to flavour the pasta well.

- Drain the pasta by pouring it into a colander. Shake to remove excess water and immediately stir it into the salad dressing.

- The salad should be chilled for 3–4 hours. Stir the salad before serving.

NOODLE BOWLS

Slurpy noodle bowls, made with prawns and vegetables, are flavourful and very easy to make

Noodle bowls were made popular by the Vietnamese. They are literally bowls filled with cooked noodles, vegetables, meat and lots of well-seasoned broth.

These bowls are sold as street food in Asian countries. The solids are eaten with chopsticks, and it's considered perfectly acceptable to slurp the broth as you eat.

The broth must be of the highest quality because it's such an important part of the recipe. Your own homemade stock is easy to make, but the newer chilled stocks on the market are of very high quality.

Each bowl should be about a quarter noodles and a quarter meat and vegetables, then filled with the broth.

Ingredients

Serves 4

2 tablespoons groundnut oil

1 onion, chopped

3 cloves garlic, crushed

1.5 litres chicken stock

3 tablespoons teriyaki sauce

¼ teaspoon dried chilli flakes

½ teaspoon ground ginger

350 g buckwheat soba noodles

225 g chopped green cabbage

450 g cooked prawns

175 g frozen petits pois, thawed

Prawn and Cabbage Noodle Bowl

- Bring a large saucepan of water to the boil. Meanwhile, heat oil in large pan over medium-high heat.

- Add onion and garlic; stir-fry for 4–5 minutes until softened. Add stock, teriyaki sauce, chilli flakes and ginger; bring to simmering point.

- Cook soba noodles as directed on package until al dente. Meanwhile, add cabbage to saucepan; simmer for 3 minutes.

- Add prawns and peas; simmer for 2 minutes. Stir in drained noodles; simmer for 2–3 minutes. Serve in deep warmed bowls.

RECIPE VARIATION

Beef Noodle Bowls: Cook 1 chopped onion, 1 tablespoon grated ginger, and 2 cloves garlic in 1 tablespoon oil. Add 75 g beef sirloin in thin strips; cook until brown; remove. Add 225 g chopped red cabbage, 150 g grated carrot, and 75 g chopped mushrooms. Add 1.5 litres beef broth and beef; simmer 5 minutes. Add 225 g noodles; simmer 5-6 minutes.

Simmer Broth

Add Noodles

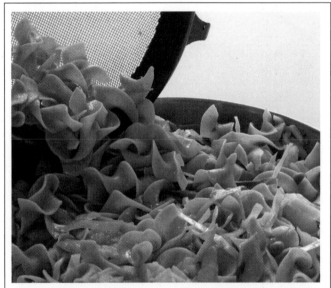

- To make your own broth, combine 900 g beef bones, 2 chopped carrots and 2 chopped onions with 2 litres water.

- Simmer for 3–4 hours until the broth tastes beefy. Strain, cool and freeze in 250-ml portions until ready to use.

- You can make chicken broth by using chicken bones. Season the broth as you like, with salt, pepper and herbs.

- Substitute hoisin sauce, soy sauce or oyster sauce for the teriyaki sauce for a different taste.

- Because the noodles absorb a lot of water when they cook, they aren't cooked in the broth with the other ingredients.

- Soba noodles are thin and are made from buckwheat flour; they are the classic bowl noodle.

- You could also use *udon,* a thick pasta made from plain wheat flour. Or substitute ordinary linguine.

- This dish has to be served immediately; it won't wait. The noodles will continue to cook in the hot broth.

PASTA

PASTA SOUPS

Tortellini is the fast food of pasta when cooked in broth and vegetables

Soup is an ideal medium for pasta. You can cook the pasta in the soup, which is not only quicker and easier, but flavours the pasta. There's a huge difference in taste and texture between pasta cooked in salted water and pasta cooked in broth.

A soup is only as good as its base. Usually, aromatics such as onions, garlic and spices are cooked in oil or with meat to start the soup. Then water or stock or other liquid is added, and ingredients such as pasta or rice are added towards the end of the cooking time.

You can make these soups with any combination of ingredients, and any additional flavourings you fancy.

Ingredients

Serves 6

450 g spicy Italian pork sausage, sliced

I onion, chopped

3 cloves garlic, crushed

350 g frozen mixed vegetables

1.2 litres chicken stock

I (400-g) can chopped tomatoes

I teaspoon dried Italian seasoning

600 g fresh cheese tortellini

40g grated Parmesan cheese

Salt and pepper to taste

Tortellini Minestrone

- In large saucepan, cook sausage with onion and garlic until sausage is browned; drain well.

- Add frozen mixed vegetables; cook and stir for 3–4 minutes until vegetables start to thaw. Then add stock; bring to a simmer. Simmer for 8–9 minutes.

- Add tomatoes, salt, pepper and Italian seasoning. Then add tortellini; simmer for 5–6 minutes until tortellini are hot and tender and vegetables are cooked.

- Stir soup gently, then sprinkle with Parmesan cheese and serve immediately.

Tomato Pasta Soup

Cook 1 onion and 3 cloves garlic in 2 tablespoons olive oil. Add 4 chopped plum tomatoes, 1 (400-g) can chopped tomatoes, 1 teaspoon dried Italian seasoning, 475 ml tomato juice, 750 ml chicken stock, and 2 sticks celery, chopped; simmer for 10 minutes. Add 200 g orzo pasta; simmer for 10–12 minutes until tender. Serve with Parmesan cheese.

Chicken Pasta Soup

Cook 1 chopped onion, 2 sticks celery, chopped, and 2 crushed garlic cloves in 2 tablespoons butter. Add 2 tablespoons flour, ½ teaspoon salt, and ¼ teaspoon cayenne pepper; cook until bubbling. Add 1.2 litres chicken stock, 250 ml single cream, 350 g cooked chicken and 200 g orzo; simmer 10 minutes; add 115 g each grated Emmental and crumbled blue cheeses.

Cook Soup Base

- Cooking onions and garlic with sausage in the first step helps flavour the whole pan of soup.

- You can add other vegetables to the soup if you like. There are many types and varieties of frozen mixed vegetables.

- Or you could chop and add fresh vegetables. Choose your own favourite combination.

- Chopped peppers, green beans, sliced mushrooms, frozen corn or sliced carrots are all good choices.

Add Remaining Ingredients

- If you'd like to substitute fresh tomatoes for the canned, just chop 6–7 plum tomatoes.

- Add them, juice and all, to the soup, along with a pinch of salt. You may need to add a few tablespoons of tomato juice.

- Fresh tortellini take only a couple of minutes to cook, so they're added to the soup at the end of cooking.

- When the tortellini are done, they float to the surface of the soup.

MICROWAVE LASAGNE

Lasagne made in the microwave is a quick and delicious main dish to make when entertaining

The microwave, believe it or not, is a great way to quickly cook almost any lasagne recipe. There is no need to precook the sheets of lasagne as long as there's enough liquid in the recipe.

It's very important to follow microwaving power, rotating, and standing instructions when you're cooking a large dish like lasagne. Be sure that your microwave has at least 800 watts of power to cook the lasagne in this time frame. If your microwave has less power than this, increase the cooking time by 30–40 per cent.

With just pasta, sauce and cheese, you can make a delicious version of lasagne quickly and easily.

Ingredients

Serves 10

1 tablespoon olive oil

450 g minced chicken

1 onion, chopped

1½ teaspoons dried Italian seasoning

1 (750-g) jar spicy tomato sauce

120 ml water

350 g ricotta cheese

2 eggs, beaten

3 tablespoons chopped chives

50 g grated Parmesan cheese

9 sheets lasagne

115 g grated mozzarella cheese

115 g grated provolone cheese

Salt and pepper to taste

Chicken Microwave Lasagne

- In microwave-safe dish, combine olive oil, chicken and onion. Microwave on high for 3 minutes, and stir. Microwave for 2 minutes longer, then drain. Stir in salt, pepper, seasoning, spaghetti sauce and water.

- Combine ricotta, eggs, chives, and 25 g of the Parmesan. In 22 x 32-cm baking dish, layer chicken sauce, 3 sheets lasagne, half the ricotta mixture and grated cheeses. Repeat layers. Sprinkle with remaining Parmesan.

- Cover; microwave on high 15–20 minutes. Leave to stand 10 minutes.

~ VARIATIONS ~

Creamy Chicken Lasagne

Combine 1 (450-g) jar four-cheese pasta sauce with 250 ml milk. Layer 9 sheets lasagne, 500 g cooked chicken, 275 g thawed and drained frozen spinach, 225 g mozzarella cheese, 225 g ricotta cheese, and sauce mixture in microwave-safe dish. Top with 25 g grated Parmesan cheese. Microwave on high for 12–20 minutes, turning once. Leave to stand for 10 minutes.

Classic Beef Lasagne

Cook 450 g minced beef, 1 chopped onion and 3 cloves garlic. Mix with 800 g tomato pasta sauce and 120 ml water. Mix 225 g cottage cheese, 115 g ricotta cheese, and 1 egg. Layer 9 sheets lasagne with beef mixture, cheese mixture, and 225 g grated mozzarella cheese. Microwave as directed.

Microwave Chicken

Prepare Ingredients

- Minced chicken has to be cooked in some kind of fat because it's so low in fat. Otherwise it will be dry.

- You can cook the chicken and onion in a saucepan on the stove if you're more comfortable with that method.

- Minced chicken, as with all minced meats, has to be thoroughly cooked.

- You could substitute minced turkey or spicy or sweet Italian pork sausage for the chicken to add extra flavour.

- You could add more vegetables to this or any lasagne recipe for more colour, flavour and nutrition. The vegetables should be cooked.

- Frozen chopped spinach, thawed and thoroughly drained, is a classic addition, as are mushrooms.

- Since the lasagne can't be stirred, standing time to let the heat travel through the entire dish is important.

- Add a layer of four-cheese pasta sauce to the lasagne for more moisture and additional flavour.

PASTA

161

COUSCOUS

Couscous is tiny pasta that cooks in a flash; stirred with chicken and vegetables, it makes a hearty meal

Many people think that couscous is a grain, but in fact it's a form of pasta. It's made from semolina wheat, and is available in two forms.

The large grains of couscous traditionally used in Moroccan cooking take a long time to prepare and cook. That's not the type of couscous called for in these recipes.

The second form is a very small grain, also made of semolina wheat, which is precooked. To prepare it, all you have to do is mix it with boiling liquid.

Because couscous has a neutral flavour, like pasta, it can be rehydrated in stock and flavoured liquids, then combined with almost any food.

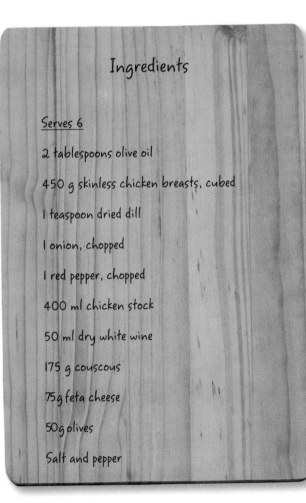

Ingredients

Serves 6

2 tablespoons olive oil

450 g skinless chicken breasts, cubed

1 teaspoon dried dill

1 onion, chopped

1 red pepper, chopped

400 ml chicken stock

50 ml dry white wine

175 g couscous

75 g feta cheese

50 g olives

Salt and pepper

Greek-Style Couscous

- In heavy pan, heat oil over medium heat. Sprinkle chicken with salt, pepper and dill; sauté until browned, about 3–4 minutes. Remove from pan.

- Add onion and pepper; cook and stir for 3 minutes. Return chicken to pan; add stock and wine.

- Bring to a simmer; simmer for 2–3 minutes until chicken is thoroughly cooked. Stir in couscous.

- Cover and remove from heat. Let stand for 7–8 minutes. Uncover, add feta and olives; fluff with fork and serve.

Tex-Mex Couscous
Cook 450 g minced beef, 1 chopped onion, 3 cloves garlic, and 2 jalapeño peppers; drain. Add 1 green pepper, 350 g sweetcorn, 120 ml salsa, and 350 ml beef stock; bring to a simmer. Stir in 175 g couscous; cover and remove from heat. Leave to stand for 5 minutes, then stir in 50 g Parmesan cheese.

French Chicken Couscous
Cook 3 cubed chicken breasts, 1 chopped onion, and 3 cloves garlic in 2 tablespoons olive oil. Add 250 g frozen green beans and 1 chopped red pepper. Add 475 ml chicken stock, 175 g couscous, and 115 g diced Brie cheese; stir, cover, and remove from heat. Leave to stand, fluff up with fork, serve.

Simmer Ingredients

- To prepare chicken breast fillets, all you need to do is cut them into 2.5-cm cubes.

- For the most tender chicken, first brown it to add flavour to the dish, then remove it while the vegetables start cooking.

- Other ingredients you could use in this dish include trimmed and chopped green beans, thinly sliced carrots and frozen peas.

- For additional authentic Greek flavour, use kalamata olives and stir in some lemon peel along with the couscous.

Add Couscous

- The couscous you use in this dish must be pre-cooked. Read the label and cooking instructions to make sure.

- The couscous will be perfectly rehydrated during the brief standing time. Fluff it with a fork when you're ready to eat.

- Make sure that the liquid is simmering before you add the couscous for the best results.

- The liquid has to be very hot in order for the couscous to absorb it properly and rehydrate.

PASTA

163

PASTA SALAD

Pasta is a natural for main dish salads, enveloped in creamy dressings with vegetables

Use your imagination when creating pasta salads. This delicious category of food is perfect for hot summer days and for when your house is full of company. You make it, put it in the fridge, and let everyone help themselves.

Be sure there's enough dressing for the salad, and that the dressing is the proper consistency. It should look like thick pancake batter. If it's thicker, it won't blend well with the other ingredients and the salad will be dry. Thinner, and the food won't be able to hold on to it, and you'll end up with a puddle of dressing in the bottom of the bowl.

Enjoy creating your own fresh pasta salads.

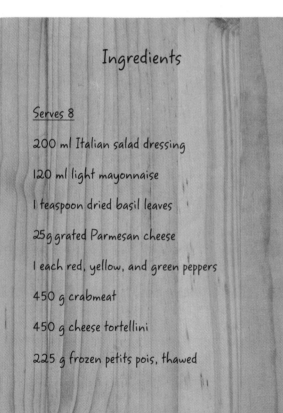

Ingredients

<u>Serves 8</u>

200 ml Italian salad dressing

120 ml light mayonnaise

1 teaspoon dried basil leaves

25 g grated Parmesan cheese

1 each red, yellow, and green peppers

450 g crabmeat

450 g cheese tortellini

225 g frozen petits pois, thawed

Italian Crab Pasta Salad

- Bring a large saucepan of salted water to a boil. In large bowl, combine salad dressing, mayonnaise, basil and cheese; mix well.

- Seed and chop the peppers; add to dressing mixture. Pick over crabmeat.

- Cook the cheese tortellini according to package directions until al dente. Place peas in colander; drain pasta over peas.

- Add to mixture in bowl and stir to coat. Serve immediately, or cover and chill for 2–3 hours before serving.

Orange Chicken Pasta Salad

Combine 120 ml mayonnaise, 120 ml plain yogurt, 50 ml orange juice, 1 teaspoon dried thyme and 1 tablespoon Dijon mustard. Stir in 350 g spiral pasta, cooked, 275 g cubed cooked chicken, 1 (425-g) can drained mandarin oranges, 225 g red grapes and 75 g walnut pieces. Mix well, chill and stir before serving.

Pasta Vegetable Salad

Combine 120 ml olive oil, 75 ml cider vinegar, 50 ml Dijon mustard, 1 teaspoon dried oregano, and 25 g Parmesan cheese. Add 350 g cooked gemelli pasta, 1 each chopped red, yellow, and orange peppers, 1 chopped red onion, 225 g frozen petits pois, 115 g diced Cheddar cheese, and 225 g cherry tomatoes. Mix, chill and serve.

Mix Dressing

Finish Salad

- It may look as if there's a lot of dressing in the recipe, but there's a lot of food for the dressing to coat. The hot pasta will absorb it.

- If you wish, make more dressing and refrigerate it along with the salad.

- If the salad is dry, you can stir in more dressing, or serve it on the side for guests to add.

- Other dressings that would be delicious in this recipe include blue cheese and Caesar salad dressings.

- To stretch this salad to feed a larger number of people, you could serve it on mixed salad greens. That would also add colour, flavour and nutrition.

- Buy fresh crab ready dressed from the fishmonger or supermarket. You will need all white crabmeat for this salad.

- Fresh crabmeat needs to be picked over. Remove any bits of cartilage and shell with your fingers.

MAIN COURSE SALADS

CHICKEN SALAD

Classic chicken salad is packed full of chicken and fruit.

Chicken salad, that popular summer lunchtime staple, is easy to make and can be made with most fruits and vegetables.

Using tender, perfectly cooked chicken is the secret of success for this salad. Poached chicken or chicken baked in baking parchment is your best bet. These cooking methods result in very moist and tender chicken. You can also marinate the cooked, cubed chicken for a short time before it's added to the rest of the salad. The chicken will absorb some of the marinade and its flavour. Use the liquid you're going to use to make the salad dressing for this purpose.

Chicken salads can be made with fruit, when it's best to use a sweet dressing, or with vegetables and a savoury dressing.

Ingredients

Serves 8

450 g cooked chicken, cubed

50 ml orange juice

120 ml half-fat crème fraîche

120 ml low-fat mayonnaise

½ teaspoon curry powder

225 g red grapes

115 g green grapes

2 nectarines, cubed

115 g dried apricots, diced

120 ml whipping cream

Salt and pepper

Creamy Fruit Chicken Salad

- In medium bowl, combine chicken with orange juice; stir and refrigerate for 10 minutes.

- In large bowl, combine crème fraîche, mayonnaise, curry powder, salt and pepper and beat until smooth with wire whisk. Stir in chicken and orange juice.

- Add grapes, nectarines and chopped dried apricots; stir gently to coat. Cover and chill for 1–2 hours.

- In small bowl, beat cream until stiff peaks form. Fold into salad, then serve.

Parchment-Wrapped Baked Chicken
Place chicken breasts on sheets of baking parchment, 1 breast per sheet. Sprinkle with dried herbs to flavour the chicken, then top each with a thin slice of lemon or orange. Fold the baking parchment around the chicken and place on baking sheets. Bake at 190°C for 20–25 minutes until cooked through.

Parmesan Chicken Salad
Combine 120 ml mayonnaise, 120 ml plain yogurt, 50 ml milk, 25 g grated Parmesan cheese and 1 teaspoon dried basil. Add 450 g cubed cooked chicken breast, 2 sticks chopped celery, 225 g cherry tomatoes, 4 spring onions, chopped, and 75 g chopped mushrooms. Stir, chill and serve on lettuce leaves.

Poach Chicken Breasts

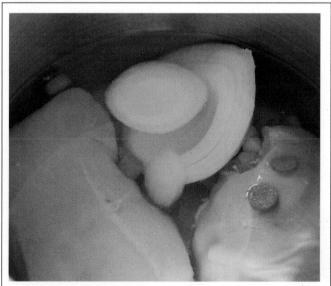

- To poach chicken breasts, place them in cold water to cover, with a halved onion and chopped carrot.

- Bring to simmering point, then reduce heat until liquid barely moves. Poach for 10–15 minutes until cooked through.

- Keeping the chicken in its cooking liquid, cool at room temperature for 20–30 minutes, then refrigerate.

- The poached chicken can be cubed or shredded and used immediately, or frozen up to 3 months.

Fold Whipped Cream into Salad

- Just a tiny bit of curry powder doesn't make the salad taste of curry, but enhances the sweet and tart flavours of the fruits.

- Fold the whipped cream into the salad just before serving so the dressing remains fluffy and light.

- You can use other fruits with the chicken if you like. Fresh mango, diced fresh peaches, or blueberries would all be good additions to the mixture.

MAIN COURSE SALADS

ROAST BEEF SALAD

Cold roast beef, in a spicy dressing with thin noodles, makes an exotic main dish salad

Beef salad makes a fantastic main dish. Cold beef has a wonderful flavour, and can be delicious with the right dressing and accompanying ingredients.

You can cook the meat and add it to the salad, or use leftover roast beef that you have cooked yourself or bought from a deli. If you're using sliced steak, it should be cooked only medium rare or medium. If you use well-done steak, it will be too chewy in a salad.

For the dressing, use your imagination. Think about flavours you like to serve with steak or hamburgers. A dressing made from steak sauce and yogurt would be delicious, as would one made from mustard, relish and mayonnaise.

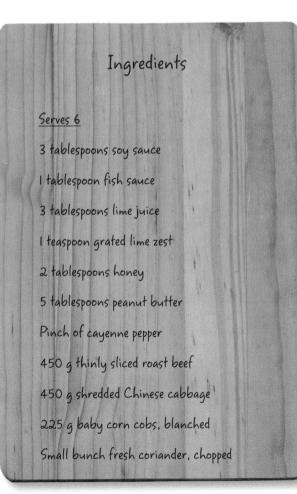

Ingredients

Serves 6

3 tablespoons soy sauce

1 tablespoon fish sauce

3 tablespoons lime juice

1 teaspoon grated lime zest

2 tablespoons honey

5 tablespoons peanut butter

Pinch of cayenne pepper

450 g thinly sliced roast beef

450 g shredded Chinese cabbage

225 g baby corn cobs, blanched

Small bunch fresh coriander, chopped

Thai Beef Salad

- In large bowl, combine soy sauce, fish sauce, lime juice, lime zest and honey.

- Stir in peanut butter and cayenne pepper and beat with wire whisk until smooth. Dressing can be made ahead of time.

- Cut the beef into thin strips and toss with the peanut butter mixture.

- Place cabbage on serving plate and top with baby corn. Spoon beef mixture on top and sprinkle with coriander. Serve immediately.

Beef and Potato Salad
In 2 tablespoons butter, sauté 450 g thinly sliced beef sirloin steak; remove. Cook 1 chopped onion, 2 crushed garlic cloves, 600 g frozen rosti potatoes. Combine 120 ml plain yogurt,120 ml mayonnaise, 50 ml French mustard, 2 tablespoons horseradish, and 50 ml beef stock. Add beef, sautéed vegetables, 225 g cherry tomatoes, and 150 g mushrooms; mix.

Taco Salad
In bowl, combine 450 g cubed roast beef, 1 (450-g) jar salsa, 350 g sweetcorn, 2 finely chopped jalapeño peppers, 1 tablespoon chilli powder, 1 red onion, 1 yellow pepper, and 4 tomatoes, all diced; mix. Serve on torn lettuce; top with 115 g crushed tortilla chips and 200 g grated Cheddar cheese.

Slice Beef into Strips

- The beef is important in this salad. Whether you slice it yourself or buy it from the deli, it needs to be about 8mm thick.

- If the beef is cut thinner than that, it will tend to fall apart when mixed in the salad.

- You can also cube the beef. An alternative would be to use leftover grilled steak.

- The beef will absorb some moisture from the dressing. You can toss the beef with the dressing ahead of time and store in the fridge.

Mix the Sauce

- Fish sauce, also called nuoc mam, is an intensely flavoured Asian sauce that adds a rich depth of flavour.

- The dressing won't taste fishy. You can substitute teriyaki or hoisin sauce for the fish sauce if you prefer.

- For an easier dressing, combine a Thai peanut sauce with some lime juice and chopped spring onion.

- The sauce can be made ahead of time and stored, covered, in the refrigerator until you're ready to use it.

MAIN COURSE SALADS

BEAN SALAD

Pulses are combined in a spicy salsa dressing for a super quick salad perfect for summer

Bean salads are so easy to make because you can start with drained canned or frozen beans.

Everybody knows about the standard three-bean or four-bean salad, made of kidney beans, green beans and chick-peas marinated in a sweet and sour dressing. But bean salads go beyond that traditional recipe.

You can combine pulses with pasta, with meats like chicken or prawns, and with just about any fresh vegetable in a salad. And the dressings can range from sweet and sour to savoury or spicy.

If you think of beans as alternatives to pasta or grains, you'll see a lot of salad possibilities open up.

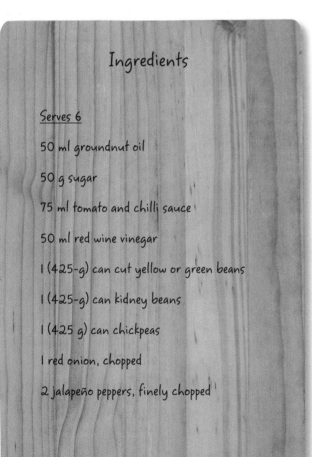

Ingredients

<u>Serves 6</u>

50 ml groundnut oil

50 g sugar

75 ml tomato and chilli sauce

50 ml red wine vinegar

1 (425-g) can cut yellow or green beans

1 (425-g) can kidney beans

1 (425 g) can chickpeas

1 red onion, chopped

2 jalapeño peppers, finely chopped

Mexican Three-Bean Salad

- In large bowl, combine oil, sugar, tomato and chilli sauce and vinegar and mix well. Leave to stand for 10 minutes, then whisk again.

- Make sure that the sugar is dissolved before adding the vegetables.

- Drain all the canned beans and rinse thoroughly; drain again. Add to sauce with the onion and jalapeños.

- Cover and refrigerate for 3–4 hours to blend flavours before serving. Add other chopped vegetables or meats to salad for variation.

~ VARIATIONS ~

Southwest Bean Salad

In bowl, combine 75 ml each olive oil and lime juice with 5 tablespoons chopped coriander, salt and cayenne pepper, 2 crushed garlic cloves, 2 finely chopped jalapeño peppers, and 2 teaspoons chilli powder. Add 425-g cans kidney, black and pinto beans, drained, along with 1 chopped red onion, 225 g thawed frozen sweetcorn and 2 chopped red peppers.

Black Bean Chicken Salad

Combine 120 ml plain yogurt, 120 ml mayonnaise, 120 ml salsa, 3 tablespoons chopped coriander, salt, pepper, and 50 ml chicken stock. Add 450 g cubed cooked chicken, 2 (425-g) cans drained black beans, 1 chopped red onion, 225-g can drained sliced mushrooms, and 4 tomatoes, chopped. Mix and chill, then stir and serve.

Drain and Rinse Beans

- Canned beans are really easy to use, but they can be very high in sodium. Look for low-sodium products.

- Always drain, rinse, then drain beans again. This will help reduce the sodium content somewhat.

- For no sodium, cook your own dried beans. Place beans in a pan, cover with water, and boil hard for 2 minutes. Leave to stand for 1 hour. Drain, cover with water again, and cook 2–3 hours until beans are tender. The cooked beans can be frozen.

Toss Salad

- The beans are fairly tender, so use care when tossing with other ingredients. Use a large spoon.

- To save more time, use a prepared salad dressing. Italian, a creamy blue cheese dressing or Caesar would be good.

- Add meats like cubed cooked chicken, cooked prawns or scallops, or grilled salmon to the salad.

- Toss the salad again before serving. Since these ingredients don't absorb dressing, it will drain to the bottom of the bowl.

MAIN COURSE SALADS

GRAIN SALADS

Tabbouleh, made from cracked wheat and quinoa, is an inexpensive and healthy summer salad

Cooked grains are some of the healthiest foods you can eat. They include wheat, cracked wheat, barley, corn, brown and wild rice and quinoa.

All of these foods are very easy to cook. They are just simmered in water, broth, or other liquid for a few minutes until tender. They are all fairly mild in flavour, too, so can be used with many different kinds of foods. Within the category of grains, there are quick-cooking options. Cracked wheat cooks more quickly than wheat berries, for example, and white rice takes less time than brown. Whatever grain you choose, make sure it's cooked properly and is still slightly chewy.

These salads are just as versatile as the others.

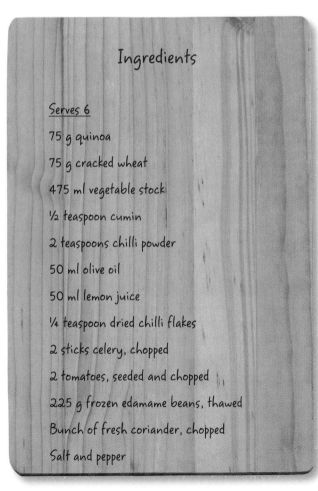

Ingredients

Serves 6

75 g quinoa

75 g cracked wheat

475 ml vegetable stock

½ teaspoon cumin

2 teaspoons chilli powder

50 ml olive oil

50 ml lemon juice

¼ teaspoon dried chilli flakes

2 sticks celery, chopped

2 tomatoes, seeded and chopped

225 g frozen edamame beans, thawed

Bunch of fresh coriander, chopped

Salt and pepper

Spicy Vegetable Tabbouleh

- Cook quinoa and cracked wheat according to package directions, using vegetable stock instead of water.

- Meanwhile, in large bowl combine cumin, chilli powder, oil, lemon juice, salt, pepper and chilli flakes.

- Add the cooked quinoa and cracked wheat and toss gently to coat.

- Prepare vegetables and stir into salad. Sprinkle with coriander. Cover and chill for 2–3 hours before serving.

Barley Black Bean Salad
Cook 175 g pearl barley as directed on package. Meanwhile, combine 50 ml each olive oil, Dijon mustard, 3 tablespoons chopped parsley, 2 tablespoons lemon juice, salt and pepper. Stir in hot cooked barley, 2 (425-g) cans drained black beans, 1 each red, yellow, and green peppers, and 65 g sliced mushrooms. Mix well, cover and chill.

Tex-Mex Wild Rice Salad
Cook 175 g wild rice according to package directions. Combine 120 ml mayonnaise, 120 ml salsa, 75 ml crème fraîche, 1 finely chopped jalapeño pepper, and 1 chopped red onion. Add 450 g cooked medium prawns, 115 g diced Cheddar cheese, 1 (425-g) can drained baby corn, and 225 g frozen edamame beans, thawed. Mix and chill; stir before serving.

Cook Quinoa and Cracked Wheat

- Quinoa is an ancient grain that provides complete protein: that is, all of the essential amino acids the body needs.

- It's a round grain that has a nutty flavour and tender texture. Be sure to rinse it before cooking because it has a bitter coating.

- The quinoa will expand to four times its volume after cooking, so plan amounts accordingly.

- Cracked wheat usually just has to be soaked in hot or boiling water until tender; follow package directions.

Add Vegetables

- Tabbouleh is usually made from just cracked wheat. Adding another grain enhances flavour, nutrition and interest. Wild rice or barley would also be good.

- Classic vegetables used in tabbouleh are parsley, cucumbers, tomatoes and spring onions.

- Edamame beans, or soya beans, are another unusual tabbouleh ingredient. Their nutty taste and slightly crunchy texture are delicious.

- You could use black beans or cannellini beans instead of the edamame beans.

MAIN COURSE SALADS

TUNA OR SALMON SALAD

Tuna salad is updated with fresh fruits in an easy and delicious main dish salad

Tuna salad is a staple of lunch boxes, while salmon salad can be a little more upscale. Either one of these oily fish is delicious in main dish salads.

These rich-tasting fish combine well with fruits and vegetables, so you can go sweet or savoury with the dressings and other ingredients.

You can use canned tuna or salmon, but you can also buy freshly cooked flaked salmon in some supermarkets, which is ideal for tossing into a salad.

For the freshest tasting salads, cook tuna or salmon yourself. Grill tuna or salmon steaks for 10–12 minutes, leave to cool, then flake and use.

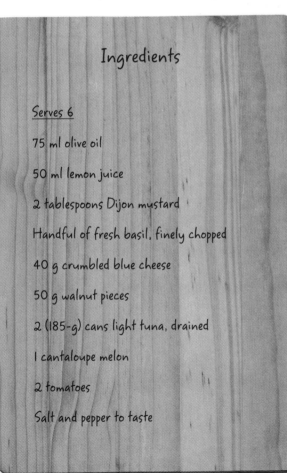

Ingredients

<u>Serves 6</u>

75 ml olive oil

50 ml lemon juice

2 tablespoons Dijon mustard

Handful of fresh basil, finely chopped

40 g crumbled blue cheese

50 g walnut pieces

2 (185-g) cans light tuna, drained

1 cantaloupe melon

2 tomatoes

Salt and pepper to taste

Cantaloupe, Tomato and Tuna Salad

- In large bowl, combine olive oil, lemon juice, mustard, basil, salt and pepper and mix well.

- Blend in blue cheese and walnuts. Flake tuna and stir into dressing; set aside.

- Cut cantaloupe melon in half and scoop out seeds. Using a melon baller, make as many balls as possible.

- Cut tomatoes into 8 wedges and cut each wedge in half. Add cantaloupe and tomato to salad; stir gently. Serve immediately or chill for 2–3 hours.

You have several options when buying canned salmon and tuna. Sockeye salmon is red salmon, which is the best quality of canned fish, and it's the most expensive with the richest flavour. Pink salmon is less expensive and is good for fish cakes. Canned tuna is packed in olive oil, sunflower oil, brine or spring water. Always look for tuna labelled 'dolphin friendly'.

Salmon Pepper Salad: Brush 1 salmon steak with 1 tablespoon olive oil. Grill for 10–12 minutes until done. Cool. Combine 250 ml creamy Italian salad dressing, 50 ml crème fraîche, 25 g grated Parmesan, salt and pepper. Add salmon along with 1 each red, green and yellow pepper, chopped, and 3 chopped spring onions. Stir, chill, then serve.

Prepare Cantaloupe and Tuna

- A melon balling tool is a handy utensil for most quick and easy kitchens.

- Not only will it make perfect balls from melons, butter and ice cream, it can also be used to core apples and pears.

- Canned tuna flakes easily. Be sure to drain it well.

- If you're using your own cooked tuna, work it with your fingers and it will flake naturally.

Blend Salad

- Don't overmix salads that use canned fish; the fish will break up into tiny pieces and won't be apparent in the salad.

- Cantaloupe melon and tomato may sound like a strange combination, but it's really delicious.

- Both 'fruits' are sweet and juicy, and the slight tartness of the tomato complements the super-sweet melon.

- Stir this salad again before serving. The ingredients don't absorb the dressing, so it needs to be redistributed before you eat it.

TOFU STIR-FRY

Tofu and noodles are stir-fried with vegetables in this hearty and healthy main dish

Tofu, that much-disparaged meat substitute, can be delicious when properly prepared. It's very good for you, so making it taste great is the way to get your family to love it.

There are several different types of tofu. Soft or silken tofu is used for puddings and dressings. The type of tofu you want for stir-frying is firm or extra-firm.

For best results, drain the tofu before you add it to the marinade. Place on a plate and top with another, resting a can on top to weight it down. Leave to drain for 15–20 minutes, then use as directed in recipe. The tofu will absorb flavours from the marinade. Then add your own flavours and favourite ingredients to create a delicious tofu dish.

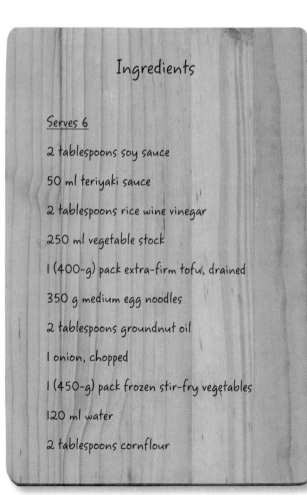

Ingredients

Serves 6

2 tablespoons soy sauce

50 ml teriyaki sauce

2 tablespoons rice wine vinegar

250 ml vegetable stock

1 (400-g) pack extra-firm tofu, drained

350 g medium egg noodles

2 tablespoons groundnut oil

1 onion, chopped

1 (450-g) pack frozen stir-fry vegetables

120 ml water

2 tablespoons cornflour

Tofu Lo Mein

- In large bowl, combine soy sauce, teriyaki sauce, vinegar and stock. Cut drained tofu into 2.5-cm pieces. Marinate in soy sauce mixture for 10 minutes.

- Bring a large saucepan of water to the boil and cook noodles according to package directions.

- Heat oil in wok or large pan over medium-high heat. Add onion and vegetables; stir-fry for 5–6 minutes. Drain tofu, reserving marinade, and stir-fry for 2 minutes.

- Add water and cornflour to marinade and add to wok with drained noodles. Stir-fry for 2–3 minutes until hot.

~ VARIATIONS ~

Garlic Tofu Stir-Fry

Prepare 400-g pack firm tofu. Combine 3 tablespoons soy sauce, 50 ml cider vinegar, and 75 ml vegetable stock; marinate tofu for 15 minutes. Drain; add 1 tablespoon cornflour to marinade. Stir-fry 200 g each sliced carrots, cauliflower florets and chopped onion with 5 cloves garlic in 1 tablespoon oil. Add tofu; stir-fry for 3 minutes. Add marinade and stir-fry until thickened.

Mushroom Tofu Stir-Fry

Prepare 400-g pack firm tofu. Mix 50 ml mushroom ketchup, 1 teaspoon chilli paste, 120 ml vegetable stock and 2 tablespoons soy sauce. Marinate tofu for 10 minutes. Drain; add 1 tablespoon cornflour to marinade. Stir-fry 65 g each sliced chestnut, button and portobello mushrooms, 1 red pepper and 150 g green beans. Add tofu, stir-fry, add marinade; stir-fry until thickened.

Marinate Tofu

- Firm and extra-firm tofu are solid enough to stir-fry and grill. Real labels carefully to make sure that's what you're buying.

- When you press out the excess liquid, these forms of tofu take on the texture of meat.

- Cut tofu using a sharp knife. Make all the cubes about the same size so they heat evenly.

- Any bottled Asian marinade can be used in place of the homemade version in this easy recipe.

Stir-Fry Vegetables

- The vegetables take longer to cook to a crisp-tender state than the tofu does to heat up, so add them first.

- Taste some of the vegetables when you think they're done. The colour will intensify as they cook.

- When they are easy to bite into but still have some texture, they're done.

- The vegetables continue to cook when the tofu is added and when the sauce cooks, so be sure to take that into account.

RISOTTO

Classic risotto is updated with soya beans and roasted garlic for a delicious vegetarian meal

Risotto is an elegant classic Italian dish that seems complicated and difficult. But not only is it easy to make, it can be prepared, from start to finish, in just 30 minutes.

The keys to risotto are to use Arborio, or short-grain rice, and to stir the dish almost constantly. Arborio rice has lots of starch, and stirring constantly makes the rice release that starch, which creates the creamy texture of the finished risotto. If you want this to be a vegan dish, you can omit the butter that's stirred in at the end. Add a tablespoon or two of olive oil instead, along with some vegan cheese.

You can add any vegetable you like to risotto, and flavour it with your favourite herbs and spices. Have fun!

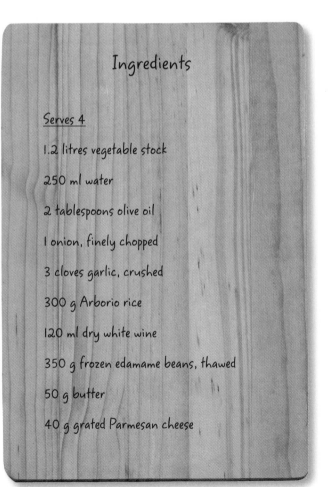

Ingredients

<u>Serves 4</u>

1.2 litres vegetable stock

250 ml water

2 tablespoons olive oil

1 onion, finely chopped

3 cloves garlic, crushed

300 g Arborio rice

120 ml dry white wine

350 g frozen edamame beans, thawed

50 g butter

40 g grated Parmesan cheese

Garlic and Edamame Risotto

- In medium saucepan, combine vegetable stock and water; heat over low heat.

- In large pan, heat oil over medium heat. Add onion and garlic; cook and stir for 6 minutes to soften.

- Add rice; cook and stir for 3–4 minutes. Add wine; cook and stir until absorbed. Gradually add the hot stock, a ladleful at a time, stirring constantly.

- After 20 minutes, the rice should be al dente and the sauce creamy. Stir in edamame beans, butter, and cheese; cover; cook 3–4 minutes, then stir and serve.

Arborio rice is an Italian short-grain rice. That means the rice contains a lot of amylopectin, a type of starch that has lots of branches. Those branches trap and hold moisture, which makes the rice sticky when it's cooked. The rice releases its starch into the liquid in the dish as it cooks, creating a creamy sauce.

• • • • RECIPE VARIATION • • • •

Asparagus Risotto: Heat 1.5 litres vegetable stock in saucepan. Cook 1 chopped onion, 2 cloves garlic, and 300 g arborio rice in 2 tablespoons olive oil. Gradually add stock, stirring constantly. When three-quarters of the stock has been added, stir in 1 bunch asparagus, trimmed and cut into short lengths. Keep cooking. When done, stir in 40 g Parmesan cheese.

Cook Onion, Garlic and Rice

- The onion and garlic flavour the oil, which in turn flavours the rice, so the whole dish tastes good.

- Be sure that the onion and garlic, and any other root vegetables you add, are thoroughly cooked before you add the rice.

- The oil you choose for the risotto can be mild, or highly flavoured to add more flavour to the finished dish.

- Sauté the rice in the oil to start the cooking process and add a nutty flavour.

Stir Risotto

- If there's one secret to risotto, it's to stir the rice almost constantly while adding the liquid.

- The physical manipulation of the rice helps break down its cells, which lets the starch release into the cooking liquid.

- Add the stock 120 ml at a time, which is about a ladleful. Then cook and stir until the liquid is absorbed.

- This method of adding the liquid also helps break down the rice, so the sauce is nice and creamy.

MICROWAVE BEANS AND RICE

Beans and rice, a classic New Orleans dish, is updated in the microwave oven

Beans and rice is a humble, rustic kind of dish, but it's been nourishing hardworking people for generations. And it's delicious, as well as being good for you.

Beans, or pulses such as kidney beans, black beans, pinto beans and cannellini beans, don't provide complete protein. You need to add grains or vegetables so your body gets all

the amino acids it needs. That's where the rice comes in. Rice provides the missing amino acids so the whole dish is hearty and nutritious.

The combination of flavours and textures is delicious, too; beans are the perfect foil to tender rice. Flavour this dish with anything from chilli to cheese.

Ingredients

Serves 6

2 tablespoons olive oil

1 onion, chopped

4 cloves garlic, crushed

750 ml vegetable stock

120 ml water

300 g medium-grain rice

2 (425-g) cans kidney beans

2 sticks celery, chopped

1 red pepper, chopped

½ teaspoon dried oregano

Bunch of fresh coriander, chopped

Dash of Tabasco sauce

Salt and pepper

New Orleans Red Beans and Rice

- In microwave-safe casserole dish, combine olive oil, onion and garlic. Microwave on high for 3–4 minutes until tender.

- Stir in vegetable stock and water along with rice. Cover and microwave on high for 14–18 minutes until rice is almost tender.

- Drain beans and rinse; drain again. Stir into rice mixture along with remaining ingredients.

- Microwave, uncovered, on high for 2–3 minutes, stirring once, until rice is tender and mixture is hot. Leave to stand for 5 minutes, then serve.

~ VARIATIONS ~

Black Beans and Rice

Cook onion and garlic in oil in microwave as directed. Add 200 g long-grain white rice and 750 ml vegetable stock. Cover and microwave on high for 15 minutes. Stir in 2 (425-g) cans rinsed and drained black beans and 75 ml seafood cocktail sauce; microwave for 3 minutes. Stir in 115 g grated Gouda cheese; leave to stand, then stir and serve.

Spicy Beans and Rice

Cook onion and 2 finely chopped jalapeños as directed. Add 200 g long-grain white rice and 750 ml vegetable stock. Cover; microwave on high for 15 minutes. Add 200 g vegetarian sausage mix, 2 (425-g) cans pinto beans, 1 tablespoon chilli powder, and 400-g can chopped tomatoes. Microwave 3–5 minutes. Stir in 4 tablespoons chopped coriander; serve.

Microwave Onion and Garlic

Add Red Beans

- The microwave cooks onions and garlic very evenly and quickly. If you want to add other root vegetables, do it now.

- Stir the vegetable mixture well so the edges don't overbrown or burn and the food cooks through.

- If your microwave is over 1,000 watts, stir the rice mixture once during the cooking time.

- Be careful; the microwave dish will be hot. Always protect your hands when you remove the dish, and watch out for steam.

- You can really only use canned beans in the microwave oven. Dried beans won't absorb the water evenly.

- Be sure to drain, rinse, and drain the beans very well. The sweet liquid they are packed in isn't desirable.

- The dish has to stand for at least 5 minutes, but no longer than 15–20, after it finishes cooking.

- The rice will absorb the last of the moisture and the flavours will blend during this standing time.

BARBECUED VEGETABLES AND TOFU

A dry rub is usually used on the barbecue, and adds superb flavour to mild tofu and vegetables

Yes, you can barbecue tofu. Extra-firm tofu can be cooked directly on the grill rack. You may want to cook softer tofu on a grill basket, so it doesn't break on the barbecue and fall into the fire.

Vegetables of all kind develop a wonderful extra dimension of flavour when they're barbecued. Root vegetables develop

a lot of sugar, and the caramelization from the heat adds complex tastes.

If you want to get grill marks on the tofu and vegetables, leave them alone for a few minutes when you place them on the rack. Pick one up with some tongs; if it releases easily, turn it over and leave it alone again.

Ingredients

Serves 6

450 g extra-firm tofu, drained

2 tablespoons olive oil

1 teaspoon ground ginger

1 tablespoon sugar

½ teaspoon ground cloves

1 teaspoon anise seeds

2 green peppers, sliced

2 onions, sliced

2 yellow courgettes, sliced

350 g baby carrots

120 ml teriyaki sauce

Salt and pepper

Asian Rubbed Tofu and Vegetables

- Drain tofu by weighting it with a plate for 20 minutes, then cut into 2.5-cm slices. Brush with olive oil.

- In medium bowl, combine ginger, sugar, cloves, anise, salt and pepper; sprinkle two-thirds of this mixture over tofu and rub in.

- Toss vegetables with the remaining mixture and place in grill basket.

- Barbecue tofu over medium direct heat, turning once, until browned, about 4–5 minutes. Barbecue vegetables in basket at same time. Toss with teriyaki sauce and serve.

~ VARIATIONS ~

Tofu Vegetable Kebabs
Drain and press 450 g extra-firm tofu. Marinate it for 15 minutes in 75 ml zesty Italian salad dressing. Thread on metal skewers along with red onion wedges, 2 peppers cut into strips, and 150 g whole chestnut mushrooms. Barbecue over direct medium heat, brushing with more salad dressing, 5–7 minutes. Serve immediately.

Chargrilled Tex-Mex Tofu
Drain and press 450 g extra-firm tofu. Rub with 1 tablespoon chilli powder, 1 teaspoon dried oregano, 1 teaspoon cumin, and ¼ teaspoon cayenne pepper. Cut into 2.5-cm slices. Barbecue along with 3 peppers, cut into strips, and 4 corn cobs, cut into 7.5-cm pieces. Brush all with 250 ml salsa while cooking.

Put Dry Rub on Tofu

- Tofu is a flavour sponge; it will absorb the flavours you cook it with. Build layers of flavour with a rub and a marinade.

- So think about your favourite barbecue flavours and add them to the recipe.

- A dry rub will add more intense flavours than a marinade. Make sure you rub it in evenly.

- There are many ready-prepared dry rubs you can buy. Keep one on hand for impromptu barbecues.

Grill Tofu and Vegetables

- To give tofu a meatier texture, freeze it and defrost it before flavouring with a dry rub or marinade and barbecuing.

- Tofu, even when cut into larger slices, cooks quickly on the barbecue. You can just warm it, or let the edges get crisp.

- The vegetables can also be threaded on skewers instead of being cooked in the grill basket.

- This recipe can be cooked ahead of time and served at room temperature if you like. There aren't any perishable ingredients.

MICROWAVE RISOTTO

The microwave cooks risotto quickly and easily, and it's less work than the classic method

You can make risotto in the microwave. Most microwaves have a turntable, so the mixture is moving as it cooks. If your microwave does not have a turntable, stir the risotto several times while it's cooking so the grains of rice are agitated a bit.

Traditional risotto usually starts with a ladle full of white wine for flavour. The wine is quickly absorbed and adds a lot

of flavour to the dish. The alcohol will not cook off, so take that into consideration. Flavoured vinegars are a good substitute for the wine.

Have fun making your own microwave risotto and experimenting with different ingredients and flavourings.

Ingredients

Serves 4

475 ml vegetable stock

350 ml water

550 ml salsa

2 teaspoons chilli powder

2 tablespoons olive oil

1 onion, chopped

4 cloves garlic, crushed

350 g Arborio rice

150 g canned black beans, drained

150 g frozen corn, thawed

40 g grated Parmesan cheese

1 avocado, peeled and chopped

Salt and pepper

Tex-Mex Risotto

- In 1.5-litre dish, combine stock, water, 120 ml of the salsa, chilli powder, salt and pepper. Microwave on high 3–4 minutes.

- Combine olive oil, onion, and garlic in 3-litre dish. Microwave on high for 2 minutes. Add rice; microwave for 1 minute.

- Add stock mixture. Cover and microwave on medium power for 10 minutes.

- Stir in remaining ingredients except cheese and avocado; cover and cook on medium power for 7–8 minutes. Stir in cheese and avocado. Cover and leave to stand for 4 minutes, stir and serve.

~ VARIATIONS ~

Classic Italian Risotto

Microwave 1 chopped onion and 3 cloves garlic in 2 tablespoons oil. Stir in 350 g Arborio rice; microwave 2 minutes longer. Add 120 ml white wine and 850 ml warmed vegetable stock; cover; microwave for 10 minutes until rice is tender. Stir in 25 g grated Parmesan cheese and 2 tablespoons cream. Cover and leave to stand for 5 minutes. Stir and serve.

French Risotto

Microwave 1 chopped onion and 4 cloves garlic in 2 tablespoons oil. Add 350 g Arborio rice; microwave for 2 minutes. Add 250 ml white wine, 1 teaspoon dried herbes de Provence, 750 ml vegetable stock. Microwave 10–12 minutes until tender. Stir in 40 g grated Parmesan cheese, 2 tablespoons fresh thyme, 3 tablespoons butter. Stir and serve.

Add Rice

- Microwave the rice for a bit before adding the stock so it absorbs some of the onion and garlic flavour.

- Because the spices and salsa are added with the stock, the rice will absorb their flavours and so will the sauce.

- Use the technique of adding spices to the liquid no matter what type or flavour of risotto you are making.

- Some spices, such as curry powder, benefit from this much cooking time because the flavours have time to develop.

Stir Risotto

- The key to risotto is tasting the rice. Take some out, blow on it because it's hot, and taste it.

- The rice should be tender, with a slight firmness in the centre. This is al dente, which literally means 'to the tooth'.

- The avocado is added at the very end, when cooking is done, because it turns bitter when heated.

- Form leftover chilled risotto into balls, roll in breadcrumbs, and deep-fry for a nice appetizer.

SLOW-COOKER VEGETARIAN SOUP

Textured vegetable protein looks and tastes like ground beef, but is much healthier

The slow cooker is a perfect vehicle for making soups, especially vegetarian ones. All you have to do is add the food, turn it on, and come back hours later to a perfectly cooked soup.

Root vegetables cook particularly well in the slow cooker. Because they are so dense, they are usually placed in the bottom of the appliance, where they are close to the heat and covered with liquid. In a soup, the root vegetables can be stirred together with all the other ingredients and they will become nice and tender.

Variations on slow cooker soups are very easy. Be sure to write down your wonderful changes to these basic recipes so you can make them again.

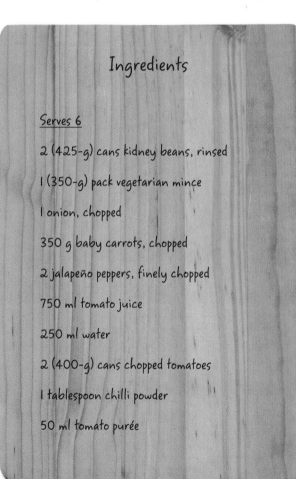

Ingredients

Serves 6

2 (425-g) cans kidney beans, rinsed

1 (350-g) pack vegetarian mince

1 onion, chopped

350 g baby carrots, chopped

2 jalapeño peppers, finely chopped

750 ml tomato juice

250 ml water

2 (400-g) cans chopped tomatoes

1 tablespoon chilli powder

50 ml tomato purée

Vegetarian Slow Cooker Chilli

- Ensure that the kidney beans are drained, rinsed, then drained again.

- Combine all ingredients in 4-litre slow cooker and stir well.

- Cover and cook on low for 7–8 hours, or on high for 3–4 hours, until chilli is blended and hot.

- You can thicken the chilli by mixing 2 tablespoons cornflour with 120 ml water. Add to the slow cooker and cook on high for 20 minutes until thick.

• • • • RECIPE VARIATION • • • •

Slow Cooker Lentil Soup: Combine 450 g lentils, 1.2 litres water, 1.4 litres vegetable stock, 250 ml salsa, 1 chopped onion, 4 cloves garlic, 3 chopped carrots, 3 peeled and diced potatoes, 1 teaspoon salt, 1 teaspoon dried basil, and 2 (400-g) cans chopped tomatoes in a 5-litre slow cooker. Cover and cook on low for 8–9 hours.

Layer Ingredients in Slow Cooker

- Soups cooked in the slow cooker are very flavourful because no evaporation takes place during the cooking process.

- Volatile flavour compounds are kept in the appliance with the food, so add spices and herbs judiciously.

- Also, since there is no evaporation, don't fill the slow cooker with liquid. The vegetables will give off liquid as they cook.

- Vary your chilli by using different types of beans, other salsas, and vegetables like peppers and mushrooms.

Add Cornflour to Chilli

- Cornflour is the best quick thickener for soups cooked in the slow cooker; flour takes longer to thicken.

- Be sure that the cornflour is thoroughly dissolved in a small amount of liquid before you add it to the soup.

- If the cornflour isn't dissolved, the soup will end up with lumps in it.

- Cook for 20–30 minutes on high to activate the cornflour. Add other tender ingredients, such as peas, at this time, too.

VEGETABLE STIR-FRY

Classic vegetable stir-fry is flavoured with ginger and hoisin sauce in this easy recipe

Vegetables stir-fry beautifully. The quick cooking method preserves their colour and texture, and all the vitamins and minerals they contain. And it's easy to add flavour to these simple stir-fry recipes. Fresh herbs and spices, and condiments such as soy sauce, mustard, hoisin sauce and teriyaki sauce can all be used in vegetarian dishes.

Vegetarian main dishes are healthy, colourful and delicious. Remember the complete proteins that your body needs? You don't need to eat them all at one sitting. Complete proteins can be spread over the day's meals. And that means you can eat a straight vegetable meal with no problem. Have fun inventing your own vegetable stir-fry recipes.

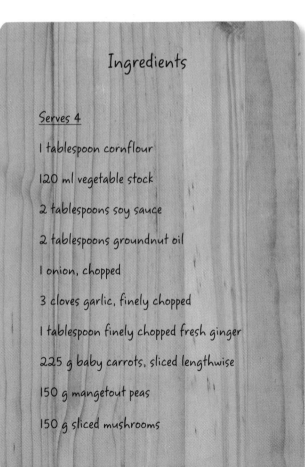

Ingredients

Serves 4

1 tablespoon cornflour

120 ml vegetable stock

2 tablespoons soy sauce

2 tablespoons groundnut oil

1 onion, chopped

3 cloves garlic, finely chopped

1 tablespoon finely chopped fresh ginger

225 g baby carrots, sliced lengthwise

150 g mangetout peas

150 g sliced mushrooms

Ginger Stir-Fried Vegetables

- In small bowl, combine cornflour, vegetable stock and soy sauce and set aside.

- In large frying pan or wok, heat groundnut oil over medium-high heat. Add onion, garlic, ginger and carrots. Stir-fry for 4–6 minutes until vegetables are crisp-tender.

- Add mangetout peas and mushrooms. Stir-fry for 2–4 minutes longer until all vegetables are crisp-tender.

- Stir soy sauce mixture and add to pan; stir-fry for 2–3 minutes until sauce bubbles.

Prepare Fresh Ginger

Stir-Fry Vegetables

- Fresh root ginger looks like a complicated creature from space, but it's quite easy to prepare.

- First cut off a piece about 2.5 cm long: this will provide you with about a tablespoon of grated or chopped ginger.

- Then use a swivel-bladed vegetable peeler or sharp paring knife to remove the rough skin and expose the juicy flesh.

- Then finely chop or grate the ginger. Add the ginger to the pan along with any juices produced.

- Vegetables like onion and garlic, which take time to mellow, and carrots and potatoes, which are hard, are added to the pan first.

- More tender vegetables, such as mushrooms, peppers and tomatoes, are added last.

- You'll know the vegetables are done when their colour is very bright and they are crisp-tender.

- That means that when you bite into one, it yields in your mouth but there's still a bit of crunch in the centre.

RICE AND TOFU STIR-FRY

Firm tofu is an excellent stir-fry ingredient; paired with rice and vegetables, it's delicious

Tofu in a stir-fry really does work as a meat substitute. Its slightly chewy texture, with crisp edges from the heat, is similar to that of meat, and the tofu can absorb any flavour you add to the dish.

When stir-frying cooked rice, the rice should always be cold. The starch in it has time to reform while it chills, making the

rice firm enough to stand up to the rigours of stir-frying. The grains will be separate and have a good texture.

Classic stir-fried rice is made with soy sauce, vegetables such as onions, garlic, grated carrots and peas, and an egg or two. You can add tofu to any stir-fried rice recipe to increase the protein content.

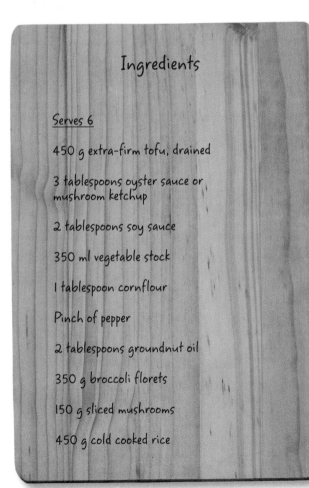

Ingredients

Serves 6

450 g extra-firm tofu, drained

3 tablespoons oyster sauce or mushroom ketchup

2 tablespoons soy sauce

350 ml vegetable stock

I tablespoon cornflour

Pinch of pepper

2 tablespoons groundnut oil

350 g broccoli florets

150 g sliced mushrooms

450 g cold cooked rice

Savoury Rice and Tofu Stir-Fry

- Drain and press tofu and cut into 2.5-cm cubes. In small bowl, combine mushroom ketchup, soy sauce, stock, cornflour and pepper; pour over tofu.

- In large frying pan or wok, heat oil over medium-high heat. Add broccoli; stir-fry for 4 minutes.

- Add mushrooms; stir-fry for 3–4 minutes longer until crisp-tender. Add rice; stir-fry for 2–3 minutes.

- Drain tofu; add to pan; stir-fry for 2–3 minutes. Stir sauce and add to pan; stir-fry for 2–3 minutes until bubbling.

190

Stir-Fried Rice with Tofu

Prepare 225 g firm tofu. Cut into 12-mm cubes; toss with 2 tablespoons soy sauce. Stir-fry 1 chopped onion and 2 crushed garlic cloves in 2 tablespoons oil. Add 150 g grated carrots and tofu; stir-fry for 3 minutes. Add 450 g cold cooked rice; stir-fry for 3 minutes. Beat 2 eggs with 1 tablespoon soy sauce and 1 teaspoon sesame oil; add to pan. Stir-fry; serve.

Peanut Rice with Tofu

Prepare 225 g firm tofu. Cut into 12-mm cubes; toss with 1 teaspoon ground ginger. Stir-fry 1 chopped onion in 2 tablespoons oil. Add 1 chopped green pepper and tofu; stir-fry 3 minutes. Add 450 g cold cooked brown rice; stir-fry 3 minutes. Add 120 ml peanut satay sauce and 115 g chopped peanuts; stir-fry and serve.

Prepare Sauce

- Oyster sauce really is made from oysters. It's a thick, highly concentrated sauce that has a rich, meaty, savoury flavour.

- For vegetarians, use mush-room ketchup, which has a similar savoury taste and texture.

- You could substitute hoisin sauce for the oyster sauce; the dish will be less savoury and sweeter.

- Don't marinate the tofu for longer than 10–15 minutes. Just leave it to marinate while you prepare the rest of the ingredients.

Stir-Fry

- Use only firm or extra-firm tofu in stir-fry recipes, and be sure to drain and press it before use.

- The rice needs to be very cold before you add it to the pan. Warm rice will just clump together and be sticky.

- Long-grain white or brown rice is a better choice for stir-frying than medium- or short-grain rice.

- The long-grain rice stays separate, while the shorter grain rice tends to clump together.

VEGETABLE AND BEAN PARCELS

Beans and vegetables are a hearty and filling combination for one-dish meal parcels

You don't need meat to make a hearty one-dish meal. A mixture of vegetables and beans is filling and delicious. These vegetable parcels are great for entertaining, too.

You can make them ahead of time and store them in the fridge, then bake them when you're ready to eat, and they can also be cooked on the barbecue. The smoky flavour added

by the barbecue enhances the vegetables and beans. If you poke some holes in the bottom of the foil parcel for recipes without sauce, that smoky flavour will permeate the food.

If you're entertaining a crowd, there's sure to be a vegetarian or two. If you're caught unawares, pull out this easy and delicious recipe.

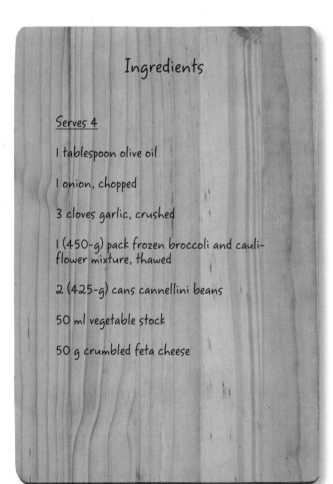

Ingredients

<u>Serves 4</u>

1 tablespoon olive oil

1 onion, chopped

3 cloves garlic, crushed

1 (450-g) pack frozen broccoli and cauliflower mixture, thawed

2 (425-g) cans cannellini beans

50 ml vegetable stock

50 g crumbled feta cheese

Feta, Bean and Vegetable Parcels

- Preheat oven to 220°C. Tear off 4 sheets of heavy-duty foil, or 4 sheets of baking parchment, 45 x 30 cm.

- Combine olive oil with onion and garlic in small bowl; toss to coat.

- Divide among foil pieces. Top with drained

vegetables and rinsed and drained cannellini beans.

- Drizzle with vegetable stock and top with feta cheese. Fold foil over or crimp baking parchment. Place on baking sheets; bake for 15–20 minutes until hot.

Potato Bean Parcels

On 4 sheets of foil, 45 x 30 cm, divide 6 small red potatoes, diced, 275 g grated carrots, 1 (425-g) can drained black beans, 1 chopped onion, 4 crushed garlic cloves and 200 g cut green beans. Combine 3 tablespoons mustard with 1 tablespoon olive oil and 1 teaspoon dried Italian seasoning; spoon over vegetables. Fold parcels and barbecue for 18–22 minutes.

Peas and Sweetcorn with Beans

On 4 sheets of foil, 45 x 30 cm, divide 225 g frozen petits pois, 400 g frozen sweetcorn kernels, 225 g frozen edamame beans, 1 chopped onion, 3 crushed garlic cloves and 1 (425-g can) drained kidney beans. Drizzle with 120 ml zesty Italian salad dressing. Fold up parcels and bake at 220°C for 20 minutes.

Layer Ingredients in Parcel

Add Cheese

- Always drain thawed vegetables; too much water from the vegetables will ruin the recipe.

- Thaw frozen vegetables by leaving them in the refrigerator overnight. Or you can thaw them under cool running water.

- Make sure you always drain canned beans, rinse the beans thoroughly, and drain again before using in recipes.

- You can drizzle a little bit of flavoured vinegar or oil on the vegetables before you close the parcels.

- If you're serving strict vegetarians or vegans, just don't add the cheese. Top the vegetables with salsa or chilli powder.

- If you cook the parcels on the barbecue, move them around several times on the rack, using a large spatula.

- Be careful when you unwrap the parcels, because a lot of steam will billow out, and steam can burn.

- The foil itself will quickly lose heat, but the food inside the parcels will be very hot.

MICROWAVE JACKET POTATOES

Stuffed potatoes are an excellent choice for a vegetarian dinner; they can be flavoured in many ways

The microwave is an excellent appliance for cooking potatoes. They don't need much preparation, and the end result is a steamed potato with fluffy flesh.

In the microwave, timing depends on how much food you put in, especially when cooking dense foods like potatoes and other root vegetables. Add 2–3 minutes for each extra potato you are cooking. Standing time after cooking is particularly important with potatoes. Because they are so dense, it takes time for the heat to travel through the potato and cook it evenly.

Stuffing ingredients are easily cooked in the microwave, and the finished potato heats in minutes.

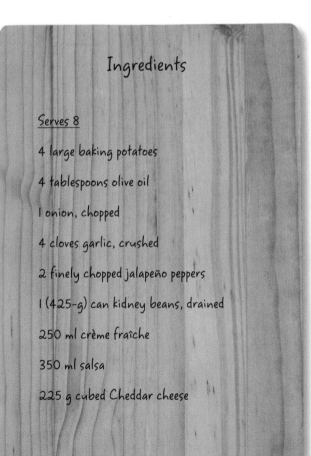

Ingredients

Serves 8

4 large baking potatoes

4 tablespoons olive oil

1 onion, chopped

4 cloves garlic, crushed

2 finely chopped jalapeño peppers

1 (425-g) can kidney beans, drained

250 ml crème fraîche

350 ml salsa

225 g cubed Cheddar cheese

Tex-Mex Stuffed Potatoes

- Scrub potatoes; prick with fork. Rub with 1 tablespoon olive oil. Microwave on high for 10–14 minutes, turning over once, until tender.

- Remove potatoes; leave to stand for 10 minutes. Cut in half and scoop out flesh; place in bowl. Beat in 2 tablespoons olive oil.

- Combine 1 tablespoon olive oil, onion, garlic and jalapeño peppers in microwave-safe dish. Microwave on high for 3–4 minutes.

- Add beans, crème fraîche, salsa and cheese, then beat into potato flesh. Stuff skins. Microwave on high for 6–8 minutes until hot.

~ VARIATIONS ~

Blue Cheese Stuffed Potatoes

Scrub 4 large potatoes and rub with olive oil. Microwave on high for 10–14 minutes; leave to stand for 10 minutes. Cut potatoes in half; scoop flesh into bowl. Beat in 50 g butter, 250 ml crème fraîche, 75 ml Louisiana-style hot sauce, 1 teaspoon Tabasco sauce, and 115 g crumbled blue cheese. Stuff skins; microwave as directed until hot.

Cheddar Stuffed Potatoes

Scrub 4 large potatoes and rub with olive oil. Microwave on high for 10–14 minutes; leave to stand for 10 minutes. Cut potatoes in half; scoop flesh into bowl. Beat in 50 g butter, 250 ml prepared onion dip, 225 g grated Cheddar cheese, and 4 spring onions, chopped. Stuff skins and microwave as directed until hot.

Prepare Filling

Hollow Out Potatoes, Mix Filling

- The microwave is a good choice for cooking foods like onions, garlic and jalapeño peppers.

- The heat will break down some of the strongest compounds in those foods and bring out the sweetness.

- Be sure to add the kidney beans, crème fraîche, and salsa to the hot onion mixture first, then add the cheese so it doesn't melt.

- You can make the filling mixture while the potatoes are cooking the first time in the microwave oven.

- The potatoes have to stand on a solid surface for 10 minutes after they finish cooking, so the heat is distributed and the flesh is evenly cooked.

- When you scoop the flesh from the skins, be sure to leave about 6 mm of flesh to make a sturdy container.

- The potato filling will have a better texture if you first add fat to the hot potato, then everything else.

- The fat coats the potato starch, separating it and preventing it from becoming gluey.

STEAMED VEGETABLES WITH RICE

Bamboo steaming baskets make a beautiful main-course dish

Steaming is one of the healthiest and easiest ways to cook vegetables, especially a large quantity. You can use one large steamer basket, or, for a prettier presentation, fill several bamboo baskets and layer them over simmering water.

The rice should be cooked before you steam the vegetables, so it's ready and waiting for them. A rice cooker is a great way to cook the grains to perfection, and takes some pressure off you as it allows you to get on with the rest of the meal.

Vegetables that steam well include mushrooms, onions, garlic, asparagus, green beans, peppers, broccoli and cauliflower, mangetout peas, sugar snap peas, thinly sliced carrots, peas and courgettes.

Steam a combination of your favourite vegetables for an easy and fresh-tasting dinner.

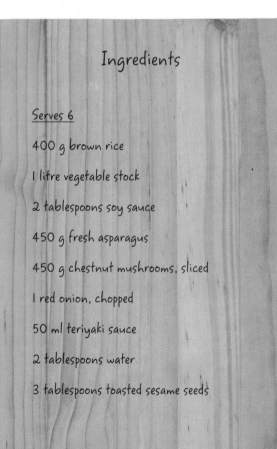

Ingredients

Serves 6

400 g brown rice

1 litre vegetable stock

2 tablespoons soy sauce

450 g fresh asparagus

450 g chestnut mushrooms, sliced

1 red onion, chopped

50 ml teriyaki sauce

2 tablespoons water

3 tablespoons toasted sesame seeds

Steamed Asparagus with Brown Rice

- In large saucepan, combine rice, stock and soy sauce. Bring to simmering point, then cover, reduce heat, and simmer for 35–40 minutes until rice is cooked.

- When rice is half cooked, prepare asparagus by snapping off tough ends. Cut into 5-cm lengths.

- Combine with mushrooms and onion in steamer basket. Set over simmering water; steam for 6–10 minutes until tender.

- When rice is done, fluff with fork and stir in steamed vegetables along with teriyaki sauce, water and sesame seeds.

Asian Steamed Broccoli with Rice

Cook 250 g brown rice in 750 ml vegetable stock. Cut 675 g fresh broccoli into florets and chop 1 onion. Place in steamer baskets along with 225 g chopped cime di rapa. Combine 2 tablespoons each olive oil and soy sauce, 2 crushed garlic cloves and a pinch of cayenne pepper; drizzle over broccoli. Steam for 10–14 minutes and serve with rice.

Steamed Cougettes with Rice

Cook 250 g brown rice in 750 ml vegetable stock. Cut 3 green and 3 yellow courgettes into 8-mm slices and place in steamer. Add 1 chopped red onion, 2 crushed garlic cloves and 2 red peppers, julienned. Drizzle with 2 tablespoons olive oil, salt and pepper. Steam for 7–10 minutes; serve with rice.

Prepare Vegetables

- If you bend asparagus toward the end of the stalk, it will naturally break where the stalk becomes tough.

- Discard the tough ends or freeze them to use when making vegetable stock.

- Always choose vegetables that have approximately the same cooking time when steaming. Or remove vegetables from the basket as they're done.

- Since vegetables cook at different rates, cook the harder vegetables before adding the tender ones, so they are all crisp-tender.

Finish Dish

- If you're steaming a large amount of vegetables, place them in separate bundles in the steamer so you can remove as they are cooked.

- For a beautiful presentation, you can mix the rice with the steamed vegetables.

- Then place in individual bamboo steamer baskets and stack over hot water until it's time to serve.

- If you have leftover rice, you have another meal! Stir-fry the rice with some garlic and add frozen peas and a beaten egg or two.

PASTA WITH VEGETABLES
A classic meatless pasta sauce is hearty and delicious

Vegetables add great colour, texture and flavour to pasta. You don't even need to add cheese! You can toss plain sautéed or steamed vegetables with pasta, or simply add more vegetables to a traditional pasta sauce.

You can use traditional pasta sauce vegetables, which include tomatoes, mushrooms, onions and garlic, or add unusual vegetables to shake up the meal. Novel spaghetti sauce add-ins include green beans, asparagus, soya beans,

kidney and black beans, courgettes and carrots. All of these foods will really increase the fibre and boost the nutritional content of the meal.

If you don't want to add cheese to top these mixtures, sauté some whole-wheat breadcrumbs in olive oil until crisp, then scatter them over the pasta. Yum.

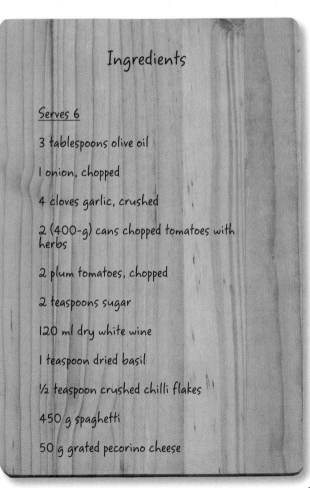

Ingredients

<u>Serves 6</u>

3 tablespoons olive oil

1 onion, chopped

4 cloves garlic, crushed

2 (400-g) cans chopped tomatoes with herbs

2 plum tomatoes, chopped

2 teaspoons sugar

120 ml dry white wine

1 teaspoon dried basil

½ teaspoon crushed chilli flakes

450 g spaghetti

50 g grated pecorino cheese

Pasta Pomodoro

- Bring a large saucepan of salted water to the boil. Meanwhile, in large pan, heat olive oil over medium heat.

- Add onion and garlic; cook and stir until tender, about 5–6 minutes. Remove pan from heat and add canned tomatoes.

- Return pan to heat and add fresh tomatoes, sugar, wine, basil and chilli flakes. Simmer for 8–10 minutes.

- Cook pasta according to package directions until al dente. Drain and add to sauce; simmer for 1–2 minutes, sprinkle with cheese.

Heavy-on-the-Veggies Pasta

Boil a saucepan of water. Sauté 1 chopped onion, 2 crushed garlic cloves, 150 g grated carrots, and 450 g asparagus pieces in 2 tablespoons olive oil. Sprinkle with salt, pepper and thyme. Cook 350 g pasta; drain, reserving 120 ml cooking water. Add pasta, water, and 2 chopped tomatoes to vegetables; cook and stir. Sprinkle with cheese; serve.

Chickpea and Vegetable Pasta

Boil a pan of water. Sauté 1 chopped onion, 4 cloves garlic, and 150 g grated carrots in 2 tablespoons olive oil. Add 1 (450-ml) jar tomato sauce, 1 chopped yellow courgette, 150 g sliced mushrooms, 1 (425-g) can drained chickpeas, 1 teaspoon Italian seasoning; simmer. Cook 350 g pasta, drain, add to sauce and season with salt and pepper.

Chop Vegetables

- Fresh chopped tomatoes in a sauce, even when you're using canned tomatoes as well, add great flavour.

- The sugar helps to counter the acidity of the tomatoes. Only add a teaspoon or two. You won't taste the sugar in the finished sauce.

- Any finely chopped vegetables, even carrots or other root vegetables, are delicious in this sauce.

- Add a few tablespoons of salt to the water you use to cook the pasta so it's well flavoured.

Top Spaghetti with Sauce

- Pomodoro sauce is usually served with angel hair pasta. That pasta can be difficult to cook correctly because it cooks so fast.

- Spaghetti or linguine are both perfectly acceptable alternatives to go with this flavourful sauce. Or use shorter pastas like penne.

- You can substitute fresh basil leaves for the dried if you have them. Use 1–2 tablespoons chopped fresh basil.

- And experiment with different cheeses to top the recipe. Try grated Havarti, Gouda or Emmental.

STORE-CUPBOARD PIZZAS
Refried beans are the secret ingredient for these rich pizzas

Pizzas are one of the best and simplest quick and easy recipes. Once you have the base – which you can buy ready-made if you like – you can top it with anything you and your family enjoy, from sautéed vegetables to grilled meats to black beans and cheese.

With your well-stocked store cupboard, you will be able to make pizzas at a moment's notice using a few simple ingredients. Some of the best store-cupboard pizza toppings include refried beans, tomato sauce, mustard and pulses such as black or pinto beans. So look through your stores, use your imagination, and have fun creating pizzas practically out of thin air!

Ingredients

Serves 6

2 tablespoons olive oil

1 onion, chopped

1 (175-g) can tomato purée

120 ml water

250 ml salsa

1 (415-g) can refried beans

1 (425-g) can pinto beans

2 large ready-made pizza bases

250 g grated Cheddar cheese

Refried Bean Pizza

- Preheat oven to 200°C. In a large pan, heat olive oil over medium heat. Add onion; cook and stir for 5 minutes, until softened.

- Add tomato purée; let it brown in spots without burning. Add water; scrape pan to deglaze.

- Add salsa, refried beans, and drained pinto beans to pan; heat through.

- Place pizza bases on baking sheets. Spread with bean mixture, and sprinkle with cheese. Bake for 25–30 minutes until cheese is melted and brown.

Bean and Vegetable Pizza

Preheat oven to 200°C. In bowl, combine 1 (425-g) can drained black beans, 1 (425-g) can drained sweetcorn, 250 ml tomato sauce, 1 (115-g) jar drained mushrooms, 1 chopped red onion, 1 teaspoon dried oregano, 2 tablespoons mustard, 40 g Parmesan cheese. Spread on one large prebaked focaccia. Bake for 20–25 minutes until pizza is hot.

Italian Flag Pizza

Preheat oven to 200°C. Drain 400-g can chopped tomatoes. Combine with 250 ml taco sauce, 50 ml tomato purée, 1 tablespoon bottled garlic, 1 teaspoon dried basil, salt and pepper. Spread on prebaked pizza base. Drain 250 g thawed frozen spinach very thoroughly; drop over sauce. Top with 75 g grated Parmesan. Bake for 20–25 minutes until hot.

Mix Sauce

Finish Dish

- You can find refried beans in cans in the supermarket.

- The beans are very thick, so they should be mixed with some kind of sauce before spreading on the crust.

- Some canned vegetables that would be good in this pizza sauce include canned corn, green beans and mushrooms.

- Don't make the sauce too wet; it should be thicker than pancake batter. If it's too wet, go on cooking it until it thickens.

- To bake the pizza base, put it on a greased baking sheet sprinkled with cornmeal, or use a pizza stone if you have one.

- The base should be about 6 mm thick. Prebake at 200°C for 10 minutes before adding the topping.

- Cheese is really the finishing touch on most pizzas.

- Cheese is a good indicator that a pizza is done. When the cheese is melted and browning in spots, the pizza is ready.

REFRIGERATOR PIZZAS

As long as you have a base, you can make pizza using items in your refrigerator

Your refrigerator is a rich source of pizza toppings. A pizza is a great way to use up leftovers, whether those leftovers are sliced hard-boiled eggs, grilled steak, cooked beans or chopped tomatoes.

If you top a pizza with foods that are already cooked, it shouldn't bake or grill very long, because you're only reheating the food. In that case, the pizza crust should be prebaked so it will become crisp in the same time.

If you top a pizza with uncooked foods, like chopped peppers or mushrooms, it should be baked or barbecued for a longer time so you can start with an unbaked crust. Enjoy making pizzas seasoned with imagination.

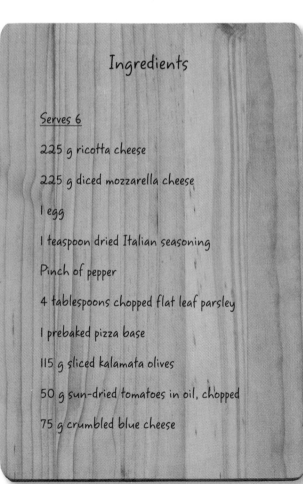

Ingredients

<u>Serves 6</u>

225 g ricotta cheese

225 g diced mozzarella cheese

1 egg

1 teaspoon dried Italian seasoning

Pinch of pepper

4 tablespoons chopped flat leaf parsley

1 prebaked pizza base

115 g sliced kalamata olives

50 g sun-dried tomatoes in oil, chopped

75 g crumbled blue cheese

Blue Cheese Olive Pizzas

- Preheat oven to 200°C. In bowl, combine ricotta, mozzarella, egg, Italian seasoning, pepper and parsley.

- Spread on to a prebaked pizza base. Top with olives, drained tomatoes, and blue cheese.

- Bake for 20–30 minutes until cheese melts and browns. Allow to cool for 5 minutes, then cut into wedges to serve.

- You can top the pizza with fresh tomatoes or salsa at this point for a contrast.

Pizza Base

Mix 225 g flour, 50 g whole-wheat flour, and 50 g corn-meal. Dissolve 2 packages yeast in 300 ml warm water; add to flour with 2 tablespoons olive oil and 1 teaspoon salt. Mix, then knead. Leave to rise for 45 minutes; shape into 2 bases. Bake at 200°C for 10 minutes, then top and bake. Freeze before topping to store.

Scrambled Egg Pizza

Roll out thawed puff pastry square to 30 x 30 cm. Place on baking sheet; bake at 200°C for 15 minutes. Beat 6 eggs with 75 ml milk, salt and pepper, and scramble in 2 tablespoons butter. Spread on pastry. Top with 115-g can drained mushrooms and 115 g each grated Havarti and Cheddar cheeses. Bake for 15–18 minutes.

Prebake the Base

Mix Filling, Top Pizza

- Prebaked pizza bases stay crisper and hold up better under heavy toppings. You can prebake bases in advance.

- If you're using focaccia bread for the base, it doesn't have to be prebaked.

- Bases should be prebaked until they are firm to the touch. Don't bake them until they are brown.

- Freeze prebaked bases by wrapping in freezer wrap after they cool. Label and freeze up to 3 months. To use, just top and bake.

- The topping on a pizza can be anything from a basic tomato sauce to a blend of cheeses to scrambled eggs and bacon.

- There should be some cheese on a pizza, simply because it helps hold everything together.

- Other choices for the bases include flour or corn tortillas, pitta breads, French bread (either sliced or halved) and refrigerated dough.

- Don't top pizzas ahead of time. The topping will soak into the crust and it will all fall apart.

BARBECUED PIZZA

Pizza cooked on the barbecue has a special smoky flavour you just can't get in the oven

Barbecued pizza is a relatively new phenomenon. Restaurants discovered it in the 1990s, and it didn't take home cooks long to catch on.

Pizza cooked on the barbecue has a fabulous smoky flavour. The crust is super-crisp and chewy, and the cheese melts to creamy, bubbly perfection. What's not to like?

When you grill dough, there are a few rules to follow. First, you need to make sure that the grill is preheated and that the rack is clean. Oil the rack and oil the pizza base.

Flip the pizza on to the rack from a baking sheet. As it cooks, move it around as soon as it's firm, so it cooks evenly. Have fun creating gourmet pizzas at home.

Barbecued Sausage Pizza

Ingredients

Serves 6

225 g Italian sausages

1 red pepper, sliced

1 green pepper, sliced

1 onion, sliced

250 ml tomato sauce

2 tablespoons Dijon mustard

1 prebaked pizza base

175 g grated mozzarella cheese

- Preheat barbecue. Scrape rack and rub with oil. Brush sausages, peppers and onions with oil.

- Cook sausages directly on barbecue rack. Cook peppers and onions in grill basket. When sausages are done and vegetables are crisp-tender, remove.

- Cut sausages into 12-mm slices; chop peppers and onion. Combine pizza sauce and mustard.

- Spread sauce mixture on base. Top with sausages, peppers, onion and cheese. Return to barbecue. Grill pizza, covered, rotating occasionally, 6–9 minutes.

If you are going to barbecue pizzas a lot, you should consider purchasing special equipment. You may want a pizza stone, which is a stoneware round that heats up on the barbecue. You just add the pizza and it cooks to perfection. You'll definitely need a pizza peel or large spatula to manipulate the pizza on the barbecue.

Red Pepper Mozzarella Pizza: Roll dough to 30-cm circle; brush with olive oil. Cook 1 chopped onion and 3 cloves garlic in 2 tablespoons olive oil. Add 1 chopped red pepper, 1 cup chopped tomatoes, 2 tablespoons chopped basil, salt and pepper. Barbecue dough; flip. Spread with onion mixture and top with 225 g grated mozzarella cheese. Grill for 8–10 minutes.

Barbecue Pizza Dough

- Focaccia doesn't have to be barbecued before it's topped.

- Start with that type of base for your first attempt so you don't have to flip it.

- When using dough, it may take a bit of practice to flip the base evenly on the rack. Even if it isn't perfect, it will still taste good.

- When the crust is brown and crisp underneath, it's time to flip. Use a pizza peel or large spatulas to flip it on to a baking sheet.

Finish Pizza

- If you work fast, you can flip the base directly back on to the barbecue rack and top it. But that's hot work!

- Once the pizza has been flipped, quickly top it with your chosen ingredients.

- Then slide it back onto the rack using the baking sheet, or grab your pizza peel or large spatulas.

- At this point, cover the barbecue and cook the pizza until the cheese is melted and browned. Then slide it on to the baking sheet, slice and serve.

GRILLED SANDWICHES

Everything is grilled in this sandwich: the vegetables, the spread and the bread

Grilled sandwiches can go beyond grilled cheese or a tuna melt, although those can be delicious if done well. Think about a grilled vegetable sandwich, or a Cobb salad in a sandwich, or luscious sliced steak grilled with melted Havarti cheese.

You can grill sandwiches in a plain old grill pan, or you can use a fancy sandwich press. In between, there's a griddle on the hob and the dual-contact grill. All you really need is a pan and a spatula.

The fillings for grilled sandwiches always have to be cooked before they go in, or be ready to eat as they are. Grill the meat, vegetables or fruits before you assemble the sandwich, finish on the grill, and enjoy.

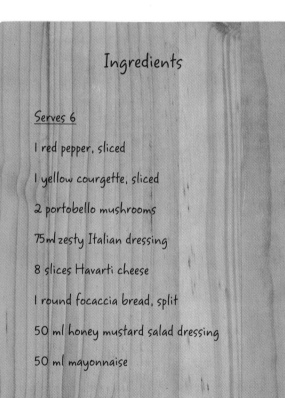

Ingredients

Serves 6

1 red pepper, sliced

1 yellow courgette, sliced

2 portobello mushrooms

75 ml zesty Italian dressing

8 slices Havarti cheese

1 round focaccia bread, split

50 ml honey mustard salad dressing

50 ml mayonnaise

Grilled Vegetable Sandwich

- Combine sliced peppers and sliced courgette with whole mushrooms and Italian dressing.

- Heat dual-contact grill. Grill vegetables in batches until crisp-tender. Let the portobello mushrooms cool for 5 minutes, then slice.

- Spread bottom of focaccia bread with mustard and top with mayonnaise. Place half of cheese, then vegetables, on bottom.

- Top vegetables with more cheese and top of focaccia. Cut into 4 wedges. Grill the sandwiches on the dual contact grill until bread is crisp.

~ VARIATIONS ~

Updated Grilled Cheese Sandwich
Spread 1 side of 8 slices whole-wheat bread with 3 table-spoons softened butter. Place bread, buttered side down, on work surface. Divide 4 slices Cheddar cheese, 4 large slices tomato, 12 fresh basil leaves, and 4 slices Emmental cheese among half the slices. Combine into sandwiches. Grill, turning once, for 5–7 minutes until cheese melts.

Grilled Brie and Cranberry Sandwich
Combine 120 ml cranberry sauce with 25 g dried cran-berries. Slice 225 g of Brie cheese into thin slices. Make sandwiches with 10 French bread slices, the cranberry mixture, cheese, and fresh basil leaves. Spread softened butter on outside of sandwiches; grill for 5–7 minutes.

Grill Vegetables

- Vegetables grill beautifully on a dual-contact grill, a panini maker, an electric griddle or a ridged griddle on the hob.

- Cut peppers and mush-rooms into strips, and onions and courgettes into circular slices, so they fit on the grill.

- The vegetables will take about 2–4 minutes on a double-sided grill; double that time on a plain grill where they need to be turned.

- Brush the vegetables with olive oil, salad dressing or a combination of herbs, oil and seasonings.

Grill Sandwiches

- When you're grilling most foods, you don't want to press down or the juices will be pressed out.

- Grilled sandwiches are different. Press down with the spatula or the top of the panini grill to melt the cheese and crisp the bread.

- For a makeshift panini grill, cover a clean brick com-pletely with several layers of foil; use that to weight the sandwiches as they cook on a griddle.

- The sandwiches are done when the bread is crisp and brown, and the cheese is completely melted.

DELUXE WRAPS

These healthy and low-fat wraps taste super-rich, and they're quick to make

Wrap sandwiches are made by literally wrapping food in a thin bread. Tortillas, whether corn or flour, are generally used, but you can also use pitta breads.

Wraps are served cold or at room temperature. They're not typically cooked before serving, although you can heat them in the microwave oven if you like.

These wraps are a great way to use up leftovers. In fact, make them with 'planovers'. When you're grilling pieces of steak, chicken or salmon, cook one extra and refrigerate it. When it's sliced, it's the perfect filling for a deluxe wrap sandwich with a spread and some vegetables. Invent your own deluxe wrap sandwich using your favourite ingredients.

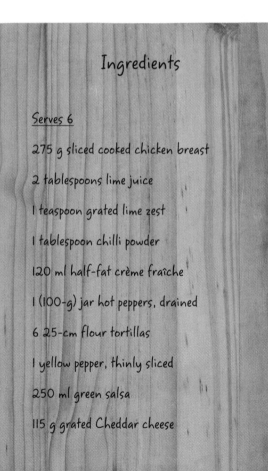

Ingredients

Serves 6

275 g sliced cooked chicken breast

2 tablespoons lime juice

I teaspoon grated lime zest

I tablespoon chilli powder

120 ml half-fat crème fraîche

I (100-g) jar hot peppers, drained

6 25-cm flour tortillas

I yellow pepper, thinly sliced

250 ml green salsa

115 g grated Cheddar cheese

Chicken Enchilada Wraps

- In medium bowl, combine chicken strips with lime juice and lime zest; toss and leave for 5 minutes.

- In small bowl, mix chilli powder, crème fraîche, and chillis. Soften tortillas by wrapping in paper towel; microwave on medium for 1–2 minutes.

- Place tortillas on work surface. Spread with the crème fraîche mixture and top with sliced chicken mixture and sliced peppers.

- Top evenly with salsa and grated cheese. Fold up bottom of tortilla one turn, fold in sides and serve.

Chutney Ham Wrap
Soften 4 (25-cm) flour tortillas in the microwave oven. Spread each with 1 tablespoon of softened cream cheese, then top each with 2 tablespoons mango chutney. Add 1 thin slice cooked ham to each tortilla, then 2 slices Havarti cheese. Roll up, folding in sides. Serve immediately.

Cobb Salad Wraps
Soften 4 (25-cm) flour tortillas in the microwave oven. Spread each with 2 tablespoons crème fraîche. Top with 2 tablespoons French salad dressing, chopped red onion, crisply cooked bacon, sliced cooked chicken breast, chopped tomatoes, chopped avocado and crumbled blue cheese. Wrap up, then wrap in microwave-safe paper towel. Microwave on medium power for 3–5 minutes until cheese melts and sandwiches are hot.

Prepare Chicken and Vegetables

Soften Tortillas

- For wrap sandwiches, slice meats and vegetables fairly thinly so they are easy to bite into. You can also chop or dice filling ingredients.

- All wrap sandwiches should have some creamy or cheesy mixture to add moisture to the meats and vegetables.

- Good creamy mixtures include flavoured crème fraîche, softened cream cheese and creamy salad dressings.

- Tender vegetables can be used as they are, but others, such as asparagus, carrots and broccoli, should be cooked first.

- Make sure that you use microwave-safe paper towels for wrapping the tortillas for warming.

- If the tortillas are very dry, sprinkle them with a little water before microwaving.

- Not all tortillas will have to be softened. Roll one up; if it rolls without cracking, it's soft enough. Add the filling and wrap it up.

- As soon as the tortillas are softened, use them. They will become hard fairly quickly since the microwave dries them out.

PIZZA & SANDWICHES

NO-BAKE COOKIES

Caramel and chocolate are perfect partners in these quick and chewy bar cookies

No-bake cookies are so easy to make and delicious. They're the perfect treat to turn to when your kitchen is being remodelled, and they're the right choice for a hot summer day.

Most of these cookie recipes do use the microwave or stovetop. They just aren't baked in the oven. There are some tricks to making the best no-bake cookies. The most important? Be sure that the sugar is completely dissolved. If it isn't, the finished cookies will be grainy instead of smooth and creamy.

Once you've mastered a no-bake cookie recipe, it's time to experiment. Add your favourite sweet ingredients – everything from white chocolate chips to dried fruit.

Ingredients

Makes 36

350 g brown sugar

250 ml golden syrup

120 ml honey

350 g peanut butter

175 g digestive biscuit crumbs

225 g chopped walnuts

175 g chopped dried cherries

175 g plain chocolate chips

175 g milk chocolate chips

Chocolate Caramel Bars

- In large saucepan, combine brown sugar, syrup and honey. Bring to the boil; cover pan and boil for 1 minute.

- Uncover pan and boil, stirring frequently, for 3 minutes. Remove from heat and stir in 300 g of the peanut butter.

- Stir in biscuit crumbs, walnuts and dried cherries. Press into a greased 33 x 22-cm shallow tin.

- In a small pan, combine chocolate chips with remaining 50 g peanut butter. Melt gently, stirring, until smooth. Pour over mixture. Leave until firm; cut into squares.

Slice and Serve No-Bake Cookies

Cut 20 large marshmallows into quarters; add 20 crushed digestive biscuits, and 60 g dried sweetened cranberries. Stir in 250 ml sweetened condensed milk until a dough forms. Spread 115 g finely chopped nuts on work surface; form dough into a log on the nuts and roll to coat. Wrap in greaseproof paper; chill for 3–4 hours. Slice to serve.

Marshmallow Peanut Butter Bars

In large bowl, combine 400 g miniature marshmallows, 115 g peanut butter, and 50 g butter. Microwave on high for 2 minutes; stir. Microwave until smooth. Stir in 115 g rice cereal flakes, 75 g chopped dried cherries, 115 g chopped pecans, 175 g miniature chocolate chips. Press into 33 x 22-cm pan; cool and cut into bars.

Cook Caramel Sauce

- Don't substitute honey for all of the golden syrup in the caramel sauce or the bars will be too hard.

- Cover the pan for a minute when the mixture starts to boil so steam can wash sugar crystals from the sides of the pan.

- Any sugar crystals remaining after the mixture boils will 'seed' new crystals and the cookies will be grainy.

- You can use crunchy or smooth peanut butter; the choice is yours. The peanut butter makes the cookies chewy and soft.

Add Nuts and Fruits

- Have all of the ingredients prepared and waiting for you before you start to cook the caramel sauce.

- If you have to stop and prepare foods, the sauce will start to set and it will be hard to mix in the other ingredients.

- Other ingredients that would be good in these cookies include flaked coconut, dried cranberries and dried currants.

- Adding peanut butter to the chocolate for the topping makes the frosting stay creamy and smooth.

DESSERTS

FRUIT SALAD

Dress up fruit salad with a white chocolate cream for an elegant last-minute dessert

Fruit salad is a refreshing and healthy choice for a quick and easy dessert. You can top it with a sweet sauce if you wish, or just drizzle with honey and add fresh herbs for an exotic taste.

And yes, herbs do combine well with fruit salads. Mint is the obvious choice, but thyme and basil bring out the sweetness of the fruits. For dessert, you want the most luscious fruits you can find. Peaches, nectarines, strawberries, blueberries and raspberries are the obvious choices. During the winter months, make a delicious dessert salad from apples, pears and exotic fruits like mangoes or kumquats.

For a finishing touch, use ice cream toppings or a dollop of whipped cream.

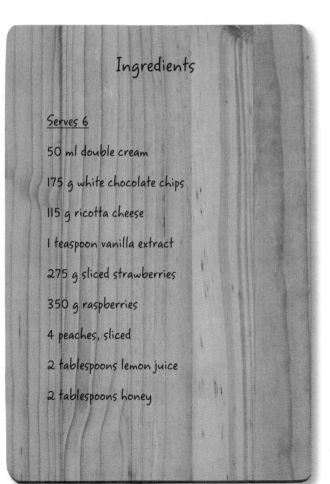

Ingredients

Serves 6

50 ml double cream

175 g white chocolate chips

115 g ricotta cheese

1 teaspoon vanilla extract

275 g sliced strawberries

350 g raspberries

4 peaches, sliced

2 tablespoons lemon juice

2 tablespoons honey

White Chocolate Fruit Salad

- In small microwave-safe dish, combine cream and chocolate. Microwave on medium power for 1–2 minutes until chocolate melts, stirring at halfway point.

- Stir mixture until smooth with wire whisk. Beat in ricotta cheese and vanilla; place in freezer 15 minutes.

- Meanwhile, prepare and combine fruits in serving bowl. In small bowl, mix lemon juice and honey until combined; drizzle over fruits.

- Remove chocolate from freezer. Beat until fluffy. Serve as a topping.

Strawberry Chocolate Salad

In serving bowl, combine 500 g sliced strawberries, 175 g miniature chocolate chips, and 350 g raspberries. Drizzle with 2 tablespoons best-quality balsamic vinegar and top with 3 tablespoons chopped fresh mint. Serve immediately or cover and chill for up to 3 hours.

Lemon Basil Fruit Salad

In serving bowl, combine 120 ml plain yogurt, 50 ml crème fraîche, 2 tablespoons lemon juice, 1 tablespoon orange juice, 2 tablespoons honey, 2 tablespoons chopped fresh basil and 1 teaspoon lemon zest. Add 300 g sliced strawberries, 300 g blueberries, 300 g blackberries, and 1 (425-g) can mandarin oranges, drained; toss. Chill or serve immediately.

Prepare Fruits

- Preparing fruits is easy; it just takes some practice. Never wash delicate fruits until just before you prepare them.

- Gently rinse the fruits under cold running water, then place on paper towels to dry.

- Hull strawberries by pulling off the leaves, stem and woody centre.

- Dip peaches in boiling water for 15 seconds. The skins will slip off easily. Remove the stone and slice.

Beat White Chocolate Cream

- Ricotta cheese cuts the sweetness of white chocolate in the dessert topping while adding a creamy texture.

- In place of the ricotta, you could use mascarpone or crème fraîche for a smoother texture.

- You can make the white chocolate topping ahead of time and keep it in the refrigerator.

- Don't beat the white chocolate topping until you're ready to eat. You can use a wire whisk, but a hand mixer is easier and faster.

DESSERTS

LAST-MINUTE CHEESECAKE

Just six ingredients make a cheesecake filling dolloped into tiny tartlet cases

Cheesecake is usually quite complicated to make, involving lots of measuring, beating and a long, delicate baking time. But there are faster ways to make a delicious, creamy cheesecake.

To make a cheesecake that doesn't require oven baking, you must use unflavoured gelatine or a combination of cream cheese, sweetened condensed milk and citrus juices.

The gelatine will firm up the sweetened cream cheese mixture in a short time, especially if you're making small cheesecakes. A few minutes in the freezer will make a soft-set cheesecake filling.

Top these cheesecakes with anything from chocolate sauce to fresh fruit to a crumbly, buttery streusel.

Berry Swirl Cheesecake

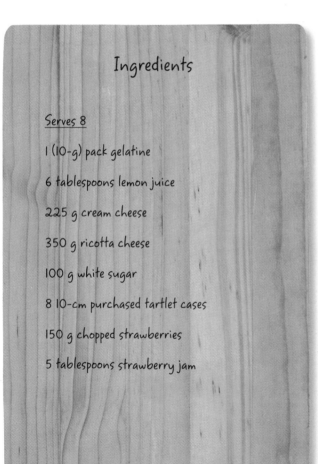

Ingredients

Serves 8

1 (10-g) pack gelatine

6 tablespoons lemon juice

225 g cream cheese

350 g ricotta cheese

100 g white sugar

8 10-cm purchased tartlet cases

150 g chopped strawberries

5 tablespoons strawberry jam

- In small microwave-safe bowl, mix gelatine with 4 tablespoons of the lemon juice; mix well and set aside.

- In food processor, mix cream cheese, ricotta and sugar; process until smooth.

- Microwave gelatine mixture on high for 30 seconds;

repeat until mixture is clear. Add to food processor; process until smooth. Dollop mixture into tartlet cases.

- In small bowl, combine strawberries, jam and remaining lemon juice; mash with fork. Drop on to cheesecakes and swirl. Cover and freeze for 20–30 minutes.

Classic Lemon Cheesecake

In bowl, beat together 225 g softened cream cheese with 2 tablespoons lemon juice, 1 tablespoon orange juice, and 50 g icing sugar until smooth. In small bowl, beat 120 ml double cream with 1 tablespoon icing sugar until stiff; fold into cream cheese mixture. Divide among 4 (10-cm) purchased tartlet cases; freeze for 20 minutes.

Quick Orange Cheesecake

In bowl, combine 300 g softened cream cheese, 1 (400-g) can sweetened condensed milk, 1 tablespoon lemon juice, and 50 ml orange juice; beat well. Pour into a purchased 22-cm pastry case and chill for 2 hours; or into 8 (10-cm) tartlet cases and chill for 30 minutes. Top with drained canned mandarin oranges and chopped mint.

Process Cheeses

Finish Cheesecake

- The food processor is the quickest way to blend the creamy cheesecake filling.

- You can also beat the mixture using a hand mixer. A wire whisk just isn't strong enough to make the mixture smooth.

- If you soften the gelatine in water instead of lemon juice, add 250 ml melted and cooled plain chocolate chips to the cheesecake.

- The cheesecake can be topped with raspberries, chocolate ice cream topping, or granola for crunch.

- To make your own biscuit crumb crusts, combine 115 g digestive biscuit crumbs with 50 g chopped nuts and 50 ml melted butter.

- Press mixture into a 22-cm flan dish and chill. Or divide among 8 (10-cm) disposable tartlet dishes and chill.

- You can make the crusts ahead of time; freeze, well wrapped, for longer storage.

- The cheesecake can be served without chilling; it will be quite soft, more like a creamy dessert than a cheesecake.

DESSERTS

215

PARFAITS

Parfaits are a wonderful quick dessert that can be made ahead of time

Parfaits are an elegant dessert. They are very easy to make if you keep just a few ingredients on hand.

All you need is something fluffy, something sweet, and an ingredient such as fruit, sweet biscuits or cake. Fluffy ingredients include silken tofu, yogurt, whipped cream, ice cream and fruit jellies.

Store-cupboard items for making parfaits include jams, biscuit crumbs, granola, canned fruit, dried fruits and pudding mixes. There are many varieties of parfaits you can make with these ingredients.

To make the prettiest parfaits, use tall, stemmed goblets, or invest in some attractive parfait glasses.

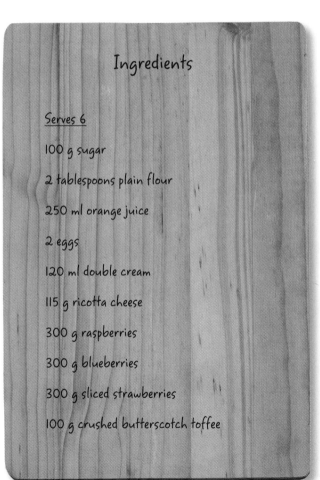

Ingredients

<u>Serves 6</u>

100 g sugar

2 tablespoons plain flour

250 ml orange juice

2 eggs

120 ml double cream

115 g ricotta cheese

300 g raspberries

300 g blueberries

300 g sliced strawberries

100 g crushed butterscotch toffee

Orange Berry Mousse Parfait

- In medium saucepan, mix sugar and flour. Beat in orange juice and eggs.

- Cook mixture over medium heat, stirring with wire whisk, until mixture comes to a boil and thickens. Chill mixture in freezer for 30 minutes, stirring occasionally.

- Whip double cream until stiff. Beat ricotta into orange mixture, and fold into the cream.

- Layer orange mixture and berries in 6 parfait glasses, ending with orange mixture. Sprinkle with toffee and serve immediately, or cover and chill for 2–3 hours.

Pineapple Crunch Parfaits

In bowl, combine 175 ml pineapple juice, 250 ml crème fraîche, 1 (47-g) pack instant butterscotch pudding mix, and 1 (200-g) can drained crushed pineapple. Cover and freeze for 20 minutes. Layer in parfait glasses with 115 g granola, 300 g peach chunks, 150 g blueberries, and 150 g sliced strawberries. Top with granola and serve.

Dark Chocolate and Strawberry Parfaits

Whisk 1 (47-g) pack instant chocolate pudding mix with 2 tablespoons cocoa powder and 250 ml milk; mix well. Layer in 4 parfait glasses with 300 g sliced strawberries and 175 g dark chocolate chips. Top with 150 ml double cream, whipped. Garnish with mint leaves.

Fold Ricotta into Orange Cream

- It's important to bring the orange cream mixture to a full boil so it thickens properly.

- A wire whisk is the best tool to use to make sure the cream mixture is completely smooth. Work the whisk so it gets into the corners of the pan.

- Beat the ricotta into the orange cream to make sure the mixture is smooth with no lumps.

- Fold the mixture gently into the double cream to keep as much volume as possible.

Layer Mousse and Berries

- There are several ways to layer the orange mousse with the berries.

- You can make berries into solid layers; use one layer of strawberries, then the mousse, then one layer of blueberries, and so on.

- Or combine all the berries in a bowl and toss gently. Layer this mixture with the orange cream.

- Add texture and crunch to your parfaits by layering toasted nuts, crushed toffee, granola, toasted coconut or streusel.

DESSERTS

217

MICROWAVE FRUIT TOPPINGS

Apples and pears are great partners in this caramel cinnamon sauce

Fruit toppings, cooked in the microwave or on the stove, are great for last-minute desserts. Not only are they good for you, but this is a great way to use seasonal produce.

Harder fruits like apples and pears are natural candidates for this type of treatment. But you can also use frozen or canned fruits; just add when the sauce is completed.

These toppings can be flavoured any way you like. Be adventurous and add some fresh herbs like thyme, mint, rosemary or basil. Add fruit juices and honey, or try spices like cinnamon, cardamom or a bit of pepper. Some chocolate, in the form of cocoa powder or melted, is always welcome too.

Ingredients

Serves 6

75 ml apple juice

115 g brown sugar

2 tablespoons golden syrup

50 ml double cream

2 tablespoons butter

2 apples, peeled, cored and chopped

1 pear, peeled, cored and chopped

2 tablespoons lemon juice

½ teaspoon cinnamon

Ice cream, to serve

Apple and Pear Fruit Topping

- In microwave-safe casserole dish, combine apple juice, brown sugar, golden syrup, cream and butter.

- Microwave on high power for 1 minute, remove and stir. Meanwhile, toss apples and pears with lemon juice and cinnamon.

- Stir fruit into sauce. Microwave on high power for 1 minutes, then stir. Continue microwaving for 30-second intervals until apples and pears are tender.

- Let mixture cool for 20–30 minutes, stirring occasionally. Serve over ice cream.

Citrus Compôte
In microwave-safe dish, combine 120 ml orange juice, 50 g sugar, 1 teaspoon vanilla and 1 tablespoon triple sec; microwave on high for 1 minute. Remove and add 1 (425-g) can drained mandarin oranges, 1 red grapefruit, cut into sections, and 1 teaspoon orange zest. Microwave on high for 1–2 minutes until hot, then serve.

Cinnamon Maple Apple Topping
In microwave-safe dish, combine 120 ml apple juice, 50 ml maple syrup, 2 tablespoons brown sugar, and ½ teaspoon cinnamon; microwave on high for 1 minute. Remove and add 2 peeled and chopped Granny Smith apples. Microwave on high for 2 minutes until apples are tender.

Microwave Caramel Sauce

- The sugar must dissolve completely in the sauce before you add the fruit.

- Spoon up a little of the sauce and look at it. If you don't see grains of sugar, it's dissolved. If you do, microwave for another minute on high.

- Be very careful with this sugar syrup. It's very hot and can burn you easily. Protect your hands when handling the dish.

- You can omit cream from the sauce, but it will harden more quickly and must be used immediately.

Microwave Fruit

- You can leave the skins on the fruit for more nutrition and fibre.

- Because the fruit is tossed with lemon juice to stop it browning, you can prepare it 30 minutes ahead.

- You can use soft fruits such as nectarines, oranges, mangoes and peaches; just microwave them for a shorter time.

- What can you do with the toppings? Serve over ice cream, sponge cake, cupcakes or waffles.

BARBECUED FRUIT KEBABS
Grilling fruit caramelizes fruit in this fun dessert

And finally, let's barbecue some fruit for an easy and healthy dessert. The fruits that grill best include apples, pears, pineapple, peaches, nectarines, strawberries and oranges.

Very delicate berries like raspberries, blueberries, or blackberries don't take well to the high heat of the barbecue. Add those fruits after the others are cooked.

Threading fruit pieces on skewers is the easiest way to handle them. Bamboo skewers, soaked in cold water for 30 minutes, are the best choice for this easy dessert. If the fruits are too hard for the bamboo to puncture, first make a hole with a metal skewer, then thread the fruits.

A bit of sugar adds a caramelized crunchy crust to the barbecued fruit.

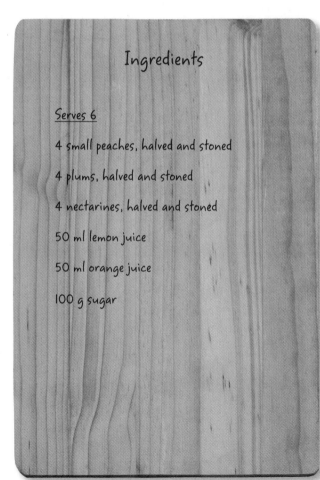

Ingredients

Serves 6

4 small peaches, halved and stoned

4 plums, halved and stoned

4 nectarines, halved and stoned

50 ml lemon juice

50 ml orange juice

100 g sugar

Barbecued Peach and Plum Kebabs

- Do not peel fruit. Place fruit, cut side down, in casserole dish.

- Pour lemon and orange juice over fruit; lift fruit so juice flows on to cut sides. Leave for 5–10 minutes.

- Prepare and preheat barbecue to medium-low. Thread the fruit on to 6 metal skewers, using 4 pieces of fruit per skewer.

- Sprinkle cut sides of fruit with sugar. Oil the grill rack, then place kebabs on barbecue, cut side down. Cook for 2–3 minutes, then turn and cook for 1 minute longer. Serve immediately.

You can marinate fruits in many different mixtures. Simple sugar solutions, with an acidic ingredient like orange juice, or a combination of fruit jam with melted butter would be delicious. You can even try a dry rub with a combination of sugar and sweet spices.

• • • • RECIPE VARIATION • • • •

Barbecued Banana Split: Cut 2 firm bananas into chunks. Thread on 6 bamboo skewers along with 18 large strawberries and 12 peach wedges. In shallow bowl, combine 120 ml pineapple juice, 2 tablespoons sugar, ½ teaspoon cinnamon and 2 tablespoons melted butter. Roll kebabs in this mixture. Grill over direct low heat for 1–2 minutes. Serve with ice cream.

Sprinkle Fruit with Juice and Sugar

Grill Fruit Kebabs

- Lemon juice stops the fruit from turning brown because the acid denatures the enzymes in the fruit cells.

- The juice also adds a fresh, tart flavour to the fruit, and adds vitamin C.

- Sprinkling the fruit with sugar not only helps protect the fruit from the heat of the barbecue, it also adds crunch.

- The sugar will caramelize in the heat, adding complex flavour and texture contrast to the soft fruit.

- If you're using large fruits, you can thread the fruit on 2 skewers at once. Place the skewers side by side.

- This technique will help prevent the heavier fruit from spinning as you turn the skewers.

- Watch the fruit kebabs closely on the barbecue, and remove them as the fruit shows grill marks.

- The fruit can burn quite easily, and the sugar coating increases that risk. Don't walk away while the fruit is cooking.

DESSERTS

GLOSSARY
Learn the language first

Al dente: Italian phrase meaning 'to the tooth', which describes desired texture of cooked pasta.

Barbecue: To cook over coals or charcoal, or over high direct heat outdoors.

Baste: To brush food with a liquid during cooking to keep it moist as it roasts or bakes.

Beat: To manipulate food with a spoon, mixer or whisk to amalgamate ingredients and incorporate air.

Blanch: To briefly cook food, primarily vegetables or fruits, to remove skin or fix colour.

Brown: To cook food so that the surface caramelizes, adding colour and flavour.

Coat: To cover food in another ingredient to provide a protective flavoured or textured surface, such as coating chicken breasts with breadcrumbs.

Chop: To cut food into small pieces, using a chef's knife or food processor.

Deglaze: To add liquid to a pan that has been used to sauté meat, fish or vegetables, to release caramelized residue stuck to the pan, which flavours the sauce.

Dice: To cut food into small, even cubes, usually about 6 mm square.

Dry rub: Spices and herbs rubbed into meats or vegetables to marinate and add flavour.

Flake: To encourage cooked fish to break into small pieces; also to cut food into thin slivers.

Fold: To combine two soft or liquid mixtures together, using a gentle over-and-under action with a large spoon, to avoid beating out previously incorporated air.

Grate: To remove small pieces or shreds of food such as cheese, chocolate or fruit zest, using a grater or microplane.

Grill: To cook food quickly close to the heat source, as under an overhead grill or on a griddle or barbecue.

Marinate: To steep meat, fish or vegetables in a mixture of an acid and oil, to tenderize and add flavour and succulence.

Melt: To turn a solid into a liquid, by the addition of heat.

Microwave: An appliance that cooks food by means of electromagnetic radio waves, which cause molecules in liquids to vibrate, creating heat.

Pan-fry: To cook quickly in a shallow pan, in a small amount of fat over relatively high heat.

Shred: To use a coarse grater, mandoline or food processor to create small strips of food, or to pull meat such as chicken apart with the hands into small pieces.

Simmer: A state of liquid cooking over very gentle heat, where the liquid stays just below boiling point.

Slow cooker: A thermostatically controlled appliance that cooks food by surrounding it with low, steady heat.

Steam: To cook food by immersing it in steam. Food is set in a perforated container over boiling liquid.

Stir-fry: To quickly cook food by manipulating it with a spoon or spatula, in a wok or pan, over high heat.

Whisk: Both a tool, which is made of loops of steel, and a method, which combines food until smooth while incorporating air in the mixture.

INDEX

INDEX

INDEX